Twenty Years of Vaudeville and a Pension

What Really Happens Behind the Badge

By

Rich Solita

Strategic Book Publishing
New York, New York

Strategic Book Publishing
An imprint of Writers Literary & Publishing Services, Inc.
845 Third Avenue, 6th Floor – 6016
New York, NY 10022
http://www.strategicbookpublishing.com

ISBN: 978-1-60693-385-5
SKU: 1-60693-385-X

Printed in the United States of America

Book Design: Bonita S. Watson

DEDICATION

To Mom and Dad, I am so sorry you are not here to join me in
my joy and elation upon completing my book.
I miss and love you both so very much.

CONTENTS

DEDICATION III

ACKNOWLEDGMENTS VII

CHAPTER 1:
THE ROOKIE.. 1

CHAPTER 2:
THE VETERAN...83

CHAPTER 3:
THE REAL POLICE 105

CHAPTER 4:
TERMINAL ILLNESS...229

CHAPTER 5:
YOU'RE ON THE AIR...I'M LISTENING 237

Acknowledgments

Special thanks given to Stephanie Spencer. For if it were not for her assistance the publication of this book would not be possible.

CHAPTER ONE

THE ROOKIE

We strolled through the gangway and I unbolted the corroded gate Dad meant to repair since my grammar school days. Its annoying squeak announced our arrival. I walked side by side with my girlfriend, the woman I would soon marry. She wished to speak to my mother, an unusual request, before we began our scheduled Friday night date.

We entered the house through the basement. Four months out of the year, the family practically lived there due to Chicago's hot and humid summers. Times were okay in those days, but Dad was somewhat thrifty on the electricity, especially when it came to the air conditioner. The basement served as my family's second home.

The area appeared darker than normal and very quiet. Unexpectedly, all appeared. The room was jam-packed with my friends, who had gathered for a surprise party. In one week, I would graduate from the Chicago Police Academy Training Division. The party was enjoyable, but nothing out of the ordinary. All of us took pleasure from the get together while we drank and devoured Mom's incredible cuisine.

The Democratic Convention had just concluded and left the city of Chicago with an angry black eye. That is not to say, my brothers in blue did not reciprocate. The final days before graduation arrived. My classmates and I were very anxious to graduate from that stink box of a school. The building had matured and the wrecking ball had the school in its site. But, the city offered nothing else for our police education. For thirteen weeks, we battled the smell of Polish sausage from the adjacent manufacturing plant as we sipped our morning brew. Unfortunately, the smell of Italian sausage was more my forte.

During those thirteen weeks, many friendships formed within this tight-knit bunch of guys. Little did we know, in fifteen years, two would be killed in the line of duty, two would be arrested for a crime and fired, two passed on from natural causes, and six would simply resign. That is twelve out of forty-five men who would, in one way or another, drop out of the picture.

The date was the 16th of September 1968, graduation day. We were positioned on stage in our new uniforms, or "monkey suits" as they were commonly called. We absorbed an abundance of skills during our training at the Police Academy, but the school lacked simulated instruction of real life situations encountered on the streets. If we heard it once, we heard it a hundred times on the street: "I know what they taught you in school, kid, but this is the way we're going to handle it on the street."

So there we stood, about to receive our certificates of graduation from the Deputy Superintendent of Police Training. We should have known the stage we were on symbolized a twenty-year journey. For on this day, we became actors, men of a hundred faces and a hundred roles. A police officer must be able to adapt instantly to situations he or she is thrust into on a daily basis. There is only one way to successfully complete your assignments safely; you must become a performer who possesses compassion and common sense. You cannot simulate a robotic police officer, for it is the robotic officer who typically ends up in the hospital, is unable to attain information from witnesses, and is even ostracized by his fellow officers. Diploma in hand, I considered myself the opening act for other veteran police officers to further my training in the field of criminal justice.

The following Monday, I reported for duty at the First Police District. Petrified, I entered the station and mostly middle-aged men surrounded me. Many carried grayish hair atop their heads with the average age about forty years.

After my new captain introduced himself, he assigned me to the midnight shift. While he peeped at me over the top of his reading glasses, I could not help but think trouble loomed. He was old enough to be my grandfather and twice as irritable.

"Rich, I'm going to keep you out of harm's way while you're on probation. Those bastards from the IAD will fire you for just about anything during this period, even if you're right. Your new assignment will be the tubes, you'll be okay down there," said the captain.

"Yes, sir," I said.

I left his office and sat in the roll call assembly room. One query popped into my mind: "What the hell are the tubes?" Everyone in the room gawked at me. I was a new breed of officer, able to take my oath of office at age twenty. The norm at that time was typically twenty-four to twenty-six years of age. My youthful appearance made it difficult to be accepted as "one of the guys." Respect and trust from my fellow officers would not come easily or quickly.

My partner for the night was Jimmy Newborn. He had one year left on the job before pension. At sixty-two years old, Jimmy stood five feet six inches tall, and all of a hundred and thirty pounds. He looked like he required an I.V. just to walk out of the room. Looks sure can deceive. Jimmy possessed the three most important traits a police officer must have to endure the jungle: common sense, a sense of humor, and compassion. If you do not possess these three characteristics, you are as good as dead, physically and mentally.

We hit the street that night, but my clothes were not adequate for the weather. After all, I thought I would be confined to a heated squad car for eight hours. Instead, we were in the tubes with winos, perverts, and rats. The platforms were covered with spent chewing gum and cigarette butts, and graffiti coated the gray cement tunnels. The tubes are what the police refer to as the mass transit system of the city. A large majority of this system runs underground where there is no heat, stagnant air, and no people after midnight. The downtown area of the city is closed at night and most train cars sped by empty. The riders who lingered utilized the trains as motels until the morning rush hour workers caused their speedy departure to the surface in order to avoid arrest.

We arrived at our post and Jim asked for my time ticket. This ticket needed time validation every thirty minutes from transfer boxes located in all stations. Since supervisors rarely verified our presence in the tubes, these tickets assured the bosses we were down in the tunnels and on our assigned post. In a flash, Jim had the time box disassembled. I stood and stared at its guts. He took his ticket, then mine, and punched us up for the entire eight-hour tour.

"There we go. We're all done for the shift. Anything you have to do tonight, kid?"

"Nope, but how 'bout some coffee?" I asked.

I wasn't a serious coffee drinker, but in the months to follow, I became one. We talked over some java and discussed many different things.

"A good policeman never gets wet or hungry, kid, even if it rains the entire shift. I actually saw it happen many times. You learn real fast to stay dry and full," said Jim.

He really had my attention now. I wanted to learn from this man.

"A smart police officer never pays for any food or drink on his post either," said Jim.

"Why is that, Jim?" I asked.

"Well, it's like an extra fringe benefit of the job. You don't bite the hand of the people who feed ya; just give them a little extra service. Sooner or later they'll need a favor and you'll be the one they know they can count on. If they charge ya for a lousy cup of coffee, get out your ammo," said Jim.

"Ammo, what the hell ya talking about?" I asked.

"Come on, kid, get out your ticket book and write his customers who are parked illegal in front of the restaurant. I guarantee they'll never charge ya again. It's similar to 'you scratched my back and I'll scratch yours.' Four or five coffee stops a night leaves a nice piece of change inside your pockets at the end your tour."

I immediately knew I was seated across from a master police officer.

"Oh, and another thing to remember is never, and I mean never, volunteer for anything on this job. It always looks like a piece of cake and then the job turns out to be a bitch. You'll kick yourself in the ass all week if that happens. If you're selected for something and it turns out to be a shitty detail, you can fault the jagoff who gave you the assignment," said Jim. "Do ya take money, kid?"

"No," I said.

"Well, I'll fill ya in anyway. Believe me, there're people out there that shove money in your face constantly. You can take it or refuse it. But, whatever you do, never accept money from a broad, a pipe smoker, bearded people, and especially someone who drives a VW wearing a tam. They're all beefers. Dagos and Pollacks are the best; they usually know what it's all about.

"Never hustle anyone, kid. There're enough assholes that screw up to fill everyone's pockets seven nights a week. Most of all, kid, don't ever trust a whore or a junkie. They'll sell out their mother if they have to save their own ass."

While Jim went on with his guidance, strictly from experience, I could not help but wonder why these words of wisdom eluded my instructors at the academy.

"Well, kid, enough coffee for now. If we don't take a break, we'll be pissing all night."

We got up and Jim grabbed the check. We walked past the register and he laid it down on top of the counter without any money.

"Thanks, Gus. See ya later. Always say thanks, kid, or they'll talk about ya when ya leave and call you a cheap mothafucker," said Jim.

The rest of the night went by tediously. We visited three more coffee shops, four hotel lobbies, and played checkers with the firemen until six in the morning. What an introduction to the world of crime fighting.

"Well, kid, it's time for breakfast. You hungry?" asked Jim.

"Yeah, let's go. These firemen whipped my ass enough. Checkers is not my game," I said.

Jim continued to call me kid at least twenty times that night. The term did not bother me. I was a twenty-year-old punk in the real world receiving a street education in police procedure.

Jim and I checked off at 7:30 a.m. and walked to our cars together. I needed to get something off my chest, so I decided to ask.

"Hey, buddy, how come the guys aren't very sociable towards me? Is there a symbol on my back that says I'm some sort of a jagoff or something?"

Jim exploded with a loud chuckle.

"Look, kid, you won't feel this way in about six or seven months. Remember, you'll probably react the same way to Johnnie New Guy someday yourself. Don't be so uptight. This job is nothing more than twenty years of vaudeville and a pension. Relax!"

"What do you mean by that, Jim?" I asked.

"I can't answer that for ya, kid; that's one you'll have to learn for yourself. But from today on, you're an actor on stage for the rest of your law enforcement career. Always remember that."

We got into our cars and drove off. His remark would frequently come to mind, but for now, it went in one ear and out the other.

I walked in the door and the phone rang. My girlfriend wanted to know all about my night. She was so concerned and curious about my new profession. I filled her in on all the particulars and hit the sack. I frequently had a rough time staying awake after working the midnight shift, even if it was sluggish. I laid in bed and, bizarrely enough, I could not wait to return to work. The academy had completed an exceptionally fine job with their brainwashing technique.

I reported for work early the next night. Jim and I were together again. The silent treatment I received the past day continued, only presently, there were some nods and very quiet hellos. The troop's greetings put me somewhat at ease on my second night of work.

Nothing out of the ordinary happened at roll call. It started off with a list of hot cars, death notices, a crime pattern in the district, and, unexpectedly, the announcement of the impending Sergeant's exam. It did not matter to me; I could not take the test anyway. I gazed around the room and a good number of the guys were excited. The chatter got very noisy.

"Don't forget to hit those books and study your general orders, men," said the captain.

He walked towards the exit.

One of the guys reached into his pocket and pulled out a dime. He tossed it to an officer related to a city alderman.

"Hey, Mark, you'll need this to do your studying. If you can't remember your uncle's phone number at City Hall, it's 744-4000, just ask the operators for the shit house," he said.

The entire room broke out in laughter. The dime represented the call needed to put your clout into action. You would not get made (promoted) if you had no one going for you during the promotional process.

Jim and I hit the street. Our tour duplicated the previous night. First, we entered the tubes and punched our tickets, drank a couple of cups of coffee, and, lastly, took a stroll through the "Loop," or the downtown area.

We strutted west on Van Buren from State Street and saw nothing but winos passed out in the doorways. Van Buren Street consisted mainly of bars, flop hotels, and pawn shops.

Suddenly, a hotel door swung open and there stood Abe, the desk clerk.

"Boy, I'm glad to see you guys. I got some jagoff in the lobby drunk as a skunk and he won't leave. I already called for a car," said Abe.

"Come on, kid, we'll handle this one and try to save someone a trip from the hole," said Jim.

I had no idea what Jim meant by the "hole," but I followed him anyway and pretended I did. We crept down the hallway and watched the roaches duck in and out of the highly visible cracks on the old plaster walls.

"Hey, Jim, what the hell is a hole?" I asked.

"Oh, that's another word for pussy," said Jim.

"Come on Jim, ya know what I mean."

"It's the spot in the district where ya can hide a squad car from the bosses and catch a couple of hours of shut eye while the action is slow, normally between two and six in the morning on weekdays and a little later on the weekends," said Jim.

Once inside the lobby, we could see the downer. He was clad in dirty blue jeans and a yellow shirt that looked gray, unshaven, and stunk like a bar room floor. Jim approached him and released a swift kick to the bottom of the bum's foot. He did not move, but an insignificant groan could be heard.

Jim's next move totally confused me. He bowed over the downer and lifted the drunk's upper lip. He examined his teeth. He glanced into his ears and then jerked down the zipper of the wino's pants and inspected his underwear. They were snow white. He nodded my way and instructed me to notify the zone operator to give the car assigned a disregard. Jim went into the wino's pocket and pulled out a handful of money. The wino came to as if an alarm started to ring in his head. Jim got Abe's attention and thrust all the money back into the pocket.

We tried to elevate the man to his feet. His impression as a drunk faded. Once upright, all stood in front of the flophouse and I started to call for a transportation wagon.

"Don't bother, kid, he'll never catch sight of the lock-up," said Jim.

Yet again, I did not understand what he meant. I trusted his judgment and kept my mouth shut. Jim straightened out the wino's clothing and asked if he would be all right.

"Yeah," said the wino.

"Go on, get the hell outta here," said Jim.

The drunk walked past us and Jim gave him a dirty look. The wino returned a snarl, as if to say, "You won this one, but I'll be back."

He wandered off and Jim muttered, "Jagoff."

The wino gestured goodbye with his middle finger.

"Hey, kid, who got the job?" asked Jim.

"Beat 112," I said.

"Do me a favor, kid, check your beat map and see what beat we're on and let's go inside and have a cup of coffee."

"You've been working here twenty years and you don't know the beat?" I asked.

"Look, kid, I can tell you what time the Englewood train arrives at the State and Madison, but since I never make any arrests in the tubes, I don't need to know the beats. Just look it up and pay attention to the old man."

I thumbed through the papers in my pocket and it took forever to locate on the map.

"Okay, partner, we're on beat 112, the same car that got the job," I said.

"Call the zone again and have beat 112 meet a P.O. at Gus's Coffee House as soon as possible," said Jim.

"You got it, partner, it's as good as done," I said.

Jim had something up his sleeve and I was in the dark on what it could be. I made the call and we entered the coffee shop.

"What's up, Jim? You look upset," I said.

"Not upset, kid, just really pissed off."

"What are ya pissed about?" I asked.

"Okay, it's school time again. The wino looked pretty scummy, didn't he? Would ya take him home for dinner?" asked Jim.

"Hell no," I said.

I still did not understand Jim's rationale.

"Those guys from IAD (Internal Affairs Division) are pretty slick, or so they think. Can't you spot a set-up when you see one? That bastard had fifty bucks in his pocket. That's plenty for a flop and bottle of wine. Why sleep in a hotel lobby? He was trying to set up Beat 112. They're the zebra team of Anthony and Johnnie. They've been together for about two years and are two sharp coppers."

"Why would they try to set those guys up?" I asked.

"They probably got a beef about grabbing money from winos and the IAD wanted to check them out."

"Are you sure, Jim?"

"Look, kid, no wino has clean teeth, clean ears, and most of all, clean underwear. Those assholes from the IAD aren't going to put on stinky dirty shorts, dirty their ears, and let scum build up on their teeth to arrest a copper. These guys want to make their job as easy as possible or they wouldn't be working in that pimp job. All of them are nothing but empty holsters," said Jim.

"I can't believe that," I said.

"If you don't believe me, kid, go find a wino with that description and I'll suck your dick at State and Madison. I'll even give you five minutes to gather a crowd," said Jim.

I agreed with Jim and sat in silence and listened. I harvested all the knowledge I could from this expert. Just then, we heard a car door slam and the bell on Gus's door jingle. Tony and Johnnie entered. Their pace appeared hurried.

"What's up, Jimbo?" asked Johnnie.

"This is my new partner, Richie. I'm breaking him in for a period or two. He's okay for a kid," said Jim.

Both said hello and shook my hand. Tony looked at my name plate and said, "You Italian, huh?"

"Yeah, a Dago with a little Pollack blood too," I answered.

"Don't cha worry, you gonna do okay under Jimbo's wing," said Tony.

"Well Tony, do ya want to know what's up, or do you think we called you here to weigh all that shiny gold around your greaseball neck?" asked Jim.

"What are you, a comedian or something?" asked Tony.

"Naw, no bullshit. The IAD tried to set you guys up," said Jim.

Both officers stared at Jim and closely paid attention to his words.

"If you don't believe me, ask the kid. We had a wino with underwear cleaner than Sister Mary Margaret and fifty bucks in his pocket."

"He's right, Tony, today's the 27th of the month. Checks don't come in until the first. There ain't no wino with that much cash in his pocket near the end of the month," said Johnnie.

Tony jumped up from the table. An expression of anger wrapped his face.

"Where did that motherfucker go?" asked Tony.

"He's west on Van Buren with a dirty yellow shirt on," said Jim.

Tony bolted for the door and Johnnie leaped from his chair to join him. Tony only looked back once to give us a wicked smile. Both jumped into their squad car and sped off.

"This jagoff likes to play bum, huh? We'll fix his stool pigeon ass," said Tony.

They located the wino down the street, and as soon as he spotted the beat tags, the wino got drunk again. Johnnie and Tony got out of their car and patted the suspect down, but neither put their hands into his pocket. Their action avoided the invisible dust located on the money.

They carried out the arrest for drunk and disorderly and threw the wino in the back seat of their cage car. This is a vehicle with four doors, where the back area is totally cut off from the front by a metal partition bolted on top of the rear of the front seat. Both back windows do not open and the fresh airflow is less than desirable.

"What do ya think, John? We're going in anyway, so let's make a sweep and pick up some downers? (Nasty, stinky drunks)" asked Tony.

"Sounds good to me, Tony, try the mission. The stinky ones should be in the alley by now and those do-gooders always call for service anyway."

The blue and white turned into the alley adjacent to the mission. The smell of urine and sour wine hung dormant in the atmosphere. The duo spotted three downers to fulfill their plan. One developed the well-known wine shits, the other had piss all over himself, and the third had so much crap in his nose it was enough to make you puke. All three were thrown in the back and arrested for disorderly conduct.

The stench filled the rear of the squad. All headed towards the station, when Tony felt a phony chill. He turned the heat to full blast. The body odors intensified three fold. None of this affected the three winos; they did not even know the day of the week.

The investigator from IAD looked ready to pass out. He could not hold out any longer. He puked his guts out all over the back seat. Sausage and pizza cheese covered the lap of the three winos. They were quite upset and started to throw the vomit at the investigator. He sat and took it so his cover would not be blown. Johnnie and Tony held their noses and continued to drive. They arrived at the station and threw all four in the lock-up. Neither Tony nor Johnnie ever received any official word from the IAD. They both survived the set up.

Things for the next few weeks were routine. I got to meet all the whores and junkies on the street and made a few bullshit arrests. This is commonplace for a street cop. The following morning, one of the guys inquired if I planned to go straight home after the tour. I said no, and he invited me to the watering hole.

The watering hole is a shot and a beer joint where the local cops stopped for a quick one after work. This type of establishment was usually a dive bar with red velvet wallpaper, dim lighting, torn barstool seat covers, and smoke-filled rooms. Not one of my usual haunts. I laughed at the thought of drinking beer at seven in the morning.

I accepted the invitation and we walked to the bar. Half the damn shift made the identical journey, bosses included. We sat and chewed the fat for quite some time, which allowed my narrow friendship an opportunity to widen with the troops. They finally spoke to me in length and in detail. Some of the war stories were unbelievable. I listened to all the tales and, as a rookie, their words fascinated me. There was no reason to doubt the validity of the stories, so I continued to take note and learn.

Eleven in the morning appeared on the clock. Dead drunk and flat broke, I made my exit. This routine occurred every morning with most of the guys on the watch. The only day they would not drink at 7:30 a.m. was Sunday. Reason being, the bars were not open yet. I made it home and tried to fall asleep. Still drunk, laughter erupted from my body. What a job!

The next night, I arrived at work with a hangover. The troops and I sat and chatted before roll call, and for some reason, the men flaunted weird looks on their faces when they gazed my way. What was up? The boss called the roll and yelled my name.

"Here, sir," I said.

The captain removed his glasses and scoped the room.

"Tonight, Officer, I'm going to take you out of the tubes and assign you with Officer Wells. His partner pulled up lame and I'm short handed. Has anyone seen Wells yet?" asked the captain.

"He'll be here shortly, sir. It's hard to find a parking place for that huge beater Cadillac he drives," someone yelled from the back of the room.

Trouble lay ahead. I now realized why everyone had funny looks on their faces. My partner was the district's recluse. This guy came straight from a horror movie. One could deduct this much from a mere glance at the man.

Officer Wells burst into the roll call room in full uniform. His head sported a Chicago Cub's baseball hat and the zipper on his pants rested in the down position. His holster lacked a weapon and his tie fashioned a string knot instead of the normal Windsor. I said a prayer. Instead of my big chance to do some police work and show the boss my capabilities, I was stuck with the laughing stock of the district. The guys advised me to put up with the setback and not make any waves. It would be over sooner than later. We got in the wagon and I plopped myself in the shotgun position. My introduction was met with a grunt and a weak handshake. We hit the street. In the early stages of the shift, we hardly spoke. Abruptly, Wells looked at his watch.

"Holy shit, it's 1:30," he said.

He activated the emergency equipment and commenced to drive west from the Loop area. I had no idea of our destination and chose not to ask. Aggravation consumed me and my mouth remained sealed in disgust. We approached Canal Street near Fulton Street and Wells stopped the truck, braking heavily. He leaped from the vehicle.

"I'll be right back," he said.

He ran up the hill that led to the commuter railroad tracks and out of my sight. Alone, I sat three or four minutes and waited for his return. The suspense grew.

Overwhelmed with curiosity, I climbed to the top of the hill. There he stood, a grown man of forty years, in full police uniform, waving at the 1:40 a.m. Silver Streak Train, which sped by every morning at this time. That was not the half of it. He removed his police hat and took from its guts a Choo-Choo Charlie engineer cap. Wrinkled, with blue and white pin stripes, he placed it atop his oversized head. What a sorry sight, but what frightened me even more was the fact that this guy had a loaded gun dangling from his hip.

When I returned to the wagon, a beam of light hit me in the face. My eyes focused on Tony and Johnnie. They chuckled at the sight of me. Johnnie threw the car into gear and they pulled away. Tony stuck his head out the window and sang.

"I've been working on the railroad, all my live long days."

The only thing left to do was climb back in the truck and wait for Wells to return. Thankfully, dinnertime approached. Wells asked where I preferred to eat. By now, I could give a rat's ass at what restaurant we dined.

We ended up in a cafeteria type eatery open twenty-four hours. I ordered two eggs, some bacon, toast, and coffee. I searched for a table some distance from any patrons. Wells returned to the table with enough food on his tray to feed three grown men. Talk about taking advantage of a freebie; he even grabbed six cartons of milk to wash down his chow.

He started to shovel the food into his mouth. He ate and grunted like a pig. After he cleaned his plate, he drank the six cartons of milk one after another. When finished, he held every carton above his tilted head and shook them to get the excess milk drops out.

The other customers enjoyed the floorshow, while my face lay buried in a coffee cup. Some patrons actually laughed out loud at the spectacle. He tore open every carton and laid them flat on his tray. He used his trigger finger as a scooper to pick up the remaining milk and sucked it like a popsicle. I could not stand it any longer and decided to wait for him in the wagon. There were only two hours left to work with this insane man. I started to think about the end of the shift and my visit to the watering hole. Wells returned and we were back on patrol.

Just then, Beat #116 called for a wagon in the railroad yards and the C.C. Room gave us the job. We arrived and the officer advised us a dead body rested inside a tiny shack in a rarely used section of the yard. His cause of death was unknown. Our job was to transport the stiff to the morgue.

The first thing that entered my mind was a stinker. Luckily, this was not the case. The body was dead approximately six months and the death odor had vanished. Both eyes were eaten out by rats and maggots, as was the inside of the mouth, which opened wide enough to engulf a league ball. A huge hole could be seen near the heart area, which appeared to be shaped as if created from the inside out. The skin on the body tightened so one could feel a bone by a simple touch. We lifted the body to set it on the stretcher. I grabbed him by the pant legs of his blue jeans and they tore in my hands like paper. A second attempt and we secured the body on its transport. Wells and I headed for the morgue.

The sun rose as we pulled into the driveway. I did not know why, but places like this always gave me the creeps. Wells beckoned the attendant and he appeared dressed in a green jumpsuit, blank facial expression, messed up hair, and unshaven. Obviously, we disturbed his snooze.

"Do you gotta good one in there, fellas?" he asked.

"Not really," said Wells.

"Why don't ya let me be the judge of that?" asked the attendant.

He opened the wagon door and glanced at the body. He smiled. I took a glimpse upward to locate the suspected full moon. It appeared quarter phased. At least I did not have to worry about hair growing from this ghoul's face and hands. The attendant asked Wells if he wanted the clothing off the body.

"You know we need them, stupid, how much do you want? Is it still five dollars?" asked Wells.

The attendant shook his head "yes" and Wells handed him a fin. We needed the clothing from the body as evidence, just in case this one turned out to be a homicide. Neither of us wanted to touch the decomposed corpse. One never knows what you can catch from a cadaver.

"Okay, partner, come up with two-fifty. You saw me give Igor a five," said Wells.

I laughed out loud and searched my pocket for the money. Granted, the joke was not that funny, but out of Well's mouth classified it as Vegas material. The attendant removed the clothing and turned them over to us. We drove to the station, inventoried all the articles, and called it a night.

The next morning, the work sheets showed Well's regular partner still on medical roll. Another night of misery and internal pain could be expected. We watched the Silver Streak zoom by as usual and then received an assignment of an outside ringer (burglar alarm). Wells and I pulled up and noticed two alarms going off simultaneously, one a liquor store, and the other a small Ma & Pa restaurant. I noticed two huge holes in the windows and immediately requested a canine unit. We sealed off the area and waited for the dogs to arrive.

Once on the scene, I filled the handlers in on the circumstances and they let the dogs do their work. This was the first time I saw the pups in action. They really knew their stuff.

In a short time, the dogs were finished and out of the buildings. They found nothing. We could now enter and not worry about some junkie knocking us over the head in his attempt to escape.

The first step in the investigation was to locate some information on the owner. He quickly arrived downtown, once notified of the break-in. Very grateful for our efforts to apprehend the bad guy; he offered us a sandwich and a drink. We accepted, and he left the room to get our snack and a six-pack.

Suddenly, the owner looked frightened. A head popped out of the counter cooler door when he opened it to get our beer. The dogs missed the burglar who squeezed himself into this airtight box and the handlers never thought to open the door due to its diminutive size. The burglar lay unconscious at the store owner's feet. We made the pinch and I had my first felony arrest.

The next day, we were to appear in court, but Wells got lost and arrived at the wrong building. He rarely made any arrests, which would explain his unfamiliarity of the court's location.

I ambled up the steps of this massive structure and the words "Criminal Court Building" stared at me. Somehow, the title just did not belong. One hears so many stories about this building, which was usually referred to as the "den of thieves" by the police (and they did not mean the criminals who were inside to stand trial). The judges, prosecutors, and defense attorneys constantly bartered with each other for the best deal possible. In the years to come, many days would be spent in this building and I would learn first hand how she acquired her many nicknames.

I located the courtroom and entered. All went well, until I reached the area of the witness stand. My knees rattled at the thought of testifying. What if I made mistakes or did not know the answer to one of those hotshot lawyer's questions? I did not like the idea of anyone making a fool out of me, especially in front of other officers.

I checked in with the clerk, but a long period of time elapsed before he called my case. No one told me to slip the guy a few bucks to get the case called sooner rather than later. The wait infuriated me, because most attorneys' cases were called in front of the judge in two minutes. Whenever this occurred, you could see the fire in the eyes of the officers who worked all night on the midnight shift. Sleepless, they sometimes sat and waited for hours for their case to be called.

I approached the bench. Obviously, the defense lawyer knew he faced a rookie from my demeanor. The state questioned first, and then came time for cross-examination.

"Officer, were these two stores located next door to each other?" asked the defense.

I hesitated to respond and the lawyer snapped at me.

"Please, Officer, just answer a simple yes or no," he said.

Why did he add the "yes or no" to the end of his first question? I could not understand his line of thinking. I felt like the axe was raised and could descend at any time.

I turned to the judge.

"Your Honor, the question can't be answered yes or no," I said.

The judge pondered a while as he glanced at the addresses of the buildings.

"658 North and 660 North, I see no reason why you cannot answer the question, officer.

Just respond yes or no," said the judge.

A slight nod at the judge assured him that I realized he controlled the courtroom. I answered, "yes."

The next words out of the lawyer's mouth stunned me.

"No further questions for this officer."

What was he up to? He had me eating out of the palm of his hand. He went on and explained to the judge how his client consumed large amounts of alcohol on the night in question and accidentally fell through both windows. He stated the alarm frightened his client and he sought shelter in the counter cooler for his own safety. The police report indicated no currency was found on his person, another fact in his client's corner.

"Your Honor, all we have here is a case of damage to property, at most. This was no burglary," said the defense attorney.

The judge gawked at all in the courtroom and stated no probable cause existed for a trial of burglary. He dismissed the case.

I was furious. No one informed the judge these buildings were separated by an alley. The bad guy entered the first building illegally, came out empty handed, and then broke into the second building. What really ticked me was how easily the judge found no probable cause. I left the courtroom and the defense lawyer followed me out. In the hallway, another lawyer approached and they shook hands.

"Hi, Barry, tough day in court?" he asked.

"You bet, Sol, they're all tough," said Barry.

When Barry and I crossed paths at the exit of the building, he flaunted an unmistakable smirk. I knew an arrangement was made prior to court and it drove me nuts the state got a raw deal.

The next night threw me back in the jungle. My desire to get my hands into any type of police work intensified daily. I ran into Jim in the lobby and he gave me the high sign to meet in the bathroom. I checked the worksheet on my way and thanked God the space cadet was not my partner. Jim and I were assigned to the tubes again. Now at the urinal, I asked Jim what's up.

"Hey, kid, two nights ago that young new sergeant checked on the whole tube detail and caught us off base. He beefed to the captain, so we're sure we'll get some time for this."

"Gee, Jim, sorry to hear that," I said.

"You're with me tonight, correct?" asked Jim.

"Yeah, why?"

"Well, that cunt-faced sergeant is on the war path again, so we'll have to play it legit."

"What's he so mad about?" I asked.

"Well, it seems during the tour last night someone cut the four tires on his 'Vette and smashed his windshield," said Jim.

"Holy fuck, the guys around here don't play games, do they?" I asked.

"You haven't been on the job long enough to understand. It wouldn't have occurred if the sergeant wasn't such an asshole. He writes guys up all the time for bullshit. You could see cum stains on his pants when he catches you dirty. If he put that much effort into cutting crime, you could walk through the district with fifties hanging out of your pockets and the only ones who'd probably fuck with you would be the police."

We let out a good laugh and headed for roll call.

The captain called the roll and ended up shorthanded to man all the beat cars. It was a holiday weekend. He changed my assignment from the tubes to working a car. I would be 10-99 the entire shift. (Alone.)

The watch went by without incident. While on patrol, I noticed a gorgeous female walking down Wacker Drive. She was alone. My intentions were merely to engage in light conversation and maybe get a phone number. I parked the vehicle and approached her and expected the uniform would do the trick. The closer I got, the more attractive she looked, until I reached a point of clear visibility. She was a he, and quite gruesome at that.

Before I knew it, he attempted to give me a hug and kiss. I pushed him away with my right hand and tried to radio for assistance with my left. I furnish a second blow to the chest area and put some distance between us. He lunged back at me and all four of my fingers became entangled in the gold chains around his neck.

I pulled and tugged, but my hand was still knotted in the necklaces. He made numerous attempts to place a juicy kiss on my lips as I continued to press on my microphone key to ask for a one-car assist. He started to yell the words "Help, Help!" The other officers in the area, who were aware of my location, mistakenly believed I needed assistance. Cars from all over responded to an officer in distress, which is a 10-1 code, as the blue and whites surrounded me.

One after another, officers exited their vehicles. Suddenly, the adrenalin rush vanished and their bodies exploded into laughter. The situation became controllable and I was able to get unraveled from the gold chains. You can imagine my embarrassment in front of the twenty officers who responded to the scene. The next visit to the watering hole was a disaster. The guys teased me for what seemed like an eternity. Did I ever want to work a beat car alone again?

The following night, I arrived at work a half an hour early. The only other officers present were the desk crew. The work sheet indicated my assignment was a walking post with six other officers. With not one officer under fifty-years of age, it appeared to be another night of loafing. My curiosity festered as to when the hell were they going to assign me to a beat car on a regular basis. I yearned to perform real police work.

The watch commander stood behind the desk and poured himself some coffee while the sound of an unanswered phone pierced his sensitive ears.

"Sergeant, get that fucking phone, will ya? My head is pounding from that drunken fest last night and you're just sitting on your ass and letting it ring off the hook," said the captain.

The desk sergeant reached for the phone, spoke a second or two, and hung up. A look of disgust materialized on his face.

"Hey, Captain, Ryan just called in sick and we're short a one-man vehicle," said the desk sergeant.

"What's wrong with him?" asked the captain.

"He's got the flu and slight fever."

"Flu and fever my ass. He was out drinking with the guys and he drank himself and that bimbo he fucks right under the table. That's all right, I'll mark him D.O.D. (day off drunk) in my black book and wait for him to ask for a favor," said the captain.

How ridiculous; some bosses remembered the D.O.D. and would hold it against you on a future date when you requested a day off. It did not seem right. The day off usually requested was your time, anyway. You merely needed his approval to get it.

"Well, Captain, who do ya want me to put on the car?" asked a deskman.

"It doesn't matter, just fill the spot," he said.

The sergeant glanced at me and turned away. I cleared my throat extremely loud, so loud that many turned to see who had the rough throat.

"Give the kid a break," said an old timer behind the desk.

"Okay, it's yours. The keys are on the board and the car is in the back lot," muttered the sergeant.

After roll call, most of the guys realized the car was cherry and they informed me not to hesitate to call for assistance. Ready for my first regular solo day in the beat car, I became excited and extremely edgy. I hit the street.

The day was unseasonably warm, about eighty-five degrees and humid. You get those days in Chicago during mid-April. The tour itself was routine and I could not wait to get my hands into some action. I felt as if the thirteen weeks of intense training went to waste.

My first job was a theft assignment. I pondered whether or not the crime had all the elements of the offense. My boss cleared the problem and ordered a reclassification to lost property. In reality, he just cut the crime stats, because, eventually,

I believed the elements did exist. But, he is the boss and I followed the order. There were two disturbances, which were both over by the time I arrived, and a lost child who ended up with the diaper dicks (Youth Officers). This was my introduction to the world of crime.One hour before the end of my shift, I received a call to check on the well-being of a resident who lived in a local flophouse. Positioned a short distance away quickened my arrival. My only thought: "Please, not a stinker."

The hotel clerk explained Mr. Beverly, who lived in apartment #308, had been ill lately. He told me he usually spends the entire afternoon lounging in the lobby glancing through the classifieds for a job, but he has not been seen for the last two days. The clerk further explained his numerous attempts to reach Mr. Beverly were unsuccessful.

"Well, what do ya want the police to do about it? Maybe he met a babe and the both are out on a binge or something," I said.

"Could you please come up to his room with me? I got the master key and I'll go in if you come with me," asked the clerk.

We started up the stairs to the third floor. Now late afternoon, the temperature rose considerably. It felt like one hundred degrees in the flophouse and the humidity seemed even higher. The clerk fumbled with the keys at the door and we finally got inside. Mr. Beverly lay there apparently asleep. He looked like a beached whale—six feet, four inches, and every bit of four hundred pounds. A pinch was not enough to wake him, nor could I get any pulse or pupil dilation. I placed a small mirror beneath his nostrils and still the breath of life eluded me.

"Yeah, I think Mr. Beverly is a member of the fat farm in the sky," I said.

The clerk tipped his chin downward and shook his head from side to side. He slowly strolled away and appeared quite distraught.

The hot temperatures lingered on. I called the wagon to handle the stiff and Shawn and Terry arrived. They found me alone in the room. Both officers were Irishmen and right off the boat, accent and all.

I related the facts of the death to both as I took short breaths to avoid the odor of Southern Comfort from their breaths. These officers were very big men themselves. Their hikes up to the third floor started the sweat to flow down their foreheads and temples. They told the clerk to check the back steps for any type of debris. As soon as he left the room, they started to search Mr. Beverly's clothing and the drawers for some type of identification, or so they said. This puzzled me, because I already had all the information about the victim. Pretty stupid, huh?

Mr. Beverly now lay strapped to the stretcher and Terry and Shawn lifted the body. Both wooden poles bowed in the middle and creaked. The light blue shirts on both officers grew darker in color as the perspiration surfaced from their body. They started down the steps, which were of the winding type, very slowly. They had a difficult time with the body due to the step width and the enormous weight of the victim.

"Hold it, Shawn, set Moby Dick down for a second. Let's rest," said Terry.

Terry took a couple of quick deep breaths and wiped the sweat from his brow. I lazily leaned on the banister and observed the two veterans at work.

"Next time we'll bring a fucking crane," said Terry.

They hoisted Mr. Beverly up again. I felt sorry for them. It was hot, sticky, and humid. Plus, they were dealing with the enormous weight on the stretcher. Terry and Shawn needed to travel down a few more steps, maybe ten or twelve.

"That's it, fuck it. I've had it with this fat ass. Come on, Terry. Throw this lard ass over the rail," said Shawn.

"My thoughts exactly, partner," said Terry.

"Hey, kid, grab the middle of this stretcher and give us a hand, or are you on furlough or something?" snapped Shawn.

I thought they were kidding, but in a flash, the man and the stretcher were airborne. They did not even wait for me to help them. They threw the stiff over the railing into the back yard. He landed with a loud thump, face down and partially implanted into the lawn.

"We should have thrown this asshole off the top right from the start and we wouldn't be sweating like this," said Shawn.

Terry just chuckled and reached into his pocket for a flask. He took a quick chug and replaced it. It dripped down his chin and added another dark stain to his already soiled police shirt.

They walked to the stretcher and each grasped an end to flip it over on its front side. A sudden jerk and Mr. Beverly once again stared up at his transporters. He had mud up both nostrils and grass stuck between his lips and teeth. What happened next can only be described as shocking. Mr. Beverly quickly wiggled and raised his bruised torso from the canvass stretcher.

"Ahhh," said Mr. Beverly.

We stood there speechless while Mr. Beverly spit grass blades and dirt from his mouth.

"What the fuck is going on?" asked Mr. Beverly.

Terry responded without a second of hesitation.

"Shut the fuck up, ya goddamn drunk. Ya fell down all the steps and we're taking ya to the fuckin' hospital," said Terry.

Mr. Beverly closed his eyes and slumped back down on the stretcher and did not say another word. All of our heads were in spin mode to see if anyone witnessed the incident; fortunately, no one had.

Terry whispered in my ear.

"You didn't see a fuckin' thing kid, right?" asked Terry.

"You got that right, buddy," I said.

"Come on, stop fuckin' around and let's get this prick to the hospital so we'll have time to stop for a quick one," said Shawn.

They brought the victim to the wagon and departed. I left the backyard nauseous as I jumped into my police car. It drove me crazy whether anyone witnessed the incident. Could you see the headline in the morning paper? "Police Throw Fat Ass Over The Railing Because He Was Too Heavy To Carry."

Now at the station, I bumped into Jim and told him the whole story. He looked at me as if nothing was wrong and told me not worry.

"It's part of the job, kid. It's your word against his. Besides, the fat ass slept during his flight anyway. Don't worry so much," said Jim.

"I don't know about this, worry is my middle name," I said.

"Look at it this way; you probably saved the asshole's life. The impact could have started up his heart again. You're a hero. You'll be in all the papers."

Being a hero did not matter to me. I did not want anyone to know of the incident. Jim told me to keep my mouth shut and forget about it.

I returned to work the next night assigned to the paddy wagon. This time, the space cadet called in sick and the captain teamed me with his regular partner, Kenny. I could not wait to meet him. I had to know what made this guy tick. Only a very strong-minded man could work with the space cadet eight hours a day, five days a week.

Finally, we met and Kenny's secret surfaced. He did not give a shit about anything. He performed his job, but only at the bare minimum. Very easygoing, nothing seemed to bother him, but no one took advantage of him either. Kenny could be mean or soft. He could turn it on or off, just like tap water.

"Hey, Kenny, how did ya get stuck with 'Space Cadet' as a partner?" I asked.

"You mean ya don't know? It's punishment duty. I had the beat car around the Hilton for about six months. What a gravy job until I stepped on my dick."

"What happened?" I asked.

"I made a stupid mistake. What a beat. The Hilton people fed me free and I could get a room anytime I wanted for a piece of ass," said Kenny.

"So how da hell did you lose it?" I asked.

"Well, I was a real bear that day. A bust out fight with the wife made me mad as a motherfucker when I headed to work. In front of the Hilton sat a limo, double-parked, but there was ample room at the curb. I asked the driver to pull over and all I got was some lip. I started to write him for obstruction of traffic.

Just then, his passenger walked up to my car. How did I know he was Vice President of the corporation? He looked at me real cocky-like and said, 'Do you know who I am?'

"I wanted to say, 'You're a fat and short Buttinski, and I don't give a fuck who you are.' But I didn't say a word. Then he muttered the typical citizen's line you hear when you're writing a ticket: 'You know I pay your salary,' he said.

"'Good, if you pay my salary, how 'bout a raise?' I wrote him the fuckin' ticket and went about my business."

"How long did it take before the captain called you in?" I asked.

"Twenty minutes. I got a call from the zone to go into the station. I walked into the captain's office and all he said was, 'You're off the car, Ken.' I must switch you with Steve; he was Space Cadet's regular partner. I stared at him for a brief moment, gave him a 10-4, and walked out. I didn't even bother to ask him why, even though I knew the reason for the switch."

"What do you think happened, Kenny?" I asked.

"Think, I know what the hell happened. The passenger either called some pussy at the 11th Street Ivory Tower or some fat ass, cigar-smoking politician down at City Hall. You know the Hilton people are always good to the police. It's my own fault. I shouldn't have written the ticket. Now it's time to pay the piper."

Just then, some of Jim's words came back to me, "Don't make waves, kid, and don't step on the wrong toes. You'll always come up with the short end of the stick."

The tour was almost over and all went well. We received an assignment of a disturbance at Soldier Field. By the time we arrived, a beat car rounded up six black teens that vandalized some stadium seats inside the grounds. Kenny and I were going to give them a break and cut them loose, but the Park District insisted on prosecution. We herded them into the wagon and the gang ringleader opened his mouth.

"Check out the rookie pig," he said.

The word pig did not upset me. My solution was to retaliate and get even with the punk who slashed this word around so freely. I would simply look him in the eyes and say his mother was a pig. It never failed. I would always get his goat, because no one ever talks about someone's mama.

Kenny grabbed the punk around the throat.

"Here's your pig right here on my hip. How would ya like it if I stuck it up your ass," asked Kenny as he clutched his revolver.

The youth did not respond.

Kenny asked for everyone's handcuffs and entered the wagon. He started to cuff the prisoners any way possible, feet to feet, wrist to wrist, and feet to wrist.

"Say honky, what you up to?" asked one of the teens.

Kenny laughed at the group and slammed the wagon door. He jumped behind the wheel and quickly took off.

"I'll be right back, gonna take these shines for the ride of their life," said Kenny.

He drove around the track that encircled the football field and got the old junk paddy wagon up to forty miles an hour. Suddenly, he slammed on the brakes. We could hear the suspect's yells and screams directed toward Kenny.

"Say, motherfucker, is you crazy or what, chump?" asked one of the gang bangers.

"Shut the fuck up, you dog motherfucker, and hold on," Kenny yelled back.

With those words, he darted off again. He drove all over the field, stops and goes, sharp turns, and even some fancy U-turns. When his joy ride ended, he returned to pick me up for the trip back to the station.

"Hey office', please let your partner drive. Ya win, man. We cool," one teen bellowed.

"What did ya say, punk? Do ya want to go for another ride?" asked Kenny.

"Okay office', just let the rookie drive," said a voice from the rear of the wagon.

Before we left for the station, I checked the back door and opened it. I took a quick glance at the punks. My action revealed such a comical sight. Lying on the floor appeared to be a gigantic bowling ball with teeth. They were all tied up in knots. It took me awhile to get them untangled, but after I did, they all calmed down. We left for the lock-up. Kenny and I arrived at the station and the teens seemed to have changed their attitude. They were now calling us "sir" instead of "motherfucker." Kenny walked in the processing room to help me with the paper and I lined the prisoners against the wall.

"Listen, guys. I don't want to hear any laughing or giggling out of your damn mouths. There certainly isn't one funny thing about being arrested. If I see any of ya laughing, we'll beat the shit out of all of you. Is that understood?" I asked.

"Yes, sir," they said.

All stood at attention and licked their lips as their eyeballs bulged out of their heads. My words must have put the fear of God in them.

Kenny, who stood about six feet three inches and weighed almost 240 pounds (most of it in his beer belly), planted himself in front of the group face to face. Suddenly, we heard a huge gasp of air and Kenny lost six inches from his waistline. His fully equipped gun belt fell to the floor. Attached to his belt were his pants, which also headed south. Kenny stood silent for a moment wearing his police hat and shirt, knee high socks, and a pair of white boxer shorts covered with hearts. The words "I Love You" overlay the front and rear.

He looked at the prisoners and inquired if something was funny. Each kid squirmed to keep from bursting out with laughter. Kenny held his ground and not a giggle could be heard from the group. Finally, Kenny chuckled and we all followed.

"You is one crazy mothafucker, office'," said one of the teens.

"I'll make off I didn't hear that," said Kenny.

It was time to get down to business. I asked to see everyone's identification, a ridiculous request. Any smart cop knows ghetto delinquents rarely carry ID so they can lie to the police as to their identity. Another fact they never taught me at the police academy.

Just then, Anthony poked his head into the room. He looked at the boys and inquired if anyone gave them their Constitutional Rights. Kenny responded "no" and told Anthony to do it because we were loaded down with paperwork.

"All right, listen up. I'll give you guys your rights all at once so I don't have to repeat myself. You have the right to remain silent. Does everyone understand this right?" asked Anthony.

The group nodded their heads "yes" and stood mute.

"Right number two, you have the right to three 'HUHS.' Do you guys understand this important right?" asked Anthony.

The ringleader looked at Anthony and responded, "HUH?"

"That's one, asshole. Now you've only got two 'HUHS' left," said Anthony.

We cracked up and the kid just muttered a long, but simple "Shiiiiiiiiiiiit." When the paper work was completed, we took all concerned to the lock-up and called it a night.

The days went on. I bounced from assignment to assignment, a car, then a wagon, details, and finally, a foot post. At least my feet were wet in all facets of police work. Plus, I met a lot of interesting people.

I reported for work the next shift. My name appeared on the detail sheet for Saint Patrick's Church. My mind blank on this one; I thought they were sending me to serve Mass or something. What kind of petty assignment could they stick me with now? The detail involved a twenty-four hour a day guard, seven days a week. Not to make any waves, I reported to the rectory of the church to relieve the other officer.

Saint Patrick's Church sat in the middle of skid row surrounded by drunks and people you would not want to take home for dinner. I rang the bell of the mansion located next to the church and police officer in full uniform answered.

"What's up, buddy? I'm your relief," I said.

"Have you had this detail before?" he asked.

"Nope, what's my job, passing out communion or something?"

"You don't do anything. Just sit in this room, answer the phone, and take incoming messages for the priest."

"Where do I eat?" I asked.

"You mean you didn't bring anything for chow?" he asked.

"Not a bite. They informed me of my assignment when I reported for work."

"Well, you'll have to call a car to bring you a sandwich. You can't leave the church. You're stuck here until your relief arrives," he said.

After his words of advice, the officer vanished from the room. It measured a mere six by ten feet. It contained a phone, a desk, and a twelve-inch black and white TV to keep me company. The chair in the room resembled an old electric chair, constructed of hard wood and lacking a sufficient pad for my butt.

I decided to snoop around and check out the mansion occupied by these humble priests. Elegance surrounded me. All the floors were solid hardwood. The oak trimmed cabinets were filled with china. Colorful stained glass windows decorated many walls along with beautiful art work. I wandered into the kitchen and noticed five one-inch steaks perched on the stove. In the dining area there were only four place settings, so I assumed the fifth steak had my name on it.

I plopped inside my cubbyhole and watched the news. The phone rang. I took messages for the priest one after another. Father McCue, O'Grady, and O'Donnell all received communications. Suddenly, a vision of boiled potatoes appeared in my mind next to my juicy steak.

"Any messages, Officer?" asked Father O'Donnell.

"Yes, Father, a couple for you and also the others," I said.

"Father, its dinner time," shouted the housekeeper.

"Okay, Mrs. Devine, I'll be right there."

Just then, a black mutt pranced into the room. He started to bark at my feet when I attempted to pet his head.

"Hi, Clover," said Father O'Donnell.

"Don't tell me, Father, ya named him after a four-leafed clover?" I asked.

"That's right, son. Pretty original, don't you think? He was an alley dog until we took him in two years ago. We keep him here for Mrs. Devine, the housekeeper. She needs the company since her dear husband passed away."

Father O'Donnell left for dinner and Mrs. Devine appeared at the door. She had a plate in her hand, which I assumed to be my supper: broiled steak, boiled potatoes, and peas. It looked mouthwatering. I found it odd she carved up my meat, but who's to judge?

"There you are, my little sweetie; I looked all over for you. Come on, it's your lunchtime. Officer, you won't mind if Clover eats his lunch in your office, do you?" she asked.

The woman did not have a can of dog food in her hands or in her apron, so I assumed the steak must be for the mutt.

"No problem, Mrs. Devine," I said.

"There you go, Clover. Enjoy your meal," she said.

She set the platter near the base of the desk. Clover began to eat and, much to my amazement, the steak sat on a china plate. I listened to my stomach serenade the room. I got pissed off. To think the housekeeper did not even offer me a cup of coffee, so much for the virtue of generosity.

The next two phone calls were for Mrs. Devine. To even the score, I made sure she did not get the messages. Suddenly, the slam of a car door pierced my ears. I peeked out the window. It was my boss. He had the responsibility to make field checks on the church and other details.

He stopped in for a little chit-chat and asked me how things were going. Puzzled, I asked how the police department got stuck with a detail on private property. The priest lived pretty damn well and the little mutt ate better than any dog I have ever known. Why were we needed here?

"Well, kid, about eight years ago one of the local scum bags around here broke in and raped and murdered the old house-keeper. Father O'Donnell, being a dear friend of the mayor, asked for police protection. The mayor granted his request. The priest became accustom to the personal service and the asshole coppers got used to doing shit for eight hours but watch TV. No one ever complained about the detail, so there are coppers here around the clock, three hundred and sixty-five days a year. Figure it out at fifteen grand a year. That's some piece of change of the taxpayer's money for private security," said the sergeant.

"What kind of shit is that, Sarge?" I asked.

"It's called political clout, kid. See you a little later," said the sergeant.

"Hey, Sarge, should I butter up to O'Donnell? Maybe I'll get promoted?" I asked.

"Forget it. Your last name ends in a vowel," he said with a smile.

"Yeah, I guess you're right Sergeant Fitzpatrick," I said.

The next day, I was assigned to another detail. This time, they sent me to Cook County Hospital. The prior evening produced a tavern robbery in the district and the offender failed to make it out the door. It never dawned on him the owner of the bar had a couple of friends who were police officers and they frequented his establishment on a regular basis.

On this particular evening, four officers were inside pounding down a few. After the robbery went down, Tyrone bolted for the exit. He took five in the back before he knew what hit him. They could not finish the job because there were too many witnesses in the bar. The ambulance arrived and transported the suspect to the hospital. My duty consisted of guarding the prisoner until he recovered and could be moved to a jail.

He laid in a room off of the emergency section of the hospital with wires and lights connected to every part of his shot up body. He resembled a Christmas tree. I sat there and stared at him. An eerie feeling of sorrow came over me, but in a couple of seconds, I jumped back to reality. I thought, to hell with him. This guy could have killed a police officer or it could be me connected to all that medical equipment.

Suddenly, red lights, buzzers, and bells interrupted my thoughts. A team of doctors, accompanied by nurses, stormed the room. I heard sounds of loud thumps, one after another. The doctor pounded on his chest in an attempt to get his ticker started. He pounded and pounded, but the patient did not respond.

Abruptly, right in front of my eyes, the doctor grabbed a scalpel and cut this guy's chest wide open. It split like a watermelon. Mom's veal began to rise from my stomach and I ran for the restroom. A cold sweat covered my body. I stood at the sink and splashed water on my face and it seemed to cool me down. I regained my composure, meal intact, and walked out of the washroom as if nothing happened.

Just then, a cart darted towards me. It materialized from the outside driveway of the emergency room entrance. Atop the cart laid a police officer with a knife that projected out of the heart area of his chest. Thank God the distance to the washroom was only a few feet away. I splashed more water on my face and neck, and once again, my quick thinking calmed me enough to retain Mom's veal. It took ten to fifteen minutes before I was back to normal when I started up a conversation with one of the hospital security guards. Suddenly, bells and buzzers rang loudly to interrupt our dialogue.

"The hell with this shit, I'm staying right here. I saw enough damn blood for the day," I said.

The guard seemed to agree. We continued to chat and noticed another cart zooming down the hall flanked by panicky doctors. We did not think anything of it, and as they passed, we glanced downward.

My eyes went from the occupant of the cart to the men's room sign. It was the officer with the knife wound. His chest was cut wide open and held apart with two huge steel clamps. We looked right inside of him and the officer's body organs stared right back. One of the doctors stuck his finger firmly in the hole of the heart that was caused by the stab wound. Later, I discovered the doctor's deed saved the police officer's life, but no time to ponder on that now. It was undetermined who sported the greener face, the security guard or I.

We looked at each other and knew exactly what was on the other's mind. We ran for the bathroom, but he arrived first. He grasped the sink and left a toilet bowl for me. I thought how long it took my poor mother to prepare her veal and now it was all for naught. My dinner filled the bowl. It was an instant cure for me, but the guard was not so fortunate. He had the dry heaves. His veins popped out of his neck with every groan. Little did I know, but in the future, the appearance of blood, guts, and human organs would become as familiar a sight as glancing through my TV Guide.

By the time I got back to my prisoner, he kicked the bucket. His death killed two birds with one stone. The crappy detail ended, and the City of Chicago got rid of a felon. I informed the watch commander of the circumstances and he instructed me to go home. Only a six-hour day, I beat the city for two hours pay. I guess that compensated for the loss of my dinner.

On the drive home, something odd struck me. I wished death on a total stranger. This man did not harm my family or me. Yet, his death meant nothing. I had no remorse whatsoever. In fact, if he survived, it would have pissed me off because that meant a return to the hospital detail.

I learned something that night. My ethics and morals were changing. Daily, I felt the alteration process. Was I that man's judge, jury, and executioner? Maybe he robbed to feed his family, or maybe he robbed to pay medical bills. Did he need money for his rent so his family would not have to live on the streets? It could have been any one of numerous reasons that society forced upon him.

A short time later, I awoke from my daydream and decided, "Naw, he's probably some lazy fuckin' jagoff who figured this was the quickest way to make a buck." I was sure of it. Yes, a change did occur. Was it for the better or for the worse?

My next shift exposed the hottest crime floating around the district. The crime pattern revealed a rash of cab robberies with the stick-up man having a very strange modus operandi. A cabby would pick up his passenger, who always carried a large box, and be directed to a warehouse area of the district. Once at their destination, the passenger would seek assistance from the cabby in order to draw him outside. When the cabby complied, that is when the robbery went down. The captain issued an order that stated anyone who apprehended this guy would receive two days off with pay. Sometimes, bosses give you those little perks for a job well done.

10-99 that day, I thought it would be great to grab this guy and do something worthwhile for a change. My mission: drive around the loop and locate a guy carrying a big cardboard box.

Do you know how many people run around the loop lugging big boxes? I trashed the theory when my count reached ten in less than thirty minutes.

The day passed by without any major incidents and my shift was about over. I needed some smokes, so I headed for a freebie joint in the skid row area. I stepped over a downer in the doorway, got the butts, and left the bar. I paused outside to light up when I noticed a man in full stride headed straight towards me. I saw him, but he did not see me. He was about to pass and I stepped out. I ordered him to stop.

"Hey, buddy, where's the fire?" I asked.

"Man, am I glad to see you," he said.

"What's the matter, you gotta problem?" I asked.

"Please, help me. I just got robbed and they're still after me," said the sprinter.

He reached into his pocket and pulled out a handful of bills. They were all crumbled.

"They didn't get it all and they want the rest," he said.

This guy was really slick. He had me convinced he spoke the truth. But where were the bad guys?

"Where did these guys stick you up, buddy?" I asked.

"Van Buren and Canal," he replied.

Those two streets were seven blocks away from our present location.

"Don't be so nervous, pal, you'll give yourself a heart attack if you keep this up. Look how fast your heart is beating," I said.

I laid my palm on his chest. My touch indicated a slightly above normal heartbeat. I became suspicious, but tried not to show it.

"Did you run all the way from Van Buren and Canal to here?" I asked.

"Sure did, I never looked back and ran all the way," he said.

That statement did it. A marathon man could not have traveled that distance without a fast heartbeat. He lied to me, but why?

I put him in the backseat and we started our hunt for the bad guys. The sprinter thought I bought his story and he thoroughly conned me. My job would be to figure out what he did, or what he was about to do. There was one piece of the puzzle missing, and it must be brought to light before I cut this guy loose.

We cruised a short time when I noticed a Yellow Cab in a load zone of an abandoned factory. A huge box balanced on the cab's trunk, but no cabby in sight. Could he have been unconscious in front of the cab and out of my view? I drove right by and paid no attention to the area.

Unaware if the man in my back seat was armed, I thought, he should have been searched before I placed him in my squad. Boy, what a dumb move on my part. I started to look for some assistance. Wouldn't you know it; there is never a cop around when you need one. I hesitated to reach for my gun. I had no knowledge if the sprinter possessed a weapon or not.

"Hey, buddy, did you ever shoot a gun?" I asked.

"Yeah, I know how to shoot a gun. Why?"

"Well, if we see the bad guys and they start to shoot, you can just take one of my weapons for protection, okay?" I asked.

"Okay, man," he said.

"On second thought, maybe you ought to take it now, in case we're pressed for time," I said.

The con completed, it was time to act. I reached to remove my service revolver from its holster.

"Here, use the big one. Hold on to this sucker with both hands so you don't drop it," I said.

He leaned over the front seat to accept the weapon. I unsnapped my holster. My main concern was both of his hands were empty. He held them out as if ready to receive winnings from a slot machine. With his hands now in my view, I quickly turned and stuck the barrel of my revolver inside his mouth. He sprung backwards against the rear of the seat. A clicking sound could be heard as the barrel slid over his teeth and left his mouth. Once again, I rammed the barrel deep into his throat and he gagged.

"Did you think I just fell off of a pumpkin truck from Iowa or something, you asshole? You're under arrest," I said.

"What the hell for?" he yelled.

I cuffed him and drove back to the area where I earlier observed the cab. There stood the driver with blood all over his head. He held a blood-saturated hanky pressed to his wound.

"That's the bastard, you got him. He took all my money," said the cabby.

"Okay, pops. Don't ya worry, he's got all your money in his pocket," I said.

I called for help and the assist cars arrived quickly. I took the offender into the station and booked him. Two days off with pay lay ahead.

The robbery dicks arrived and I supplied them with the facts of the case. They listened, but I could not help but notice something was not right. The proper papers completed, the offender was sent to Felony Court. I appeared the following morning to testify.

I arrived at the 26th street courthouse at 8:30 a.m. and proceeded to the courtroom. I passed the dicks in the hallway and they gave me a friendly nod. My loyal brothers in blue were about to play "pin the tails on the donkey." If I glanced in the mirror, would it reflect long pointed ears atop my head?

The clerk called the case and I sat in the hot seat. The offender could not afford an attorney, so the judge appointed a Public Defender. Most of these P.D.s were good, but some thought in their minds that their "shit didn't stink." Their goal was to get their client a probation period as a sentence, no matter what the crime. But their motivation lacked righteousness.

If the offender beats the rap, he assumes this lawyer has some smarts. He will remember the P.D. in months to come, and to help his memory; the Public Defender slips him a card for future reference. Most of these attorneys only practice a short time and then proceed to private practice. This is where the big bucks are earned. This practice is strictly forbidden, but they do it anyway.

The first motion by the defense was for dismissal on the grounds of an improper ID. The State's Attorney fumbled through the file and a confused look appeared on his baby face. He leaned over the rail of the witness stand, covered the microphone with his hand, and started to mumble.

"Why in the hell did you bring him back to the crime scene for a goddamn ID? Didn't you ever hear of a line-up?" he whispered.

"I didn't bring him back to the crime scene. I was on normal patrol. The cabby saw me and flagged down the car," I said.

I panicked and lied to the prosecutor for fear of blowing the case, big mistake.

"Your Honor, this wasn't an intentional return to the crime scene. The officer had no idea a crime was committed," the State's Attorney shouted.

"Is that so, Officer?" asked the judge.

"Well, not really, Judge. He was up to no good, but I didn't know why or how. Maybe you can call it a hunch, but I did not have a victim to confirm my thoughts," I said.

With that statement, I reversed the earlier lie.

"Due to the officer's honest testimony, I'll have to grant the defense's motion. I'm afraid we have an improper ID, case dismissed," said the judge.

The State's Attorney looked at me, bit his lower lip, and covered his face with his hands. He requested my presence in the back office. I entered the small conference room and, before a calm word could be said, he started to ream me out. He blamed his failure to show probable cause on me. He rattled on and cut me up into little pieces. Finally, my temper flared.

"Okay, enough is enough. You keep this shit up and I'll take off this badge and we'll step outside. You're such a hotshot lawyer. If you weren't so stupid, ya would've known it was a loser when ya got it. Ya should've pleaded the guy out. Then you'd have your precious conviction for your stats come election time. Every cop knows ya have to produce, but that's not my problem. It's yours."

The two dicks entered the room. The situation was tense, but both dicks displayed smirks on their faces, which confused the both of us.

"Don't worry about the kid blowing the case. Our friend will be back tomorrow after we pinch him when he's released. This time, he'll cop out and be looking at a lot of time. We have sixteen more robberies we can pin on him. Ya did a fine job, kid; ya just didn't know the law. Now ya do," said the old timer of the two.

"Yeah, these judges in Washington have been making the laws for the last ten years, instead of interpreting them the way they're supposed to. Just a few years ago, they ruled having a victim view a suspect one on one, even though the crime had just been committed, a constitutional violation," said his partner.

"What do these senile judges think, Americans have mashed potatoes for brains? I could understand their justification if a long period of time elapsed, but an hour or so shouldn't make a difference," I said

"In most cases, the offender is in the area, the clothing description matches, he has evidence on his person, and he's frightened enough to give himself away. It's a very costly decision for the law abiding citizen," said the State's Attorney.

The court would make numerous unfavorable decisions in the future, which many felt tied the hands of law enforcement. However, in years to come, this ruling would be overturned with the seating of a much more conservative Supreme Court.

The next day, I filled in Jim on what went down at the trial. He laughed, but I did not know why. I stood dumbfounded.

"Don't ya realize what they pulled on ya, kid? They stole your pinch. The dicks are famous for it," said Jim.

"I don't know what the hell you're talking about," I said.

"Look, ya made the pinch and only one robbery got cleared that night. The dicks knew this was the guy in the robbery pattern by his MO. They could've taken steps to book him on every robbery listed in the crime pattern, but they didn't push it. They knew the case was a loser due to the Supreme Court ruling on IDs. They only appeared to re-arrest him for one reason. They needed their names on the paper to receive credit for the pinches."

My hunch was right.

"I knew I didn't like those two dicks," I said.

Before I walked away, Jim asked if I heard about the shooting that occurred on the North Side the other day. He told me Johnny the Nose, a known stick-up man, got killed in an attempted armed robbery. Peculiar thing about Johnny, he was a Born Again Christian, and instead of packing a pistol on his side like normal stick-up men, he carried a Bible.

Johnny attempted to rob a store with a toy gun in broad daylight. The storekeeper thwarted the crime and shot at Johnny in the middle of the hold-up.

"Yeah, Rich, the Bible saved Johnny's life. He tucked it in his shirt, and the book prevented the bullet from entering his heart when it struck him in the chest," said Jim.

"Jim, if the Bible saved his life, how did Johnny wind up dead from the shootout?" I asked.

"Well, our friend Johnny needed two Bibles that day, because the first bullet hit him in the chest, and the storekeeper, an expert marksman, placed the second bullet right between his eyes. He should've been reading the Bible instead of carrying it in his shirt," said Jim.

"Well, the Lord works in mysterious ways," I said.

The months went by quickly and my relationship with everyone on the watch grew. I was finally part of the clique, but the problem of no regular partner still existed. This uncertainty wore down my nerves. When would I get a steady guy to work with?

I walked into the roll call room and everyone was excited. The new promotional list dangled on a portion of the wall for all to inspect. I had little concern because I did not have enough time on the job to take the exam. Everyone read over the list to see if any friends were in the top one hundred. These were the officers who were shoe-ins to be made (promoted). Next to some of the names officers wrote a few choice personal comments.

"Hey, Tony, check out some of the names on the exam results," said Jim.

Tony walked over to the wall where the scores were posted and started to read the comments.

"You're right, Jim. It's the who's who of the department, alderman's kid, alderman's nephew, deputy's son, alderman's son-in-law, and must know somebody because he's so fucking stupid he can't spell sergeant. Isn't it remarkable how these people are so smart? They must have studied so hard to pass the test," said Tony .

In the early seventies, a minority police officer would sue the city claiming the test discriminated against minorities and women. A federal judge heard the case and ruled against the city. No doubt minorities and women were not promoted, but not due to their gender or race. They simply had no clout. The ruling led the public to believe women and minorities were not treated fairly concerning promotions. The city did not care what race or sex you were. The officers with the clout got the promotions, male or female, black or white. This fact could have been determined if the judge examined names on past promotional lists. A simple comparison of the names of prominent government officials of the City of Chicago, Cook County, and the State of Illinois to the names of the top two hundred officers would have would exposed the clout theory.

But, be that as it may, the judge imposed a quota system on all upcoming promotional exams and new hires. Actually, he initiated reversed discrimination. Minorities and women were promoted who were down near the bottom of the list. Many male white candidates were passed up during this process. Police morale reached its lowest point in years and the nickname of "quota sergeant" came into being.

We were about to hit afternoons in a few days and my steady partner for the month was Billy. What a relief! We got along very well, probably because we were both single. The first night was very slow and we could hardly keep our eyes open. Neither of us felt like doing anything, so we stopped for a cup of java.

In the middle of our conversation, a character walked up to our booth and related he wanted to report a murder. I asked him who was the bad guy and he implicated himself.

He told us he killed someone about an hour ago. Billy and I ignored him and continued to drink our coffee, but he continued to annoy us.

"Okay, listen. We're on lunch now and we really can't help you. Go over to the phone and call PO-5-1313 and they'll send a car to help you," said Billy.

Billy sent him on his way and directed him to a pay phone across the street and not in our beat boundary. Billy anticipated, if what our friend said turned out true, another car would get stuck with the job. What we did not know was this nut case did kill someone and the dead body lay on our beat. The murderer informed the zone the location of the victim and we got stuck with the job.

Billy was really upset, a murder investigation at this time of night. He knew it entailed a huge amount of paperwork, especially when you have the offender. We did not feel like writing a parking ticket, let alone investigate a murder. We left the restaurant and found the imbecile who ruined our night.

"Okay, jagoff. Where did you put the body?" asked Billy.

"It's about four blocks down," he said.

We drove over the Madison Street Bridge and our friend told us to stop.

"He's down there," he said, pointing to the river's edge.

We questioned this guy and informed him if he did not tell us the truth, we would beat the shit out of him. He told his story.

"Okay, I just got in town from Georgia and this nigger been following me everywhere I went. He first spotted me in the train station."

"Why was he following you anyway?" asked Billy.

"Don't know, but about seven o'clock tonight, I grabbed him around the throat and asked him myself. He told me he wanted to suck my dick and pay me for the chance on top of it. I told him to shove those lips into park and punched him right in the eye."

"What happened next?" I asked.

"About an hour ago, he spotted me on the bridge. He kept bugging me to suck my dick. I figure the only way to get rid of this guy is to fuck him up good. I talked him into going somewhere quiet. He said okay and we headed for the river. He pointed out a docking post and told to me to sit my ass down. I sat on the post and he knelt in front of me. I unzipped my pants and the asshole got a hard-on and a big smile on his face. He started to go down on me and I gave him a little shove. He fell in the river and I never saw him again. I got worried and I saw you guys. The rest is history."

We both illustrated a look of skepticism on our faces. It just sounded a bit far-fetched to be true.

"Hey, look, Officer, if you don't believe me, have a diver search for the body. He'll be easy to find," said the killer.

"What do you mean?" asked Billy.

"Just look for a nigger with a smile on his face and a big stiff dick," he said.

"This prick is telling the truth. Call the divers," I said to Billy.

The divers arrived in a short time and Billy ran down the facts.

"You guys are crazy. You called us out at three in the morning over a cock and bull story like this? This is bullshit," said one of the divers.

Billy looked at both divers and became agitated.

"Look, Flipper, we don't need your fuckin' advice. Just dive. We've gotta cover our ass," said Billy.

"Okay, Officer, you got it. But, not a chance we'll find anything down there," said the other diver.

We put the offender in the car and waited at the river's edge for the divers to return to the surface. The water was cold and stinky dirty. In about ten minutes, one diver popped his head out of the water. He was clinging to a rope. He discovered the body.

"Well, Officers, you guys were right and I was wrong," said the diver.

"That's him, that's the guy. See if he still got a hard-on," yelled our killer through the squad window.

I glanced at the top of the bridge.

"Put your head back in the car, asshole, or we'll come up there and throw you in the fuckin' river ourselves," I said.

We affected the arrest and officially charged him with murder.

The next day, we appeared at the Coroner's Inquest. I testified in front of the board concerning the facts and the men loved the part about the hard-on. They were about to rule on the fate of the offender when one of the members requested to speak to the prisoner.

They solicited one question. The board's concern was whether or not the bad guy knew if the victim could swim or not. His response was "No." The sheriff escorted him out of the room. The board possessed the authority to change the charge and they did. The murder rap was dropped and reduced to involuntary manslaughter. This first time felon later pleaded guilty and received five years felony probation.

The next shift bordered zilch as far as action was concerned. Billy and I continued our employment relationship, and most importantly, my knowledge of police work grew substantially. I learned all the little police tidbits omitted during my training at the police academy.

For example, Billy and I made traffic stop that night with a Spanish driver and a female white passenger. Billy said he would handle it and I observed his extraordinary technique of interviewing traffic violators.

"Let's see your driver's license, Juan," said Billy.

"No speak Ingles," said the driver.

Billy peeped into the car and asked the passenger if the driver spoke English.

"Hardly any at all," she said.

He asked the woman if she understood Spanish. She said no. Billy knew someone in the car was a liar and went into his own wallet to show Juan his license.

"Oh, si," said the driver.

The driver reached into his wallet and handed Billy a license. Billy returned to the squad, but had concerns about the language barrier.

"I think we should give this guy a pass. I don't like writing people tickets if they don't know why they're getting one. But, first let's check out something," said Billy.

Billy walked back to the car with Juan's license concealed in his shirt pocket.

"Well, Juan, you got yourself a pass," said Billy.

With those words, non-English speaking Juan removed both his hands from atop the steering wheel and reached outside the driver's window to retrieve his license.

"Looking for something, Senor Asshole? You probably speak English better than your senorita. Wait here, I've got a little present for you," said Billy.

Billy stepped back from the vehicle and returned to the squad car laughing.

"Hey, Officer, it almost worked, didn't it?" yelled the driver.

"Yeah, you almost had yourself a pass," said Billy.

Juan got his ticket and a court date. Billy sent him on his way.

"Hey, Billy, I'm curious. What was his name?" I asked.

"Juan Gonzales, why?"

"How in the hell did you know his name was Juan before you looked at his license?"

"If they ain't named Juan, Pedro, or Jose, they're liars. If they're not telling the truth, it means they don't have a green card, and if they don't have a green card, they don't belong in this fuckin' country. But, if they weren't here, so many of us wouldn't be needed on this job," said Billy

After Billy's unique explanation of the United States Immigration policy, we drove off and continued our tour.

A couple of hours went by and we spotted a car in a secluded part of the railroad yards. The windows were steamed, which usually indicated a couple of backseat lovers.

"Come on, let's have some fun," said Billy.

"Naw, Bill, give the poor guy a break. Maybe he can't afford a hotel room or something," I said.

"Yeah right, a brand new car and he can't afford a hotel room. He's probably a cheap motherfucker. That's even more reason to fuck with him. You never know, she might be a whore and maybe we can get some head ourselves."

We approached the car in silence, and once we reached the rear, Billy banged his nightstick on the metal bumper. It made a deafening noise and two heads popped up from the backseat. To our surprise, both were male.

"Having fun with these two will make our night. Okay, you assholes, get out of the fuckin' car," said Billy.

"But Officer, I don't have any pants on," a voice said from the rear seat.

"That's your problem, buddy, now get out," said Billy.

Out stepped a male black he-she, with no pants on, shivering from the extreme cold. He wore red knee high socks with underwear to match, silk of course. It was like a drag show. I ordered his partner out of the car and obviously he was the female of the duo. All he wore was a pair of yellow silk bikini underpants. She, I mean he, was also freezing and kept mysteriously jumping up and down in place.

"Office', I's sick. I's gots to go to the hospital," said the female of the two.

"You look okay to me, sweetheart," I answered.

"Naw, really, I's fuckin' sick. Take me to the motherfuckin' hospital."

Through the entire conversation, we could not help but hear a strange humming sound. Neither of us could figure out what it could possibly be. The passenger continued to hop and demanded transportation to the hospital. Finally, Billy advised him that if he did not tell us the problem, we were not going to take him anywhere but jail.

"Well, Leroy and I's were having sex and he was sticking the dildo in my ass. You two came up on us and scared Leroy. He let go of the motherfuckin' dildo and it's in my ass. It's still running, office'."

"You mean to tell me the dildo is your ass right now?" asked Billy.

"That's right office'. I's gotta go to the hospital. Please."

Both of us giggled and I told the guy to bend over. We placed our ears as close to his butt as possible and listened. The sound emitted resembled the purring of a finely tuned engine. Billy grabbed him by the arm and escorted him to the police car.

"Come on, fuck face, we'll take you to County Hospital. See, these guys did make our night. Can't wait to tell the troops this one at the watering hole," said Billy.

We headed for the hospital and Billy made sure to hit every pothole on the way. We pulled in the emergency room driveway with our friend still buzzing away. We had to check in with the nurse before doing anything, so we told the patient to be seated and keep quiet.

"Good morning, Officers. What's the problem?" asked Nurse Bloom.

"Oh, nothing a little Vaseline can't cure," I said.

"He's got an eight-inch dildo trapped up his ass and it's been running now for about an hour," said Billy.

She, being a nurse at Cook County Hospital, has seen just about everything in the medical field. But we did manage to get a chuckle out of her with this one.

"Okay, fellas, you can go. I'll get him a doctor," said the nurse.

We strolled to the exit and Billy turned for one last look at the patient. He blew him a kiss and left with a smile. The gesture was romantically returned.

The tour was over and we headed in for check off roll call. We stopped at the desk to see who would be making a pit stop at the watering hole. A few guys joined us, but all we had were a couple of quickies. I arrived home sober for a change and had a hard time falling asleep. That is the problem with working the 12:00 a.m. to 8:00 a.m. shift. You go home, sleep, have dinner, and before you know it, it is time to return to work. Talk about screwing up your social life. The good part about midnights is you did not have any of the brass around to screw things up. There is nothing worse than being second-guessed by someone with twenty years on the job, with only five of the twenty on the street.

On patrol again, we drank our coffee at Billy's usual spot. Why we always went to this restaurant puzzled me. This cheap Greek would charge us every night for a lousy cup of coffee, but Billy remained a loyal patron. Not that we had it coming, but we were locked in as he counted his money. We sat and drank our java and Gus got complimentary security. Who would pull a stickup with two cops seated at the coffee counter?

The mystery continued to haunt me, so I asked Billy why we frequented the Greek's place so much. He told me it is a matter of principle.

"We'll catch this Zorba prick dirty one day and he won't have a leg to stand on. It may take some time, but it will happen. It always does, trust me on this one," said Billy.

As usual, his prediction came true. Three months later, we were driving west on a one-way street. Approaching from the west, a vehicle headed straight for us. We killed our lights and pulled over until he got closer. We did not want to spook him and we needed the mover. Just one more block and we would be able to effortlessly curb him. He fell into the trap and we had him. We could read his lips through the windshield as he swore either at us or at himself for being so stupid.

"Well I'll be a monkey's ass. It's that asshole from the restaurant. Let me use your hanky. I'm about to cry. Why don't you step out and listen to this one. You'll get a big kick out of it," said Billy.

We approached the car and the driver exited. He did not recognize us at first, but when he did, you could see a sign of relief on his face. Boy, was he in for a surprise.

"Officer, my friends, how you are?" he asked.

"May I see your driver's license, sir?" asked Billy.

"Sure, sure, Officer. No problem," said the Greek.

"This is a one way street, and even though you were only going one way, it's the wrong way," said Billy.

"I know, I know, you know Gus in big hurry. I own restaurant on State Street. You know me. Please, you give Gus break, no?"

"Yeah, I know you," said Billy.

"Good, then you give Gus break, no?" the driver repeated.

"No. We come in your restaurant, we have coffee, and we pay. Now you're in our restaurant, and you just had some of our wrong-way on a one-way street special blend. In a minute, I'm going to give you a check and you can pay in court or appear to fight the charge. Now, why don't you go back to your booth, I mean car, and I'll bring you your check," said Billy.

We went back to the car and I could not stand it any longer. I started laughing and Gus could hear me. He was so mad I could not see Billy or myself ever returning to his restaurant for coffee again. Billy gave him his ticket and once again street justice prevailed.

Only ten minutes elapsed, when we observed a big caddy blowing red lights one after another. We pursued and pulled up to the auto at the next red light. Billy signaled the driver to roll down his window.

"Listen, pal, when the light turns green, grab a hunk of that curb and pull over. Better yet, you just blew four lights in a row, so just go through this one and park it," said Billy.

The driver parked and got out of the caddy. He approached us rather quickly.

"Hello, Officer. Look, I realize what I did was improper, but I'm an attorney and on my way to see a client who was just arrested. I want to speak to him before he goes in front of the judge at Night Court."

"So, what's your hurry?" I asked.

"I'm not in any hurry," he answered.

"Maybe if you didn't have lipstick all over your face and a dolly in the car, I'd believe you. But since you do, I think you're full of shit," said Billy.

"You know, Officer, you can't give me a ticket. It's the law."

"I'll show you who can't, just watch me," said Billy.

"It's true. An Officer of the court can't be detained for a misdemeanor traffic violation traveling to and from official court business," said the attorney.

The lawyer returned to his vehicle and Billy looked at me kind of funny. Neither of us was aware of any such law. He wrote the lawyer the ticket and tossed it on his lap.

The attorney grabbed it and crumbled it up right in Billy's face.

"Throw that ticket on the fuckin' street and you're going to jail for littering," said Billy.

"Okay, fellas, if you want to look like fools, just show up in court and I'll prove it to you," said the lawyer.

He chuckled, started the engine, and floored the pedal. His tires squealed in place and stunk up the early morning air.

"Hey, why don't you just beat it and stop showing off for the bitch. The cheap hotel rooms are about three blocks down. Just stay here on LaSalle Street," said Billy from the window of the squad.

The lawyer sped away. We were certain no judge would ever believe such a bullshit story at four in the morning, especially with a broad in the car. Odds are, he would get slapped with a heavy fine come the court date.

Later that morning, we grabbed Chapter 38 to ascertain if such a law existed. We could not believe our eyes. The attorney quoted the law practically verbatim.

"How in the fuck did this even get on the books?" asked Billy.

"The politicians down in Springfield make the laws. Most of them are lawyers," I said.

"How could I have been so dumb? Looks like I'll be eating some shit come court time," said Billy.

"Better bring some Charmin. You might need a napkin," I said.

Billy walked away quite upset, probably because he knew the lawyer would get even about the wise crack concerning his female companion.

With only a couple of hours left on the shift, we hit the streets just to get out of the station. You never hang around because if the boss needs something done, you get stuck with it. We decided to hit the hole and sleep until the tour ended.

We were about to pull into an alley when we noticed another traffic violator. This guy ran reds left and right with our squad in full view. It was not our night. We gave chase and hit his rear view mirror with our spotlight. He pulled over out of the traffic lane. The driver leaped from the car and ran back to us. He nervously mumbled something in Spanish.

"You know what this fucking taco bender is trying to tell us?" said Billy.

"Nope," I said.

He finally gave us a signal that indicated we should proceed to his auto. We obliged and walked up to the rear of the car. I peeked inside the backseat area. There lay his wife on her back with what appeared to be a basketball stuffed under her dress. She screamed from the severe labor pains.

"Holy shit, Billy, she's having a baby," I said.

"Naw, she ain't havin' any kid," said Billy.

"Naw my ass," I said.

I stepped in front of Billy to get a closer look at my soon to be patient.

"Okay, partner, you handle this. You're not out of school that long and I know they taught you this shit," said Billy.

"But Billy, all they showed us was a fucking movie and most of us slept through the damn thing anyway."

"Well then, just fake it and let Juanita do the rest. You can handle it, kid."

I could not believe he just called the woman Juanita

The pain persisted, and in just seconds, it intensified. I took a towel off the front seat and wiped her forehead. She grabbed my hand and smiled. It appeared I was her only hope and she knew it. I panicked. I did not want her to know my wisdom in this area was somewhat limited.

The pains started once more and she lifted both legs in a spread eagle position. One locked on the rear of the front seat and the other lay on the top of the backseat. This position seemed to give her some comfort, but not for long. She looked like the wishbone of a turkey.

This was it. I rolled up my sleeves, ready for the birth. I instructed the husband to get into the squad. Billy stood to my rear and peeked over my shoulder. He would be my coach in the delivery.

"OYE! OYE!"

She began to scream very loud and right in my face.

"What the hell does 'OYE' mean?" I asked Billy.

"Shut up, stupid, it's Spanish for 'OW.' Now prepare yourself, doctor," said Billy.

I knelt between her thighs and put my hands out. All of a sudden, a gush of fluid hit my face. Evidently, this must have been the part of the training movie I slept through or my head would not have been so close to her pelvic area.

"Sit tight, partner. Don't give up. I got some totes and a rain cap in the trunk of the squad. I'll get them for you," said Billy.

"Very funny, asshole. Oh shit, here it comes," I said.

I hoped what was about to emerge from her body resembled the kid's head and not the feet. Who knows what could happen if the birth ended up breach. The top portion of the kid's skull popped out. The image was beautiful. But, my problems were not over yet.

It appeared she stopped doing whatever it took to get the kid born into the world. Both of us were confused and bewildered. What should I do? I couldn't count on Ben Casey standing behind me for help. He was useless. For some reason, I became angry.

"Come on, lady. Don't stop now, just a few more pushes and the kid will be out. You can do it," I yelled at the top of my voice.

The perspiration rolled down my brow into my eye sockets. It burned and my sight blurred. Suddenly, with one last push, the kid lay in my hands. His body covered with all sorts of weird liquid, I became somewhat standoffish. The child lacked his birth cry and I hesitated to clutch his feet. He was so slippery and I was so nervous. Billy just stood behind me and watched. Three seconds went by, which felt like ten minutes. Suddenly, he screamed. I set him on his mother's stomach and backed out.

"I heard when you were born, the fucking doctor slapped your mother instead of you," said Billy, snickering.

"It's always a pleasure to work with a good cop, especially when he thinks he's a comedian," I said.

With that comment, we all took off for the hospital. It really felt good inside to help this woman. The whole experience was gratifying and we were actually proud of ourselves.At the end of the tour, I asked Billy why the lack of participation on his part during the delivery.

"Hey, partner, I was your back up," he said.

"Back up shit. I didn't need a back up, I needed an assistant," I answered.

"Oh yeah, smart ass, what if there were two beaners instead of one? Then what would you do? That's right, looked for a back up, and it would've been me."

"Let's go home, Bill, I'm flat out exhausted," I said.

The parents named the child Ricardo.

We were rolling again on the next shift. They came around so fast when you were on midnights. It seemed there was not even enough time to sleep. Billy and I left the station and began the tour.

"Man, I'm fucking horny tonight. Let's hassle a couple of whores for a blow job," said Billy.

"Naw, partner, I'll take a pass on that one."

"Come on, partner, it wouldn't feel right leaving you out in the cold while I got some skull."

"Boy, what a partner, I wouldn't know what to do without you watching over me," I said.

Hours passed and we could not find a prostitute anywhere. Just then, we turned the corner, and to our surprise, a lone female waved us down. In police jargon, she is classified as a hand-waver.

Billy glanced at her and said, "Hey, look at this bitch and she ain't no whore. Now let me handle this, 10-4?"

"In other words, you want me to keep my mouth shut and observe the master at work?" I asked.

We pulled up to get a closer look at the hand-waver. Not bad. A female, white, about twenty-four years old, brown hair, fairly attractive, and a set of thighs that traveled all the way up to her neck. Billy rolled down the window and asked if she needed any assistance.

"I sure do, fellas. I got about six hours to kill before my Greyhound leaves the city. You guys need another partner?" she asked.

"Absolutely. The one I got doesn't have legs anywhere near as pretty as yours. What's your name?" asked Billy with an enormous sense of anticipation.

"It's Paula. Some guys call me 'Pax-Phone Paula.'"

The Pax-Phone is an inter-departmental communication system only used by the police and personnel with security clearance. Evidently, that is where she got her nickname.

With that remark, Billy almost swallowed his cigarette. He knew something I did not. I expected to be left standing in the cold that night while Billy took care of business. We drove around for some time and finally stopped for coffee. Billy instructed Paula that if an inspector approached, she was to tell him some pervert assaulted her and we were combing the area for the bad guy. The only pervert in the area was Billy. She agreed on the excuse for her presence and excused herself to the ladies' room.

"Do you know who this cunt is?" asked Billy.

"Partner, I haven't the foggiest idea."

"That's PAX-PHONE PAULA. She's a cop freak and all she ever does is fuck and suck policemen. I heard she did the entire 020th District, from the captain right on down. She's probably looking for some dick right now. Did you notice certain things she said could've been taken more ways than one?"

"Yeah, some remarks did seem a bit weird," I said.

"Well, enough of this nice guy shit. It's time to get down to the business at hand," said Billy.

We were in the squad again, when Billy pointed to his crotch and held his side. A look of pain appeared on his face. By now, I knew Billy and his charade language. The signal technique was his way of telling me to say I needed to take a piss, even though we just left the restaurant. He cleared his throat and gave me a nod.

"Hey, Billy, can you find an out of the way spot? I gotta take a piss," I said.

In two minutes, we were in the railroad yards, out of the public's view and looking for a place to take a leak. I left the vehicle and walked from the squad. It was very cold and dark, and to make matters worse, I forgot my gloves in the station locker. I shoved both hands into my pockets and hoped Billy was as horny as he said.

I approached an underpass, when I decided to give Billy just five more minutes to change his oil before I returned.

His time elapsed and I started back to the squad. Lying in front of me, unnoticed, was a two-foot pile of frozen asphalt. Some idiot railroad employee had failed to clean up his mess. I stumbled on its base and fell. I managed to get both hands out of my pockets before I hit the ground and they somewhat broke my momentum. I slid down the frozen asphalt, hands first. Slivers of the substance were embedded in my palms. It was very painful and bloody. I sprinted to the car for help when I heard Billy yell.

"Aw, you dumb bitch, what's the matter, are you sick?" asked Billy.

"I couldn't help it. I gagged. Have ya been storing that shit up for a rainy day?" she asked.

Billy sat in the squad with puke all over his lap.

"The bitch puked all over ya. You smell like shit," I said.

"Give me your fuckin' hanky," said Billy.

"I can't. It's covered with blood."

"What the fuck happened to you?" asked Billy.

"Get me to County," I said.

"Fuck the hospital. I gotta get this puke off of me," said Billy.

"Look, Billy, I'm sorry," said Paula.

"That's okay, babe. Here's some cab fare. Can we do this again?" asked Billy.

"No problem. I'll be looking for you guys. Take care," said Paula.

Paula left the squad to look for a cab or maybe another police car. After all, the night was young and I am sure her hormones went unsatisfied.

"I don't believe she did this to you," I said.

"You better shut your mouth on this one," said Billy.

"If you think I'm not gonna tell the guys, you're fuckin' crazy," I said.

"So what happened to you?" asked Billy.

"I tripped and fell, that's it," I said.

"You're bleeding all over the place. Did you fall off a bridge?" asked Billy.

"Will you please get me to the hospital?" I asked.

"Okay, partner, we're on the way. Boy, what a night. We're gonna have to cover up this one. We can't tell the sergeant I was getting a blowjob and you tripped while waiting for me to get off. Let me handle this," said Billy.

Billy picked up the transmitter and, with a smirk on his face, told the Communications Center we were going to check out two suspicious suspects at Madison Street and Clinton. The operator gave us a 10-4. Billy paused and put his finger to his mouth as if to say, "Shhhh." He let thirty seconds elapse and, once again, spoke into the microphone.

"Beat #102, Beat #102 emergency."

"Go ahead Beat #102, what's your situation?" asked the C.C. Room.

"Yeah, squad, my surefooted partner slipped on a patch of ice and cut his hand pretty bad. I'm gonna have to rush him over to County before he bleeds all over me."

"10-4, beat #102, I'll send a supervisor there shortly," said the operator.

Billy turned, gave me a huge smile, and laughed.

"And that's how it's done," he said.

We drove directly to the hospital. The doctor removed each sliver of asphalt from my palms while Billy hit on the nurse. The pain intensified with each pluck until all were removed. After the treatment ended, my hands did not feel as bad as they looked, so Billy and I returned to our duties.

"So, let's sum up the night, partner," I said.

"What do ya mean, buddy?" asked Billy.

"Well, you got your dick sucked, puked on, lied to the sergeant, and conned a nurse out of her phone number. I ended up cold, tired, cut, bleeding, and scarred for life. Something is just not right here."

"Ah, forgetta 'bout it. It's just another day of vaudeville," said Billy.

The funny thing about his remark was he was right.

The next evening, tragedy struck the city. There had been a mass murder of student nurses with very few clues left behind.

Only one witness surfaced. The dicks had a composite of the suspect, but a murder such as this is very difficult to solve. The offender had no motive and no ties to any of the victims. It was a crime of sex ending with murder.

One of the biggest manhunts in Chicago's history began to apprehend the killer. His composite could be seen on every TV station and in all the papers. After two days, he was still at large. Billy and I were both off those two particular days and returned to work on the afternoon shift. The tour started off like any other.

"Partner, we're going to catch this perverted prick and get promoted," said Billy.

"What do ya think, he's going to jump into the backseat of our car because he likes our looks?" I asked.

"No, really. I'm dead serious. We're gonna catch him. This guy is probably the transient type, and if he needs a flop, he'll be in the skid row area. I'll bet my shorts on it."

"I hope to God they're not the ones the bitch puked all over," I said, laughing.

"There are only about eight flop hotels to check. Hopefully, we'll spook out this guy if we start to get too close," said Billy.

It sounded like a long shot to me, but Billy being the senior man on the car, we put the idea into action. During the course of the tour, we eliminated five flops and their newly registered guests. I could not believe how easy it was to locate these people. If they were not in their room, we went to the bar and yelled out their name. Of course, no one responded until we asked who dropped a pint of Ripple while waving it in the air. Each individual staggered up to claim his prize. All suspects were checked out and released. We had no luck that day.

After the shift, we gathered at the watering hole for beers. Billy ran down his plan to the guys and all had a big laugh.

"You won't be laughing when we catch this prick and the Mayor puts stripes on our arms," said Billy.

"Hey, Billy, you might be right. I know you don't have any clout and we all know how legit the sergeant's exam is. That's probably the only way you two can get made. Go for it, man," said one of the guys.

Billy proceeded to order another round for the boys when he noticed the pile of money in front of him had decreased in size. He had yelled at the bartender.

"Hey, Nick, did you change your religion from Catholic to Jew or are you gonna buy the boys a fuckin' cocktail?" asked Billy.

Nick laughed and poured everyone a freebie. Just about all of us left drunk that night, but made it home without incident.

The next day, I woke up with a hangover and clicked on the TV. The killer had been caught, recognized by a doctor at County Hospital while being treated for a self-inflicted injury. He arrived at the hospital via paddy wagon from the Moon Hotel, one of the three establishments that remained to be checked on our next tour. This guy could not wait one more day before trying to take his own life. I know we could have pinched him that night. I felt it in my bones. There went our stripes out the window and Richard Speck went behind bars.

When I showed up for work that night, Billy strutted around the station with his head in the clouds. He knew we would have grabbed this guy, but it was not meant to be.

"You guys thought I was blowing hot air last night, huh?" asked Billy.

"Aw, you just had a lucky hunch, don't get so cocky," said one of the deskmen.

For some reason, I knew Billy's hunch was not luck. It is a skill one develops over the years from street experiences, good common sense, and logic. You have to think it out the way Billy did. Many officers have it, but they do not take the time to let it blossom. I was determined not to let this sixth sense slip away. In the years to come, I found it, never let it go, and was one of the best at it. The combination of street savvy, basic logic, and common sense makes for one hell of a cop.

We were on patrol that night and the shift ran smoothly. A few drunken disorderly arrests, a theft victim, and a couple of movers (traffic tickets) made up our activity thus far. Funny thing about movers, you could apprehend a rapist and the brass could care less, but bring in three movers a day and you could have anything you asked for in the district. The hierarchy would never admit a quota existed for tickets, nor could you ever find it in writing, but believe me, it's bona fide. We only had two more hours to go and we could call it a night.

Billy looked at some guy walking down the street that rubbed him the wrong way.

"Hey, partner, let's check this asshole out. He just doesn't fit in the area," said Billy.

We pulled to the curb and requested the suspect to come over to the squad car.

"Why don't you two dickheads go find a toilet and fall in," he said.

"Hey, jagoff, do you know who the hell we are?" I asked.

"Yeah, a couple of pig motherfuckers," he said.

Obviously, he was not from Chicago with his strong southern accent. Billy exited, stick in hand, and I thought the hick could look forward to a beating. He called us every name in the book. Just then, Johnnie and Tony pulled up and they could see Billy's body language indicating his anger.

"What do ya got, Billy?" asked Johnnie

"This guy is new on the street and wants to take a ride to the gym," said Billy.

"We'll meet you there in a minute," said Tony.

I had no idea what the "gym" meant. This was the first time I heard Billy even mention the word.

"Get in the car, Jethro, we're gonna take ya for a ride," said Billy.

"Okay, asshole, drive on," said the hick.

"I'm gonna give you an asshole in about five minutes," said Billy, chuckling.

We drove to the railroad yards and parked the car. I thought of Paula and my bruised hands. All exited and walked through a closed loading dock area when the hick started to mouth off again.

"Man, you Yankee assholes got some shit looking jails up here. Can't you afford anything better?" asked the hillbilly.

We kept walking a distance from the squad car and all I could think of was this poor guy had the idea he was going to jail. He was in for a real surprise. Billy had this shit-eating grin on his face as we approached a right angle turn at the end of the dock area. I felt a tug on my shirt and slowed my pace. This allowed the hick to pass me. We started to make the turn and Jethro started to "motherfuck" us again, when "POW." Jethro got whacked and lay flat on this back. He was knocked unconscious.

This was the first time Billy displayed real anger and pure meanness. It took a lot to get him hot, but when you did, he was vicious. It dawned on me Billy was human like everyone else and also had emotions like the rest of us. We were supposed to restrain these emotions better than Joe Q. Citizen, but what society must realize is we are not robots. We have feelings and sometimes it is impossible to control them if, for example, an officer is going through a bitter divorce or just lost a loved one. This poor guy came in contact with Billy at the wrong time and he caught a beating. Maybe Billy fought with his girl that night or he had some unexpected financial problems. Who knows? We left the hick lying on the cobblestone street of the railroad yard.

We were back on patrol with thirty minutes to check off.

"Hey, Billy, you don't think ya really hurt that guy?" I asked.

"Fuck no; I hit him in the head. One of the hardest objects on this earth is a hillbilly's head. You've heard the saying, 'if ya want to kill a hillbilly, shoot him anywhere but in the head?' We'll see that jagoff on the street again, guaranteed."

"Speaking of the devil, ain't that Jethro standing on the corner?" I asked.

"It sure is. Watch his attitude adjustment, partner. He'll be a new man," said Billy.

We pulled up to the curb and called Jethro over to the car. He looked at us and spoke extremely courteous.

"Hey, buddy, where ya from?" asked Billy.

"Just got in from Nashville, Tennessee," he said.

"Well, I want to let ya know we ain't putting up with no fucking jack rolling on the street. Got it?" asked Billy.

He stared at Billy and said, "Yes, sir, I understand everythin' you is saying. You police boys up here don't fuck around. I'm not here to cause no trouble."

Billy laughed.

"We sure straightened that hillbilly out. He's talking like a fucking Boy Scout," said Billy.

"I don't think he was our man, partner. He was just too nice of a guy," I said.

"You can kiss my ass, you know that was him. Now let's go home. I'm beat."

"10-4, partner." I said.

Whatever caused Billy to erupt seemed to have vanished. Too bad police psychologists could not predict street justice in their diagnosis. If this were possible, the city would probably excuse the officer with pay like any other sick day. It would save a whole lot of CR numbers (numbers issued by the IAD when a complaint has been initiated against a police officer for brutality). The problem with this scenario is that there are hundreds of officers stressed out who would correspond with the imaginary psychologist's projection. The city would always be shorthanded as far as manpower needs.

The next day, we were on the wagon together because the two regular men were involved in a minor fender bender on the way to work. They both suffered unexplained back injuries.

"Ah shit, I hope they don't keep us on the wagon for a long time," I said to Billy.

"You never know. The brother of one of those coppers is an attorney and you know he'll tell them to lie down for at least a month, or the case won't be worth shit. Them fucking attorneys can squeeze blood from a scab on your arm," said Billy.

The night went by normal as far as wagon work is concerned. Basically, all we did was transport other prisoners for the guys. Our assignments were crimeless.

Just then, we got a call to proceed to the Concord Hotel. We were to see the desk clerk about a strange odor. We could not believe it, just three hours to go and we drew a stinker.

"Maybe it's a gas leak," I said.

"You asshole, if it's a gas leak, they'd call the gas company. Pull over at Tom's bar. We gotta buy some bad smelling cigars," said Billy.

I had not yet experienced the true smell of a stinker, but if it's worse than a bad smelling cigar, one can only imagine.

The Concord was a skuzzy flop with rooms that measured six by six. Each contained a footlocker, a ceiling constructed out of chicken wire, four unpainted walls, and a backbreaking bed. There were two hundred rooms on each floor and seven floors to the building. The smell of live people in these confined quarters, let alone dead ones, left something to be desired.

Each floor only had one bathroom, which was in such dire need of repair that you could grasp the stench in the air. I could not believe the city health inspectors would allow this to exist. The owners must have dropped some big dough at city hall.

We cautiously entered the lobby and tried not to step on the non-registered guest lying on the floor. Some of them appeared to be dead themselves.

"What's up, Willie?" asked Billy.

"Bad news, Officer, stinker up on the fourth floor," said the clerk.

Billy asked how many days Willie figured the body was dead. The desk clerk estimated six.

"Ah, fuck. I don't believe this is happening to me," said Billy as he looked to the heavens.

"It can't be that bad, partner. Why don't we just go up and take a peek?" I said.

"Okay, smartass, you go up with Willie and come back down and tell me what we need," said Billy.

"No problem. Let's go, Willie," I said.

Willie and I got in the elevator and proceeded to the fourth floor. He asked if I ever handled a stinker before. I told him no. Willie reached into his shirt pocket and gave me two cigarettes with instructions to put one in each nostril. He told me to take deep breaths only through my nose, and under no circumstances take in any air by mouth. This guy scared the shit out of me.

"Is the creature from the Black Lagoon up there?" I asked.

Willie smiled and told me not to discount his advice.

The elevator door slowly opened and the unpleasant odor

punched us in the face. Goosebumps swallowed up both my arms. I looked at Willie and reached into my pocket to retrieve the two Lucky Strike cigarettes. I jammed them in my nose. He would not go any further, but instructed me how to find the body. At 150 feet from the corpse, the odor overwhelmed me. What lurked at the end of the hall?

I walked closer to the room and the odor intensified. I sucked air through my nostrils as fast as I could. The cigarette trick sufficed, but how long would it last? I pushed open the door, glanced down at the body, and froze in my tracks. There he lay. Each eye socket contained a rat competing for dinner with the maggots. Other bugs blanketed his entire body.

I gagged and both cigarettes blasted from my nose. I felt like a diver who just lost his air tanks at fifty feet. I panicked and forgot Willie's instructions. I took in a gulp of air through my mouth as I turned away from the body. There is only one description of the sensation that passed through the rear of my mouth. Imagine someone sticking his fist down your throat and grabbing the base of your tongue. Instant vomit resulted from only one breath. I hurled all over the body and ran for the elevator. My vomit caused the bugs to scatter to adjoining rooms, but they soon returned and continued their feast. I finally arrived at the elevator and went downstairs. Billy and Willie were waiting and laughing out loud at the sight of me. The odor imbedded itself in my uniform.

"Is he bad, partner?" asked Billy.

"Bad, that motherfucker is from a Frankenstein movie," I said.

Billy looked at me and asked for five dollars. Was he going to send the dead guy some flowers? I came on this job to make money, not to give it away. I complied. He handed the cash to Willie for the purchase of a can of Raid. Billy and I went outside for some fresh air and to retrieve the body bag from the wagon.

"Billy, do we gotta touch that creepy looking bastard?" I asked.

"You think I'm gonna touch him, partner?" asked Billy.

"Well, he won't walk into the body bag by himself. I learned that at the Academy."

"I'm the senior man on the car. Will ya just let me handle this? Can I have five more bucks, buddy?" asked Billy.

"Hey, cocksucker, does it say First National Bank on my back?" I asked.

"Either come up with five more bucks or we'll have to pick that prick up and stuff him in the bag ourselves," said Billy.

Immediately, I reached in my pockets and handed Billy five singles.

"Now, all we've gotta do is find three wine-heads who look thirsty enough to kill their own mother for a drink. Oh, here comes candidate number one right now. Hey, Pops, are you thirsty?" asked Billy.

"Sure, Officer. Could you spare some change for a drink?" asked the bum.

"I'll do better than that, old-timer. We'll give you a half-pint and a pack of smokes," I said. (Police get free smokes; at least I don't have to pay for those.)

"I don't know, Officer. Who do I have to kill?" asked the bum.

"Oh, it's nothing like that. We got a stinker upstairs and we'd like you and two of your associates to stuff the prick in a body bag," said Billy.

"That's all I gotta do?" asked the bum.

"That's it, Pops," said Billy.

I asked Billy if we should tell the bum about the odor. It would be obvious the minute he reached the floor where the body lay. The hobo overheard my comment.

"Don't worry, kid. I've slept in boxcars next to assholes all over the country. Some of them hadn't showered in months. You guys wait here and I'll get two buddies. The deal goes for them, too, doesn't it?" asked the bum.

Before long, we had our strike force and were ready to attack. Billy instructed me to handle the rear and he would go in with the troops. He told the bums of the forceful odor and how they must work fast. We gave them the Raid with instructions to spray the body before stuffing it into the bag. Each bum had an assignment. Two were assigned the head and feet for placement into the bag, the third had to seal the bag. The agreement was if they brought the body out of the room with the bag unzipped, all bets were off. Pops tried to get some cash up front from Billy and that pissed him off.

"Go fuck yourself. Just think of that wine trickling down your throat when the job is complete," said Billy.

We approached the door all of a sudden; the smell attacked and knocked out our bagman. The vomit gushed from his mouth and nose. He started his retreat. We yelled words of support at the two remaining troops in the trenches, from a safe distance, of course.

The offensive began with the Raid. The maggots and roaches again leaped off the body and entered adjoining rooms from under the inadequate baseboards. This caused a stampede down the hall of other residents from the floor. The bums lifted the body and dropped it in the bag. The first battle was over.

The war stormed on, and another casualty succumbed to the stench. We lost him to the dry heaves. Billy yelled.

"Get out of Pops's way, you pussy motherfucker. Let him finish the job. You got it in the bag, Pops, just zip it up."

Pops slithered from the room with his stomach still intact. The body was in the bag, but it remained unzipped. I refreshed Pops's memory of the deal and told him to return to the battlefield.

"Fuck your deal, man. That motherfucker stinks," he said.

"We'll give you all the money, Pops, just go back and finish the job. Fuck your friends. They left you in there to die. Just think, Pops, you could buy a whole fifth of CC and still have some cash for butts. Just zip it and we'll drag him out. The cash will be all yours," said Billy.

Pops ran in, zipped up the bag, and ran out with his hand open. Billy placed the money in his palm as he scrambled for some clean air. Billy seemed relieved. He probably realized I was not going in there to zip up that damn bag. He knew the job would have been his. We grabbed the bag and dragged it down the hall towards the elevator. We passed many rooms and the remaining occupants opened their doors to inquire about the commotion that disturbed their hangover.

"Hey, Officer, who checked out?" asked one of the residents.

"Never mind, just get back in your room, it's none of your business," I said.

"I knew that fucking guy was dead two days ago. I could smell him," he said.

"So, why didn't you call the police then, you dumb ass-hole? He wouldn't have smelled this bad two days ago," said Billy.

"He sure did," said the bum.

The stench still prevailed in the air. It seeped its way right through the thick rubber body bag. My only thought was get this guy to the morgue so we could disinfect the bag. It felt as if the maggots were crawling all over me.

"I sure hope Igor works today or we'll have to remove this prick from the bag ourselves," said Billy.

"I told you, partner, not me. Here, take all my fuckin' money. You're gonna ask for it anyway at the morgue," I said.

Billy refused to take the money.

We arrived at the morgue and parked right next to the loading dock. It felt as if we were delivering a slab of beef or something. A second smell attacked us as Igor appeared. He had the odor of the morgue embedded in his clothing.

"What's up, Igor? How ya doing today?" asked Billy.

"Oh, just fine," he said.

"Is the going rate still three bucks or what?" asked Billy.

"Naw, Billy, it's up to five for a good stinker, and by the looks of your partner's face, I can tell you guys got a pretty bad one in the wagon."

"Okay, buddy, here's the five bucks. He's all yours," I said.

Igor pulled a hose from the loading dock, entered the wagon, and slightly unzipped the bag. He inserted the noz-zle in the opening. The bag flooded and all the debris inside rushed out the wagon door and down the sewer. He grabbed the body and yanked it out of its temporary coffin. This poor guy resembled a wet washcloth. Igor stripped the victim and turned over the clothing. Each piece had to be inventoried.

We left the morgue for the station. On the way, we stopped at the hotel and I sealed off the room in case the incident turned out to be a homicide. I told Billy the room was already picked to pieces by the vultures that lived on the floor. He suggested we should have called a car to sit and guard the premises prior to our departure for the morgue. This would be something to remember for similar incidents in the future. Always secure a potential crime scene.

I arrived home that night and left all my clothes in the garage. The stench remained quite detectable. The next morning, while at the dry cleaners, I told the clerk the source of the odor. She immediately turned her head away. She did not want to touch the clothing and acted quite upset. I told her to be careful when she went through the pockets for anything that crawled. The clerk looked at me and mumbled something about me being crazy. I just laughed.

Time was really flying now. Two years under my belt and I finally had a regular partner. Fantastic! Despite the age difference, we worked well together. Honestly, Billy taught me almost everything I know to date about police beat work. During the months to come, we picked up a third man on the car and he was as sharp as Billy. Not only did we share our police work, the happy times, and sad times, but we also shared something else very important on the job. We were comrades in the brotherhood of police officers, a very special bonding. The job does have its drawbacks, primarily stress, but we stressed out as a team. We all possessed a must quality concerning stress-related employment. A police officer must strive to leave his job at work and never take it home with him. The stress will destroy you and your family. This fact is so important to survive the police jungle. Exceptionally high divorce rates of police prove my point.

Perched in the watering hole, I pondered the thought of becoming an alcoholic at the young age of twenty-two. It frightened me. Excepting the day shift, I could not remember a night when I did not observe an officer drinking on duty or arriving at work a little tipsy. Most of the men could handle it well and cover it up, but for some, the masquerade was difficult.

One midnight, Ray came to work so drunk he could hardly stand up. John, his partner, always covered for him and allowed him to sleep it off in the squad. To get past roll call was not a problem. Half the time the cherry nose bosses were tipsy themselves. But on this particular nigh, Ray was in his John Wayne syndrome and did not feel like sleeping off the drunk.

About 2:30 in the morning, they got a job of burglary in progress and Billy and I took the back up. We arrived at the same time, and before we entered the premises, Billy told Mr. Johnny Walker and Soda to stay put in the car. John and I took the front and Billy covered the rear. It seemed routine, until we located an open window. I ran to the car and told Ray to call for more help. I should have known better; Ray could not find the radio, much less operate it. I assumed he made the call and the rest of us entered the building. Ray stumbled out of the squad and somehow located the rear entrance of the premises. The door ajar, Ray entered.

Suddenly, a figure dashed across the room and Billy ordered him to halt. The offender took a shot at us while in full stride. John was the first to return fire and I know he hit the punk in the head because I saw it whip back as if he got clotheslined. The body fell forward and managed to wedge itself between a desk and a filing cabinet. This kept the bad guy upright. The gun still in his grasp, we started to fire. This guy would not go down. In a matter of seconds, our weapons were empty.

We looked at his lifeless body and realized the desk and filing cabinet supported his stance and that is why our friend lingered in a vertical position. Ray suddenly appeared.

"Did we get the asshole or what?" asked Ray.

"Yeah, we sure did," said Johnny.

Ray staggered over to the body to examine it. He gave the suspect a swift kick to the head to reassure he was dead and then asked if we could go for a drink. His partner declined and informed him they had about six hours of paperwork ahead and he wanted him semi-sober. Johnny knew the brass and nosy reporters would arrive soon as we called in the kill. I went for coffee and Billy notified homicide. The kill appeared justified.

The first to arrive were the vultures from the IAD. They licked their chops as they tried to determine who they would screw on this one to put a feather in their cap. They threw questions at us left and right, but we were too slick for them. We simply told the truth. All went well until Ray opened his mouth. We had to back him up or they would have nabbed him for filing a false report. Thank God he told only a few white lies.

This drunken copper told the guys from downtown that when the offender turned to fire, he pushed him. This caused the offender's shot to stray. All returned fire and killed him. The problem with this statement, Ray still had all six bullets in his weapon.

In five seconds, this drunk made himself a hero and saved our lives, and an hour ago, he was drunk at the rear of the building. We backed up his story, sort of a code among good cops. Bottom line, the burglar attempted to kill us first. Self-defense prevailed.

It appeared we were in the clear until Napoleon from the 11th floor attempted to play super sleuth.

He wanted to know why so many bullet holes were in the body. Billy told him we kept shooting because the burglar would not go down. The eleven wounds in the body still concerned the investigator. He thought the bullet hole in the forehead represented the last shot to finish him off. This would mean we murdered the guy in cold blood.

Just then, John approached the investigator.

"Over here, Dick Tracy, I'm going to teach you something about investigation."

I wondered what John had up his sleeve. I took note because something was about to be learned. They walked over to the body.

"Why don't you unbutton his shirt and take a look at the holes in his chest and compare their size to the hole in his forehead," said John.

"So what the hell is that supposed to mean?" asked the IAD detective.

"Aren't the holes all about the same size? So, if we were gonna kill him with a last shot to the forehead, do ya think we'd do it from the same spot where we first fired, or walk up to the body, put the gun close to his forehead, and pull the trigger?"

"Logically, the thing to do would be to walk up to the body to make sure you don't miss," said the investigator.

"Very good, so have the lab check for powder burns on his forehead and maybe you'll get the answer. Case closed," said John.

The IAD investigator shook his head and walked away.

We headed back to the station to complete the necessary forms and Ray ran out the back door to make sure no one stole his bar stool at the watering hole. This was the first time I had shot at a human being, let alone killed one. It baffled me why I remained so calm. Probably the fact that the bad guy shot first put my nerves at easy. I went home that night, got into bed, and slept like a baby. I am sure Ray did, too, if he made it home at all.The next day started no different than any other, something serious, something sad and funny at the same time, and something crazy. A car with out of state plates blew a red light right in front of Billy and me. It seemed to be a normal traffic stop, but no such luck.

The two females in the car would not pull over and began to run. We tried everything, lights, siren, hand signals, and even a few choice words out the window. Finally, we cut them off and curbed them. We approached the vehicle.

"Get out of the car, lady," I yelled.

She looked at me and raised her middle finger.

"I'm gonna kill this little cunt," I said.

"Take it easy, you used the wrong approach. Let a pro show you how to handle these broads. Okay, sweetie, roll down your window and show me your driver's license," said Billy.

"Take a flying fuck, asshole," she shouted.

"Hey, lady, we're police officers. Open up this goddamn door right now," said Billy.

"How do we know you're police officers? I demand to see your ID right this minute," said the driver.

"Hey lady, ID this," said Billy.

He grasped his crotch.

"We're in full uniform and this is a marked police car, so open the fucking door," I said.

"Fat chance, asshole," she said.

I could not help but chuckle a bit, even though the woman aggravated the shit out of me. She left us no choice but to order a tow truck.

"I'll get a tow truck and fix this bitch real quick," snapped Billy.

"Don't worry, Samantha, I know they're bluffing," said the driver to her companion.

Furious, Billy snatched the microphone from the dash holder. "Squad, I need a tow truck at Canal and Lake Street, code #1."

"What do ya got, Beat #102?" asked the zone operator.

Billy mumbled his words because he did not want to tell the C.C. Room and others listening that we had two bimbos who refused to let us in their car. He thought a second.

"Ah, squad, we have a vehicle that is a hazard and it's blocking an intersection. It's also blocking a bus route, has no lights, and is facing the wrong way on a one way street."

An unknown voice yelled on the radio, "Who the fuck is driving that car, Ma Barker?"

The C.C. operator copied the info and dispatched our tow. We were going to tow the car with both broads inside.

"Okay, lady, the truck is on the way. Now are you gonna open the door?" asked Billy.

"Now are you going to open the door," she mocked. "I told you to fuck off. I don't believe you guys are cops."

The truck arrived and Billy explained the situation, but the driver couldn't care less. He hooked the car; all were on the way to the lock-up.

Billy and I pulled up in front of the district. The tow truck driver arrived and wanted to know where to dump the load. Billy attempted to communicate to the two dumbbells one more time.

"Miss, will you please open the door? We're right in front of a police station," he said.

The driver glanced around and finally complied. They exited the car and we went into the station. We wrote Mary a ton of tickets, but she charmed us into not towing her car to the pound. Both seemed to be good people, and after we talked, they apologized for the insults. The four of us met after work for a drink and Billy introduced them to the guys. I told the story and we all had a big laugh. In the future, Mary would appear in court and the tickets would be dismissed due to the unusual circumstances of the stop. Billy ended up with her phone number.

The next night, I was off and decided to take my girl to a basketball game at one of the local high schools. We ran a little late, so I parked a few blocks from the entrance of the gym. We walked and I could see people in the distance approaching. Once closer, I realized they were three drunken teenagers.

A strange feeling about the situation overwhelmed me. I took my weapon out of its holster and put it in my coat pocket. My girl suggested my reaction bordered craziness, but it is an instinct one develops on the police force.

"Don't tell me how to do my job, and I won't tell you how to take shorthand, agreed?" I asked.

We passed the group and one of the teens intentionally bumped me. We did not stop.

"Hey, jagoff, why the fuck don't ya watch where you're going?" he yelled.

He spit a honker in our direction. I stopped and debated what action to take. My girl begged me to continue on because there were three of them.

"Three of them, I don't care. There are seven of us," I said patting my coat pocket.

"Did you say something to me, you punk motherfucker?" I snapped back.

"How would ya like us to beat your ass right here in front of your bitch?" asked one teen.

Not a car or person in sight, I reached into my pocket and pulled out my weapon. I fired three shots into the ground. But what they did not know was that, even with a weapon, I was afraid. Did they have a weapon? Could they overpower me and take my weapon? These thoughts go through a policeman's mind in a nanosecond when the use of deadly force is concerned.

"There's still three left, punk, one each," I said.

"Fuck this crazy motherfucker, let's get outta here," said one of the teens.

I grabbed my girlfriend's hand and we ran back to my vehicle. Curiously, she wanted to know why we fled because righteousness appeared to be on our side. I told her even though we were right, the guys on the 11th floor would still scrutinize my actions.

"Your word wouldn't hold much weight in an investigation. You're my girlfriend," I said

Silence accompanied us during the ride home. She seemed quite upset and something told me it was not the incident. Her impression of me began to change. She did not like my mobster attitude. Maybe a change did occur; after all, three people were merely walking towards us, and the first thing that came to mind was to be on guard. My personality was changing and I believed the process irreversible. Back to work.

On patrol again, Billy and I gabbed over a cup of coffee when we heard a call of a domestic disturbance at 400 N. Michigan Ave. We decided to give the car a backup because we were curious as to the nature of the beef. The address indicated an upper class building and we wanted to see if the rich beat their wives the same as the poor.

We pulled up to the high-rise with two other cars in front of us, thus, a total of six officers at the scene. This amount of men should have been sufficient to handle a domestic disturbance.

A knock on the door. "Police, open up," I said.

"Don't open that door, bitch," came a voice from inside.

We heard a "fuck you" as the locks turned and the heavy oak door swung open. There stood a black woman, nicely dressed, with a blood-stained fat lip. To her rear hid the husband, a big man, forty years old, and sophisticatedly attired.

"I want this crazy motherfucker locked up," she snapped.

We looked at her and calmly inquired if her husband assaulted her.

"No, I always bleed from the motherfuckin' lip like this," she yelled.

"Miss, will you sign a complaint against this man for battery?" I asked.

At this time, no such charge as domestic violence existed; this was a simple battery.

"Yes, Officer, I will," she said.

"Okay, buddy, let's go. You're under arrest," said Billy.

"Just one minute, Officer, let me explain. I'm a doctor and I'm on call. May I notify the hospital, please?" asked the husband.

"Sure, Doc, be my guest," said Billy.

While the doctor notified the hospital, his wife, who happened to be a nurse, signed a complaint against him for battery. Two policemen started to put the cuffs on the prisoner when this crazy lady jumped on the back of one officer and started to beat him.

"Let my husband go, you no good bastard," she said.

The officer reacted and punched the woman in her already swollen lip.

"Now both of you assholes are under arrest," he said.

I thought it strange we had so many problems and were treated so poorly by such highly educated people. All concerned arrived in the station, and to my amazement, processing went smoothly.

Two weeks later, I received a call to go into the station. The captain informed me two F.B.I. agents were in the back and they wanted to speak to me. Quite impressive, the F.B.I. wanted to talk to me. Would they be like those guys on TV? No such luck. They were two rednecks, slick and square at the same time. They waited in the back room, clothed in their polyester walking suits and black patent leather shoes. Not a great combination for what seemed to be the norm of our stylish F.B.I. agents at that time.

They informed me of their business. It concerned a criminal investigation, but I was not required to speak to them. The captain was also briefed. I decided to waive Miranda and at least listen to what they would say.

They explained a complaint had been filed from a Mr. and Mrs. Watson concerning an incident, which took place two weeks ago in their Michigan Avenue apartment. They believed the complaint touched on craziness, or so they said, but it still required an investigation. Neither knew my captain positioned himself down the hall and listened to the entire conversation; for that matter, neither did I.

"I still don't know what the hell this is all about," I said.

"Officer, the allegation is against you and the other five who responded to a call at the Watson's apartment. She claims the six of you beat and raped her," said one of the F.B.I. men.

My mouth dropped wide open, and then anger set in.

"You mean, she didn't even mention the guys and I laughed the entire time?" I asked.

"This is not funny, Officer," said the other agent.

"You're right," I said.

"You're wasting my time. All we need is a written statement from you. We already have statements from the other officers involved," said an agent.

The captain burst into the room and instructed the G-Men to leave immediately. They lied to me as to how many other officers had made statements. I was the first, not the last, and all they wanted were some facts on paper to start their investigation against the police. I told both agents if they wanted any info about the incident, they were to get it from the reports on file in the Records Division. I left the room. Always remember, NEVER, NEVER, NEVER talk to the F.B.I. if you are a suspect. Get an attorney. They can, and will, screw you every time to suit their needs.

I went into the captain's office to thank him for his help on the matter.

"Do you believe this shit, Captain? They actually took a phony beef like that. Those government guys have no balls," I said.

"Well, I'll tell you, Officer, with all this civil rights shit going on, everyone is afraid of getting sued. I'll have to agree with you. No legitimate investigator would've believed the

events actually happened the way the Watson family reported they did. Some political shit is going on with this one,"
said the captain.

That was my first run in with the federal government and
quite unpleasant.

Back on nights again, Billy remained as my other half. Would
this be another month of unusual events and fun and games? Both
of us had hot dates that night and prayed we would not to get a
last minute job. No such luck. With one hour to go, we received
an assignment of a man stabbed in one of the flop hotels.

"Dirty motherfucker, I knew this would happen. This bitch
will never believe me if I stand her up again," said Billy.

"Why, partner, how many times did ya leave her stranded?"
I asked.

"Three times in the last six weeks," said Billy.

"Boy, that's one shitty track record. Remind me not to let
you date my sister."

We sped to the flop and screeched to a halt. The victim waited
in the front lobby for our arrival. Sure enough, he had a small stab
wound just below the nipple area of the chest. Billy examined the
wound and asked the victim the circumstances of the crime.

"Well, it was my roommate, Maurice. I told him I'd replace
his hair spray, but no, he had to have it right now. He went nuts
and stabbed me."

This guy was as queer as a three-dollar bill. The victim and
the offender were lovers, one of the worst kind of calls to get late
in the shift. Could it be possible to blow the job off? We went up
to the room and knocked on the door. From the other side, we
heard a sweet, soft, and long response, "Whoooo is it?"

The lock turned and the door opened. The offender appeared
clad in thigh-high web stockings, an empty red silk bra, and zebra panties. The biggest hair rollers one could imagine balanced
precariously on the top of his head.

"Can I be of any assistance to you, Officer?" Maurice asked.

"Why did you stab your roommate?" I asked.

"I did it because he used up all my hair spray," said Maurice

"I suppose if he fucked up your hair rollers, you would've blown his head off?" I asked.

"Oh, don't be silly. I love him," said Maurice.

Reconciliation became our only option. We did not want to make paper on the job. If we were successful, both of us could make our dates. We convinced each of them to drop the whole thing, basically after we told the victim that he would sleep alone tonight if we took Maurice to jail. Immediately, the thought of aloneness and no one to cuddle caused the anger to drain from his body. We took the victim to the hospital and it was registered as an accidental stabbing. Accordingly, we killed another crime for the district statistics. This always made the brass happy.

The next shift came around quickly. We received a call of a battery victim in a high-class downtown bar. We arrived and were met by an elderly couple. The gentleman exhibited a large bump on his head and his wife could not stop sobbing because it was in the area of a World War II head wound. A metal plate had been inserted in the gentleman's skull as part of the recovery process.

The couple explained they were having a drink in the lounge and this guy at the bar started to use foul language. They quoted words such as "fuck," "dick," and "asshole".

"I asked him to refrain from the bad language on two different occasions and he refused. When I asked again, he was all over me. His friends dragged him off to keep me from getting beaten any further," said the victim.

We called for a backup. Once they arrived, all entered and immediately we could hear the loudmouth in the rear of the lounge.

"Hey, buddy, would you please step outside with us? We would like to talk to you," said Billy.

"Go fuck yourself," said the unruly customer.

Billy looked around and leaned over toward the gentleman's ear.

"Listen, you fucking asshole, if you don't come peacefully, we're gonna beat the shit out of you right here in the bar, in front of everyone. You're under arrest. Now, you've got the ball, run with it, or punt, fuckhead."

With those words, the customer struck Billy in the head and he fell to the floor. I took a baseball swing at the offender with my baton. A ping rang out through the lounge from the impact, but he did not go down.

This guy took on all four of us and did not feel a thing due to the amount of alcohol he had consumed. After a few minutes, we cuffed him and he cooled down. He looked like a beefer, so we collected names of all the witnesses. We knew there would be a problem with those guys from Internal Affairs.

Once in the station, we ran a name check that indicated the offender had three arrests for battery in the last two years and two resisting arrest charges, but no convictions. The guy did beef to the IAD, but we had so many witnesses in our corner, the investigators were helpless.

When it came time for trial, our barfly brawler appeared elegantly dressed. I knew his head still buzzed from my baton and that would explain the expression of hatred and anger displayed on his face.

Once on the stand, Billy was an excellent witness. The offender's high-priced lawyer could not confuse him and the case looked good. Billy convinced the jury what a real troublemaker the offender was that night. The trial lasted for three days. The jury found him not guilty for the original battery on the citizen but guilty of all counts against the police. He went crazy after he heard the verdict. We smirked at him and left the courtroom.

For the next six years, this man tried every known appeal that existed in our state criminal justice system. After that, he initiated a federal lawsuit for the violations of his civil rights. He was a real pain in the ass, but we decided to fight him all the way. We had no idea why he became so obsessed and determined to reverse the decision.

The city offered this guy a ten thousand dollar out of court settlement to drop the mess. He refused to buckle for the money. He did not deserve a penny, and he could have made ten big ones. He dragged the poor couple that started the incident into federal court. I felt like a member of their family. Billy and I even received Christmas gifts from them.

Finally, the lawsuit came to trial. This idiot, who studied numerous law books for the past six years, decided to represent himself. Needless to say, after a five-day trial, at the taxpayers' expense, the jury awarded him a big goose egg. Justice was served.

Months later, I accidentally discovered a flaw in the State's case that would have assured a reversal in the offender's trial. I kept my mouth shut and the conviction still stands today.

The next few weeks went by without any unusual occurrences. The weather got freaky and hotter than normal. This is when everyone comes out of the woodwork like roaches. About 7:30 p.m., we got a job of disturbance in a bar. The dispatcher sent us an assist immediately, so we knew something was up. Billy and I entered and spotted the trouble right away at mid bar. The unruly patrons were seven ironworkers who just finished work at the construction site of Sears Tower. They were all drunk, displayed huge beer bellies, and red whisky noses.

Outward appearances indicated all were very, very, strong. Two more cops arrived to even the odds a little, but we were still at a disadvantage. We discussed the situation for about two minutes and, after we took a little shit from them, we thought we possibly avoided a major incident. More troops were on the way, but had not arrived yet.

Just then, one of the drunks put his hand on the bar and swept everything off as he walked toward the exit. We had to take action, so we grabbed him and the fight commenced. Punches and kicks flew as more help arrived. A sergeant leaped on one of the brawler's back and I swung my baton. I missed the brawler and struck the sergeant. My blow knocked him out and he slid down the wall to the barroom floor. The brawler put a death grip around my neck. A swift kick to the jewels and the drunk found both balls up around his chest. He let go and I slumped atop the nearest table. It took a few seconds to catch my breath, but I swiftly recovered.

The brawl more or less concluded, now relocated onto the street. Two more guys needed to be secured. Tony and John had trouble cuffing one arrestee due to the size of his wrists. They had him spread eagle across the hood of a brand new 'Vette. The owner swiftly appeared. He was a stockbroker from the Exchange Building across the street.

He started to whine and, with eight policemen in full uniform present, he grabbed Tony around the neck and attempted to pull him away from his car. Ten seconds later, his body laid horizontal next to his vehicle. Tony charged him with battery and interference with the police. All were taken into the station and allowed to make their phone calls.

Surely, it is no secret the police department in Chicago is very Irish and very political. Clout is the department's middle name. Six of the arrestees were of Irish descent except the gentleman from Skokie. The phones rang off the wall at the front desk. Six of the seven lived in the infamous 11th ward. The 11th ward is where the mayor lived. It was time for clout to be put in motion, and in motion it went. The commander himself wanted all released without charges. These guys turned out to be a pretty good bunch of Joes, but it was foolish not to charge any of them. They all struck a police officer in full uniform.

Why was I upset? Some politician, who sat at home and chomped on a cigar, assumed the drunks were above the law because of the way they voted. But there are more than two ways to skin a politician. Someone picked up the phone and beefed to the press. Within minutes, there were inquires as to the circumstances of the arrest. The captain became nervous. It would not look good for city hall or the police department if this incident hit the papers. The outcome: they were charged with a lesser offense and all were happy. Who said you cannot beat city hall. I learned that day the press can be a valuable tool when up against the adversary entitled "clout."

The next day, the captain was upset because he was unable to provide the favor for the politician who placed the phone call. He felt it necessary to keep his men in line, due to the fact union talk filled the air for the first time in the history of the department. At roll call, he passed out papers and demanded that anyone who had information about the call to the press must report it immediately. He had no idea what a tightlipped watch we were.

He read the papers in silence and blushed. He took the scrap papers and discarded them into the wastebasket. We could not wait for him to leave the room. He abruptly walked out and we charged the receptacle.

"Hey, look at this one," said one of the officers.

We passed the papers around and read the insults. We laughed out loud. I think every swear word in the dictionary could be found on the papers. The responses showed the unpopularity of the captain, due to his negative stance on the formation of a police union.

Today, Chicago expected some Washington big wig from the Labor Department to visit the city. The union organizers of the CPD thought this would be a great chance for some TV coverage. They decided to organize a labor march. Many other groups appeared to protest other labor issues, but there were plenty of real police on hand to avoid any type of confrontation. The commander of the district oversaw the entire detail. He ordered every off-duty police officers in the demonstration to relocate across the street where they were out of the representative's view. The other protesters were left alone. All but three officers moved across the street. They were placed under arrest.

Once the protest ended, the commander returned to the district to assure the officers were charged properly. They were allowed to wait in the roll call room and not a cell for the duration of the processing. After their paperwork was completed and their name checks cleared, by law, they must be given the opportunity to post bail, a measly twenty-five dollar bond.

The three were at the front desk prepared to bail out. The commander curiously appeared. He was furious. He ordered the bond process be halted in front of the entire shift of officers who were ready to end their tour.

"Sergeant, not one of these men can make bond unless they return to the roll call room and pick up the cigarette butts on the floor," said the commander.

Silence and uncertainty crammed the room. How could someone be denied bond over cigarette butts? None of the arrestees even smoked. The three officers stood their ground and eyeballed the commander.

"Officers, I order all three of you to go back into that room and pick up the cigarette butts before you bond out," said the commander.

One of the officers slowly moved toward the room, but the other two disregarded the order.

"Did you hear me, Officer? I gave you a direct order," hollered the commander.

"You know what you can do with your direct orders, fat ass. I'm not a police officer," said one of the arrestees.

"Commander, I suggest you authorize the bond without delay. I'm an attorney, not a police officer," said the other arrestee.

The boss's blood boiled, but he was not above the law. He reluctantly allowed the private citizens to bond out. The supporters of the union productively demonstrated the elitist attitude of some command personnel towards subordinates. Word of the confrontation spread throughout the department and the mindset of the men and women leaned more and more towards the creation of a union. Eventually, we would have our union and working conditions would improve immensely.

CHAPTER TWO

THE VETERAN

The days turned to weeks, then to months, and finally years. I now had five years seniority on the job. In those five years, I had learned a great deal about life, as well as police work, but, most of all, I had a firm grip on how politics infiltrated the police community. In actuality, it had been five years of vaudeville, limited only by one's imagination. The assignments, the exams, the shifts, the vacations, the suspensions, and even my actions were all influenced, in one way or another, by clout.

I reported for work one day, assigned to the desk detail. I thought, no big deal; the job is nothing but shuffling papers. Wrong! Some days, the deskmen worked their butts off, because police work is seventy percent paper work. Another fact omitted in my training days at the police academy.

We had a brand new sergeant that day. He portrayed himself as someone who thought the job was legit and wanted all to know how hard he studied for his promotion. What a bullshitter, I knew his clout.

Two little kids entered the station and one held a cardboard box in his hands. They found a full-grown alley cat. Their mother advised them they could not keep animal, so they tried to sell it to the police. None of us desired a cat at the time, so the sergeant asked if I could handle the job. Thinking he was joking, I agreed to accept the assignment.

I rose from the desk and escorted the two kids outside. I handed them a buck for the cat and returned to the station. I strolled past the sergeant with the cat still in the box and exited the back door. I released the feline. I returned and the sergeant asked the whereabouts of the cat.

"I don't know where he is by now. I let the little shit go in the alley," I said.

He went nuts and started to chew my ass off. One would think I just released Capone. He calmed down and instructed me never to violate department general orders under his command. From that day on, the sergeant was known as "old puss and boots."

This same sergeant, who worried so much about the rules and regulations, happened to get nabbed months later residing outside the city. The police department rigidly enforces this violation. He took a thirty-day suspension. Police brass ordered him to sell his home and relocate within the city limits at his own expense. What a hypocrite!

I checked the worksheets the following day and my partner was new to the district. Word around the CPD, he liked to make waves. He filed a lawsuit for discrimination against the city as mentioned earlier in the book. This lawsuit protested how the city of Chicago promoted its police officers.

The written exam consisted of one-third of the entire promotional procedure. The city refused to grade this exam in your presence. City officials marked your paper in private, no reason given, they just did. When one takes the detective's exam, a much more difficult test, it is graded right in front of you. There is no hanky panky, you passed or failed.

Step two of the promotional process consists of an oral exam. A ninety-five or better must be scored on this segment of the test. If you have no one going for you (clout), you get an eighty-five and that will knock you right out of the box, even with a well-written exam. They would ask questions like, "What do you do if you witness a child get struck by a car?" Of course, you would call for an ambulance and render assistance to the child. These idiotic questions justify the high scores given to the officers with clout.

Finally, the most important part of the test is the forever-changing efficiency cards. You are graded on such things as appearance (I've seen slobs get ninety-seven), punctuality (I banged on doors to get some ninety-five scores out of bed), medical roll abuse (ninety-six scores would call in ailing every other week-end with a hangover), and number of arrests (some sergeants can't even fill out an arrest slip properly). The unwritten rule of thumb is every unit must maintain an average of eighty-five percent, although the top brass will never admit it.

What this means is if you give a clout officer a ninety-seven percent, an aggressive officer must receive about a seventy-seven percent. This will eliminate the hard working officer's chance of promotion. Sometimes, a sharp sergeant would ask who planned to take the exam. Consequently, the low score would not hurt these officers, and the patrolman participating in the exam can be given a higher evaluation. These efficiency marks are only used for promotional purposes. They do not have zilch to do with how well you execute your job, nor would they generate a dismissal on the basis of a low grade.

Please, do not think all sergeants are unqualified. This is not factual. Chicago certainly has some of the most intelligent sergeants in the country and quite a few with college degrees. They attended school and worked at the same time. The difference, these men rarely were assigned to patrol. Most worked easy desk jobs, which allowed them to study while at their job. You cannot study very well and answer a robbery in progress call at the same time. The rules give the supervisors the responsibility to grade you and that is the way it is. Each sergeant has his own method. The following will explain the latitude of the process.

A sergeant and a gang detective rode together on the four to twelve shifts. They observed a group of teens hanging on a street corner and one held a rifle in his hand. The duo pulled up and made the arrest without incident. During the drive to the station, the rifle mysteriously fired as the sergeant amused himself playing with the weapon. It struck the officer seated behind the wheel in the big toe. This officer missed work for six months and the incident was categorized as accidental.

The injured officer returned to work just prior to his six-month evaluation. The grader happened to be the same sergeant involved with the arrest of the teen and the rifle. Here is how the conversation went when the sergeant cautiously tendered the officer his efficiency card for review.

"Officer, I have your efficiency card for the last six month period. Will you please read it and sign it?" asked the sergeant.

The officer grabbed the card and read his marks. He shook his head in disbelief. He rose from the desk and yelled at the sergeant.

"Hey, Sarge, you only gave me a seventy-four. Is this a mistake? This will fuck up any chance of a promotion. You know I took the sergeant's exam."

"I'm sorry, Officer; I had to give you that grade. You spent 180 days on medical roll," said the sergeant.

"Why, you pompous prick," screamed the officer. "You're the asshole who shot me in the foot and put me on the medical roll."

The state rests its case.

So, if the federal judge mentioned earlier portrayed himself as such a righteous individual, he would have noticed the exact same thing everyone else did when it came to promotional exams. CLOUT! But then again, the people do not elect federal judges; they are nominated and appointed by none other than politicians.

The next day's assignment had me breaking in a rookie. My regular partner was on furlough time, so I had to babysit. It seemed like yesterday I stood in this kid's shoes. Some kid, I was twenty-five and he was thirty-five, with a daughter almost eighteen. But, he still held a rookie label as far as the police department was concerned.

John and I did not live far from each other, so I inquired if he needed a pick-up for the upcoming St. Jude Parade that would take place in a few days. This parade is held in honor of all slain policemen. The Chicago Police Department is very Irish and very Catholic. The city also realizes the religious needs of their men. So, on a Sunday morning at 9:00 a.m., they allow police officers, in full dress, to have a parade down the middle of State Street that Great Street. The funny thing about this parade is the lack of spectators. Who gets up that early on a Sunday morning but police officers? The audience consisted of winos and bums left over from their Saturday night drunk. Some honor. Not even the participants wanted to be there. It is somewhat of a disgraceful situation because most are forced to attend.

Afterward, all are expected to participate at mass in honor of their slain brothers and sisters. While five thousand of us walk up the steps of the church, which only seats two thousand, news cameras roll. We walk in the front doors and right out the back ones and a large majority head for the nearest watering hole. The bulk of participants at mass are politicians, the brass of the police department, and the suck-ass patrolmen who must attend to maintain their cushy jobs. John related he did not want to attend because he spends Sunday mornings with his family.

"John, you don't understand. You gotta go," I said

"Fuck them and their phony parade," he said.

If John did not grace the parade with his presence, he would have been marked absent by one of the commander's suck-ass friends. The commanders would use this roll as a reference when one of the men would ask for a favor, wanted to work a special shift, or take time due. For example, they would deny a time due request and tell you a shortage of manpower existed that particular day. When you arrive at work, there would be so many men; you could roll with three-man cars for the shift.

I enlightened John that these political patsy bosses repeated the scenario if you failed to sign up for payroll deduction when it came to donations for the Crusade of Mercy Charity Fund. The Mayor always strived to look good and this was another route to accomplish his goal. A satisfactory turnout at the parade made the city look good. He was as sharp and intelligent as they come, plus a master politician. One must always bow to the demands of City Hall without a strong union, and at that time, we did not have a union at all.

We hit the street. The truth be told, John seemed to know police work. I believe his upbringing contributed to his unique sense of street smarts. Plus, John possessed common sense, a must-have trait for a police officer. I later found out he had a brother on the job. I am sure that fact had something to do with his ability to outshine the average rookie.

Around 9:00 p.m., we agreed on pizza for dinner, but hesitated to dine in a restaurant. It seems you always get some loudmouth who approaches and inquires about something stupid or complains about a ticket he received a month ago. We pulled into a tri-level parking lot with the pizza and a six-pack and started to chow down. John, being a rookie, asked a million questions and I answered all to the best of my ability. Somehow, we lost track of time, and before we knew, the shift ended. A problem arose. We tried to leave the lot, but the attendant must have forgotten we were on top. He locked down the iron mesh gate and we were trapped inside.

"How in the fuck do we solve this one? The watch commander will never believe it," said John.

"You're right, we're not going to explain it, put on your seatbelt," I said.

"No, you're not going to do what I think you are, are you?" asked John.

"Beat #105 to tower, ready for take off," I said, chuckling.

"Come on, don't fuck around," yelled John.

"Do you want to explain this to the captain, rookie? It won't look too good if he writes you up on this one," I said.

John thought out loud the idea of ramming the gate or taking another route. He looked at me and took a very deep breath.

"Co-pilot ready for takeoff, sir, seatbelts buckled," said John.

I floored the pedal, squealing both tires, and we rammed the gate. It popped right open and the lock ended up across the street on the sidewalk. We were free and not a scratch on the police car. We arrived at the station on time and no one seemed to be the wiser.

"Is this what the hell goes on every night around here?" asked John.

"Well, not every night, but I can't remember a time this job did not generate a good night of laughter," I said.

The next evening, John and I were partners again and ready to roll. Nothing exciting happened and he began to bitch from the boredom.

"Pretty slow for a Friday night, isn't it?" asked John.

"It's only 8:30. Don't worry. The shit will hit the fan as it always does, just don't get any on your face."

Ten minutes later, a call came over the radio. "NAKED WOMAN ON THE FIFTH FLOOR AT THE OAKLAND HOTEL." Another car got the job, but we decided to respond anyway. We did not go down on the air.

"Here comes our laugh, John. This will be a beauty," I said.

We pulled up, along with six other cars, and could not wait to see the floor show. We entered the hotel and went up to the fifth floor. The elevator doors opened and revealed an attractive black hooker, totally naked, and clutched in her hand, a chrome plated snub nose 38. Just like in the movies, it appeared the smoke was still flowing from the tip of the barrel.

"Two crazy honky motherfuckers just tried to rob me. They're in room 510 right now," said the hooker.

We gave the whore something to wear, as slowly as possible of course, and ran to the room. All of us turned the corner and there lay the honky, half naked and shot in the ass. Suddenly, he looked up at us and we started to laugh. George was one of us. He even worked our shift, but today was his day off.

"George, what the fuck happened to you?" I asked.

"The fucking whore shot me while I brushed my teeth, right in the ass!" he said.

We called an ambulance and got George to the hospital A.S.A.P. The rest of us went back to the station with the whore to ascertain her version of the incident.

George and his buddy were on the hunt for a little action, so they picked up a lady of the evening. The three headed for the Oakland Hotel because it was a freebie for all the police officers that worked in the district. George, the hornier of the two, went first. Finished, he began to clean up. George's friend went next.

The second customer started to undress and accidentally knocked George's coat on to the floor. George's snub nose fell out of his pocket and onto the carpet. Before his buddy could explain George's profession, she panicked and thought rip off. She whacked George's friend in the head with the weapon and knocked him down. George heard the commotion and came out of the bathroom bare-assed naked. The frightened whore fired three rounds at George. She could have killed him. Luckily, he only ended up with an ass wound. She was charged with the crime and poor George went home with an additional hole in his ass.

The word "whore" was never mentioned in any of the official police reports, thus saving our fellow officer any suspension time. That ended the tour and we called it a night.

The next night was routine and, once again, boredom set in. We volunteered to back up cars on jobs to keep awake. The C.C. Room finally gave us an assignment of an activated silent alarm at the Art Museum. Two other cars arrived and the six of us entered the building along with a security guard. No intruder could be located, so we informed the C.C. Room we were back up and clear. It appeared to be a false alarm.

Ten minutes later, we received a second call to return. The alarm was ringing again and, this time, in more than one location. On a stormy night, it is not uncommon for alarms to go off in this manner. We walked through the building and sought the source of the possible malfunction. The museum was enormous.

I stupidly wandered off alone down a hallway and no longer heard the chatter of walkie-talkies or the laughter of other police officers as they critiqued the art. I was about to place myself into a precarious situation.

I heard an unidentifiable tapping sound that recoiled off the marble floor. It puzzled me at first, but in a few seconds, I identified the source. The echo of a dog's paw slipping and sliding on a freshly waxed surface of marble became louder.

"Holy fuck, they called the dogs in," I whispered to myself.

I rummaged around for a place to hide. My only option appeared to be long narrow hallway a short distance away. I broke into a full stride. The keys jingled on my gun belt and serenaded the sensitive ears of the police dogs. I could now hear the dog's bark as they pursued the sound. Quickly, I realized the pooches were not on their twenty-foot leads.

At the end of the hallway was an area under construction. Was this my only chance for safety? The last thing I wanted was to get bit by theses vicious animals. My shelter consisted of a row of makeshift offices. They were constructed with eight-foot high plasterboard walls, no ceilings, and flimsy balsa wood doors. There were no doorknobs on any of the doors.

I burst into an office and tried to close the door, but it would not click shut. I managed to brace it closed with my own body weight. The canines actually threw their bodies against the other side of the door in an attempt to push it open. The impact almost knocked me to the ground. With the entrance secured again, the dogs scratched, barked, and pounded in an attempt to enter.

I had the ability to use my police walkie-talkie, but poor technology and tons of cement prevented my cries of help from reaching the airwaves. About five feet from the wall stood an office desk with a phone atop. I stretched for the receiver, but it was just out of my reach. If I released my body weight from the door it would no longer be secured. I decided the phone was out of the question.

I knew the handlers were close behind. One minute seemed like an hour in this situation. Abruptly, the pounding stopped and I heard a very bizarre noise. The plasterboard wall quivered. It appeared to be breathing. I heard a loud snort, a growl, and all of a sudden, the drywall cracked. A moistened black nose, decorated with plaster dust, poked through a very small hole. A huge set of front teeth and an eyeball materialized next. I gawked at the intruder and it stared back. The dog started to chomp again and it would only be a matter of time before its powerful jaws produced an opening large enough for its body to crawl through. Funny thing, the thumping on the door from the other side stopped. Sure, the second mutt just sat in the hall and thought, "To hell with throwing my body into the door, I'll let Jaws break through the wall and prance in behind him."

Time ran out and only one option remained. I must shoot the beast. Its entire head was nearly through the hole as I stepped back and drew my revolver. If I fired a shot into the air, it would not scare the dog. These animals are trained not to fear loud noises. In a matter of seconds, my attacker would burst through the barrier. Just then, a voice rang out, "Max, Yield!" The animal withdrew his head, sat, and did not move a muscle. His handler approached. My revolver was still in my hand when I exited the office.

"Hey, Officer, put that thing away. What the fuck were ya gonna do, shoot my dog?" asked the handler.

"Yeah, asshole, you're the one I should shoot. Why did you let him off his leash?"

"Do you know how fucking big this place is? It would've have taken all night to search on a twenty-foot lead," said the handler.

"Are you okay, Officer, you're walking kinda funny," said the handler's partner.

"I guess so, but I think I need some toilet paper."

We walked out together. The trained killer now licked my hand when ten minutes earlier he wanted to devour it. My partner and I got back in the car and we went in to check off. Immediately, I went to the restroom to wipe off.

The watering hole was a definite that night. I had to unwind. My partner and I entered to down a few cold ones and most of the shift had already arrived. Everyone had smirks on their mugs; so apparently, someone let the cat out of the bag about my canine story. All flung out jokes, one crack after another, which put the entire joint in a laughing mood.

The beer glided down our throats very effortlessly. By now, an hour and a half passed and we all showed a little buzz. This is usually the time police officers start a discussion about sucking and fucking and who is going to stop on the way home to get a blowjob from the first street walker they see (free of charge, of course).

The bartender set up another round as the door flung open. Jeannie, the district groupie, entered the establishment. She was an easy lady who fucked and sucked anything that walked, as long as it was clean and wore a police uniform. For a police whore, Jeannie was quite attractive. Only twenty-four years old, she would brag to the troops how she already traveled through two miles of police dick.

"Hey, Jeannie, how about a drink?" one officer asked.

"Thought you'd never ask, you cheap Pollack," she said.

"I got your Pollack right here," said Stan as he pointed to his crotch.

"Yeah, if everybody was as cheap as you, I'd die of thirst," she said smiling.

When the hilarity calmed from the put down session, the horny vultures moved in for a piece of the carcass. A couple more drinks under Jeannie's pantyhose and she would be geared up for anything. Tony gave me wink as he slipped the bartender a sawbuck for the use of the closed section of the restaurant. A velvet booth for six, in all probability, would be better suited for the mission than the backseat of Tony's car. Well, it appeared Tony was going first as he asked Jeannie if he could speak to her about something private.

"Sure, Tony, as long as that something private is your dick," she said.

Ten minutes elapsed and Jeanie walked out from the back. Tony trailed a short distance as he attempted to zip his pants and walk at the same time.

"Next," Tony yelled like a counterman at a deli screaming for a customer.

"Let me go, guys. The old lady is at home and gawking at the clock by now," said Stan.

The guys moaned somewhat, but allowed Stan to go next. He jumped up from the barstool as if he just sat on a tack. He sped toward the rear and a bulge disfigured the normal shape of his groin area. Comments soared at Stan because he thought he deserved to go next.

"Aw, come on, guys. Don't fuck around, I'm already late," said Stan.

"Okay, go ahead, you motherfucker, before you drown us with your drool," said Tony.

Stan disappeared into the darkness of the backroom and we drank on.

Not everyone visited Jeanie, and when she ran out of play-mates, she would return to the bar front and kid with the men. She was always good for a few laughs. Just then, the lights went on.

"Last call," bellowed the bartender.

It was already past the legal drinking time, but who in the hell was going to arrest us? The only patrons left were police officers. We chugged the last drink and left half intoxicated for the ride home. Married now for about a year, I prayed my wife slept when I arrived. I did not want to listen to the whining concerning my excessive drinking the second I entered the valley of death.

I made it home safely and quietly undressed. There was a new addition to my family. I was the proud father of a new baby girl. My wife and I named her Jennifer and she could not have been more loved.

Most officers will tell you that when a child is born into a working police officer's family, his attitude toward the job changes. He becomes much more cautious and thorough, especially when he deals with a suspected felon. But, I had extra motivation that caused such feelings. My daughter was born with some complications. I often wondered what would happen to her if anything happened to me. How would she survive in this dog eat dog world with the birth defect of cerebral palsy? I decided the only way for a secure future was the best education possible. My wife and I decided to send her to a private school. Due to childcare issues, my wife quit her job. We returned to one-income with the bills of a two-income family.

A few years later, I added another bundle of joy to my family. I became the proud father of a baby boy. No one had any doubts what to name the child, and Richard Jr. joined Jennifer as the loves of my life. But, with Richard came another mouth to feed and more future tuition bills.

I had two options. Start to steal, or find a second job that would contribute to Jen's medical bills and both children's future tuition cost. I entered the world of private security and worked an additional sixteen hours a week. I felt the easiest way to carry out this feat was to work one of my days off and put in a double shift one day a week. I would leave the police job after working eight hours and go straight to work on the private security job. For the next fifteen years, this grueling schedule doubled the stress in my life, but I knew my efforts would pay off in the long run and my children would get the best education possible.

By now, patrol became tedious. Each shift seemed routine and nonproductive. Back at work, Billy and I decided to break up the boredom with a cup of java. We ended up at a coffee shop the Rush St. bar people frequented prior to their drunken journey home. We sat at the counter in the restaurant because everything the police ordered there was a freebie.

Out of the corner of my eye, I spotted three friends from my old neighborhood. I grew up with these guys and they were bad actors when it came to a street fight. I approached them to say hello, but could not help but notice the occupants in the booth to their right. It contained seven fags who were loud and quite rowdy. I returned to my partner without saying hello, and told him it was time to leave. In this situation, I could predict the future.

"I'm not done with my coffee yet," he snapped.

"Leave it, and just follow me out the fucking door," I said.

The minute we got outside, Billy wanted to know what the hell the problem was. I explained and we drove off to distance ourselves from the restaurant.

"The shit is going to hit the fan in the restaurant, so let's make a traffic stop and go down on the air to avoid the job," I said.

We curbed the first car we saw for a routine check and went off the air on the stop. No sooner than the microphone was replaced in its holder, a call came over the radio that announced a fight in the same restaurant we just left. We rushed back to the scene, but the melee was already over. Sprawled everywhere were the seven fags.

My friends immediately recognized me, but I gave them a wink and avoided eye contact. As expected, the fags wanted the straights arrested because they assumed the only reason they were beaten was due to the fact they were gay. We interviewed people who were not involved and they verified my friends did not instigate the fight.

My friends dined quietly, until one of the fags dipped a napkin in a glass of water and tossed it at one of his buddies. He missed, strike one, hit one of my buddies in the face, strike two, and then told my friends "fuck off" when they complained about the flying napkin, strike three, you're out. Ketchup bottles and metal napkin holders were employed to beat the shit out of the seven.

"Sounds even to me, three against seven, looks like the bottles made it a fair fight," said Billy.

The wagon transported all to the station. I instructed my friends, if the fags insisted on signing a complaint, they also should sign cross-complaints. The situation grew calmer. One of the fag arrestees requested to speak to me in confidence. I checked to verify my zipper was in the locked position and we walked into an empty room.

"Listen, Officer, an arrest is out of the question," he said.

"Why, are you God or something?" I asked.

"No, silly, you don't understand. My father is…" and he whispered his name.

The mystery man was one of the richest people in the country.

"Could you see the headlines? 'Millionaire's flaming fag son arrested in restaurant brawl.' The press would tear my father apart," he said.

He requested a phone to contact his dad. The other police officers could not wait to see what politician the kid's old man would wake at 4:00 a.m. in the morning. Who ever said politics and police, never the two shall meet.

It did not take very long for the interaction to occur. Within twenty minutes, the captain walked in the back, all heavy-eyed, and wanted to know what the hell was going on. We explained, and to our amazement, the captain told us the governor's office phoned and wanted the whole thing squashed. We could not believe our ears. The kid's old man called the governor's mansion. Now that's "CLOUT."

The captain instructed us to handle the matter or our next assignment would be in a rowboat counting barges on Lake Michigan. I wanted to tell him to go to hell for exerting so much power over us, but I did not. Instead, my friends were told to sit down, keep their mouths shut, and they would walk in an hour.

Both parties, after some convincing, agreed to drop the complaints and were set free as if the incident never happened. Fascinating what MA BELL does for our criminal justice system. It would be a good wager the governor could expect a healthy contribution toward his next election.

The following day orders came down from the Ivory Tower for one hundred officers to report to the U.S. Armory for in-service training. The training served two purposes. One, it warranted the jobs of the empty holster policeman at the academy when there were no recruits to instruct. Secondly, we received riot control instruction and the city used the Feds to foot the bill.

The next five days were certainly entertaining. We watched law enforcement movies so ancient Clark Gable could have had the leading role. We practiced gun range techniques where some of the old timers could not even hit the paper, let alone the body image of the bad guy. Finally, three full days of riot control, which consisted of thrusting a baton at thin air.

This exercise took place at an armory because it had enough room for one hundred men to march in something drill instructors tried to call a formation. The idea was to use this tactic in actual riot conditions. After drinking lunch, half of us could not even find the front door of the armory, let alone march in step. Once inside, they made us parade around with gas masks on our faces. These same masks were the actual ones to be worn in real riot situations, but there were no filters in the mask to screen out the gas. If called out immediately, the police would drop just as quickly as the rioters.

I remember the first time we tried to put this drum and bugle stuff into action. It was Puerto Rican Day and a civil disturbance erupted at Humboldt Park caused by the excessive amount of alcohol one consumes during this type of function.

The day was so hot that the blistering heat caused the street asphalt to actually stick to our shoes like bubble gum. On one side of the road stood about two hundred drunken Puerto Ricans, half unable to speak the English language, and on the other side stood a hundred police officers. They were in full uniform, sixty yards away, helmets and batons ready for battle and all fashioned in a configuration known as the "wedge."

Amid both groups, a high-ranking police official, bullhorn in hand, actually tried to communicate with these drunken idiots. Every time he issued a command, beer bottles soared from the crowd like raindrops. In the back-up wedge, we were about eighty strong and in plain clothes. Our group already decided we were not going to allow this crowd to hurt any of us, no matter what orders the commander issued with his bullhorn. He was very open-minded towards this unruly mob. The commander's liberal approach upset the men and the tension mounted.

The crowd started to move closer and so did the bottles and bricks, but our leader ordered us to hold our ground. The officers in front started to go down, one after the other, from the hurled debris. Suddenly, I felt a blow to the right side of my chest. I laid in the street looking up at the sky. Quickly, I jumped back up on my feet. You could see the steam coming out of my nostrils and the pain on my face. Some of the other officers tried to get me out of the area but to no avail.

It would be only a matter of seconds before we could not avoid the incoming missiles. We had two choices: run and avoid injury, or attack the crowd and clear the area. We broke through the front wedge and ran by the commander with the bullhorn. In a situation such as this, pick out one bad guy and go for him. Next, whack him in the head. Pick out another and whack him, too. In a matter of minutes, we had the psychological edge. The sea of blue helmets showed unity and strength and the officers behind us decided to follow in our footsteps. Our attack left Mr. Bull Horn positioned in the middle of the street with no one to command.

He finally gave the order to disperse the crowd. Funny thing, they were already dispersed and half of them were on the ground with some part of their body either soaked in blood or very sore.

With our job incomplete, the troops darted through the park and swung at anyone in a rowdy gang who smelled like a taco and appeared loaded with rum. We broke up the horde and returned to the staging area to attend to our wounded. There were many officers hurt that day. A peculiar thing about the aftermath, the same people who threw the bottles and bricks now had the balls to ask for assistance to get to a hospital. We took them, it was our job, but we made sure the doctors knew injured police officers were en route and no way would the rioters be treated before our brother in blue.

The crowd dispersed and broke into twenty small clusters spread out through the neighborhood. The bullhorn man was at a loss for words, but his boss, the one with two balls, gave an order to clear the streets. We effortlessly carried out the order and returned to our police vehicles.

While en route, a Puerto Rican rioter who evaded our sweep through the park chucked a stereo speaker out of a third floor window of his residence. It hit one of our guys on the base of the neck and the blood gushed out before he hit the ground. A concerned woman approached and pointed to the window where the speaker became airborne. We looked up and could see the bastard. He laughed at us and closed the window. Six officers bolted up the back steps and kicked in the door. They grabbed the offender and placed him under arrest.

"Hey, asshole, you like throwin' things out of windows? Watch this," said one officer.

First, he launched the kitchen table out the window. The chairs were next, a few dishes, and even the wall clock. I think this will be the last time our prisoner heaves anything out of a window with a police officer as the target.

We walked into the station with the bad guy. The place was a madhouse; people were planted all over and waiting to bail out the rioters arrested earlier in the park. The station resembled a Greyhound Bus Station at Christmas.

"What kinda shit is this? All we need are a few chickens to complete the scene," said Greg, the deskman.

Greg appeared quite upset and was overwhelmed with paperwork piled in front of him. I told him to take it easy and relax.

"Fuck this job, I got writer's cramp," said Greg.

Just then, some poor guy moseyed into the station to get a theft report completed. He approached Greg.

"I's work everyday and some mothafucker brokes into my car. I's need a report for my insurance company," he said.

The expression on Greg's face let me know this bullshit was about to come to a halt. He grabbed a scratch pad from the desk and wrote the number "52" on the paper. Greg handed the paper to the man.

"I'll get to ya as soon as I can. Take a seat and I'll call out your number. Number three, who has number three?" asked Greg.

The man gazed at all of the people and assumed they were also in the station to make out reports. He looked at Greg and mumbled something while he walked out the door. Got to hand it to Greg, if there is a way to get around something, he could find it. One thing a Chicago cop can always manage is a way to figure out how to get something accomplished with the least amount of effort.

Today was Saturday and my day off. In summer months, for the recreation of the troops, the police department sponsored a softball league. This ball was sixteen inches in circumference and the game is played without any mitts. Any police officer is invited to play for the District or Area in which they work. The problem with the Saturday games is policemen happen to work on that day.

Officers from all over the city would drive their police vehicles to Grant Park, even though on duty. They would hide their police cars on the inner driveway of the park out of the public's view. The police who were not at the ball game would cover for the officers who were. This scenario existed for weeks without any problems, until, one day, a situation bloomed. A police officer, on duty at the time, broke his ankle during a ball game.

According to department regulations, a police officer gets full pay if he or she is injured on duty. Is participating in a city-sponsored event on duty? The weeks went by and injuries to the police skyrocketed. The city decided to take action. Their conclusion was to discontinue on-duty officers from participating in any of the ball games. Teams forfeited game after game and the league bordered extinction.

The brass devised a very creative solution. Officers who wanted to play ball, when they actually were on duty, merely would submit a time-due slip. This would allow them to leave the district and play the game without breaking any department rules. But, time-due was scarce in those days because everyone wanted the overtime pay instead. Officers decided not to play ball and retain their precious time-due.

The league seemed doomed once again until the bosses came up with another great idea. They would just tear up the slips if the officers returned to work in one piece. The only one who loses out in this situation is the taxpayer. Twenty dollars an hour to play baseball is not a lot of pay by professional standards, but for police officers, its easy money. Once again, the police solved a problem to their advantage. I now had six years under my belt in the career of policing. The time I spent in the patrol division was quite educational, but it was time to move on. There were many opportunities to transfer, but none were ever acted upon. The sense of satisfaction at my present assignment remained strong. My job was very enjoyable. That is, until now.

I was on the afternoon shift and 10-99 (solo). A rapid transit station situated on my beat needed periodical safety checks by the police. In recent months, stick-up men preyed on the passengers and were able to escape practically every time before the police arrived. This fact compelled "Mr. Top Cop" to form a unit of undercover policemen who called themselves the Decoy Unit. They were an instant success. The press played up their presence and L-station robberies dropped dramatically, dropped not stopped.

Around nine o'clock one night, I received a call of a man shot at the L-station located at Halsted and Lake Street. Just around the corner, I arrived in seconds. There on the platform laid the bad guy. He had two clean bullet holes in the facial area. Perched over the body were three decoy officers, one a friend of mine.

"Isn't that a pretty sight? Tough luck, my camera is at home," said one of the officers.

"Yeah, the only good stick up man is a dead stick up man," said another officer.

This was the conversation of two of the three officers. My friend Tom just stood there mute. Tom bagged the kill. He had an elongated scratch on his throat from the switchblade of the offender and both hands trembled as he attempted to light a smoke. Obviously shaken, the thought of the kill worried him.

The wagon took the stiff to the morgue and the three officers went into the station to complete their paperwork. I was to check off at 11:20 p. m., but had some concern for Tommy and his two buddies. I left my post early to get coffee for the three.

My timing could not have been shoddier. I dropped off the coffee for the guys and called it a night. Little did I know the street deputy had pulled in behind me to investigate the homicide. Deputies are various exempt ranked officers who alternate to work the streets as the officer in charge of the tour. They have the final decision on any street situation. But most try to avoid any major decisions, because if it is the wrong one, it could be a political disaster. When you upset City Hall and are in a position of exempt rank, you can be demoted at anytime for any reason, especially a wrong decision that upsets a community or ethnic group involved.

This particular night, the street deputy happened to be my district commander. Instead of immediately investigating the shooting, he took note of the fact my car logged in prior to the official end of my shift. When I reported for work the next day, he instructed my sergeant to check on my status for the prior shift. The C. C. Room confirmed I was up, clear, and on my beat. Since the deputy observed my car in the back of the station, its presence contradicted my status. The boss recommended a one-day suspension without pay, and never gave me a chance to explain my actions.

My personality did not allow me to respect or work for this man any longer. Feelers were sent out for a transfer, but it was not going to be easy. I had the clout to move, but where would I go? I hated to ask for the favor and represent myself as an ass kisser, but I had no choice. I made the call and arranged an interview with the commander of the new Gang Crimes Unit.

This man was a real gentleman and a class act. The interview went without a hitch and I believed he was somewhat impressed with my responses. Possibly, the fact that he knew a call had been made on my behalf may have clouded his judgment in my favor. It really did not matter one way or the other to me. I liked the man and it would just be a matter of time before I became a member of one the best units the Chicago Police Department had ever created, The Gang Crimes Division.

CHAPTER THREE

THE REAL POLICE

Transfer orders are issued every twenty-eight days and my name appeared on the subsequent order. My instructions were to report to Lieutenant Green, Gang Crimes West Division. Assigned to the day shift, I became energized at the thought of entering a new world of police work. Daily, I dealt with criminals who could be considered the scum of the earth. They would slit your throat in a minute, if they thought they could avoid arrest. But these were the days the old time homicide dicks brought you in on a slab if you were a cop killer.

I reported a few minutes early and the butterflies fluttered in my stomach. The building appeared it should have been condemned by city officials years ago, and to make things worse, insufficient air conditioning throughout fueled my anxiety.

The deskman greeted me first. His name was Bob. In the years to come, he would cover my ass many times, from ducking out early to bullshitting broads to reporting in late. Bob had a million excuses and he is what we consider in the trade as a "great paper man." If you needed the proper wording on a report to cover your ass, you would see Bob. He ran the show, along with his counter part Gino on the afternoon shift.

The office resembled the set of the old Barney Miller Show, lacking the cell. I could not believe my eyes. The lieutenant came over and introduced himself. It felt strange. I had met my boss and liked him immediately. It took three months in the patrol division before I warmed up to any of those bosses.

"Come inside my office. I'd like to explain a few things to you, and find out a little about yourself," said the lieutenant.

He put the key in his office door and pushed it open. Two steps inside and he immediately paused. His action caused me to walk into his backside. I peeked over his shoulder and was shocked; for that matter, the lieutenant was taken back himself. The room looked as bare as the aftermath of a sale at Marshall Field's Bargain Basement. Desk, chairs, filing cabinet, and locker had disappeared. Perched in the middle of the room sat a dirty toilet bowl that had been left behind. I remained tightlipped and afraid to laugh. The lieutenant turned and looked at me.

"My boys must've had a good night. They would've never pulled this stuff on me if they didn't know what kinda mood I'd be in this morning."

He looked at Bob with a smile on his face.

"Bob, does this mean they think I'm a piece of shit, or a big asshole?" asked the boss.

"Come on, Lieutenant, you know they're only fucking with you," said Bob.

I could not believe it; the man was not angry at all. Bob looked at me and smirked.

"Sorry, Officer, not a very good impression on your first day in a new unit."

Still stunned, I thought this has to be my kind of unit.

The boss requested the stats for the previous evening. Bob stood up tall and proud.

"One homicide pinch, one robbery pinch, three guns, one simple battery, and a search warrant which netted one kilo of smoke," said Bob.

The lieutenant inquired how many men worked the shift.

"Just eight men, boss, not bad, huh?" asked Bob.

The entire watch I came from did not accomplish that much work in one –month, much less in one night. Suddenly, the troops started to trickle in for roll call. The atmosphere seemed very casual. I introduced myself to everyone and my nerves calmed down. Out of the ten men who were to report for work, three were late. No big deal. If I were back in patrol, they would have been on the phone immediately questioning the tardiness.

There were three sergeants at roll call and I slipped up with my immediate negative judgment of them. At one point or another, all three said, "Don't call me on the streets, guys, I'll call you." It took a couple days to realize what they meant and what the other guys already knew. Simply, do not bother me with any bullshit and waste my time.

They accepted us as grown men and knowledgeable investigators. The sergeants required the men to make their own decisions and would stand behind us whether we were right or wrong, similar to the code of silence concerning police misconduct.

This newly created unit selected most of its supervisors from the detective division rather than the patrol division. Detective division supervisors seemed to have a different attitude about the job than patrol sergeants. They were mellower. The commander handpicked all his supervisors and most of them were former detectives. Many of the troops also came from the detective division. I was an exception and from the patrol. I felt very fortunate about my transfer; it gave me the opportunity to further my police knowledge and experience with these seasoned veterans.

Any Chicago cop will tell you, no matter how good your job is, if you get an asshole for a boss, the job is only worth fifty percent of its potential. These bosses appeared to be great, except for one. He was heavy enough to get transferred in from the patrol division. All he needed to do was open his mouth and you could tell he lacked detective division training. He was an administrator. Every time he spoke, the looks on the other officers' faces illustrated discontent. My past experiences with Billy gave me the sense to observe first and then make a decision. The trick was to roll with the punches and keep my mouth shut. After all, six years of seniority under my belt in patrol did not make me a seasoned veteran. I still considered myself a "rookie" in this division until I could prove to be an effective investigator.

The function of the Gang Unit's day shift consisted of gathering intelligence about the gangs and their members. We collected certain information on these punks and documented the info for future reference. I made one or two pinches a period. The rest of the time was free. Quite the opposite case on nights, these gang dicks worked very hard.

My first assignment was nil, as far as police intelligence is concerned. A couple of punks posed as leaders of a phony boys' club in an attempt to extort money from the local businesses. Enough evidence existed to pinch these guys for the crime, but my partner, being the senior man, stretched out the job. One month turned into three months of investigation, just to arrest these two imposters. They were sentenced to three years probation.

I finally realized why it took three months to complete the job. My partner knew they would not receive any prison time, and the brass downtown told him to take as much time as needed to clear the case. We could have walked across the country in three months, but I learned if you complete a job hastily, the brass would expect the next job completed even faster. If not accomplished as quickly as the last, their suspicion figures you dogged it.

In this unique unit, you could work on any gang related crime that came to your attention. If the guys made an exceptional arrest and not gang related, they would just put the offender in a gang to keep the downtown brass off their back. The problem with this procedure is the statistics become inaccurate, but nobody seemed to care. As long as you brought in a head for the time spent on the investigation, the downtown people were content. This tactic continued for the entire time I spent in the unit.

As in any small unit, you cannot accomplish much until you hook up with a steady partner. I felt like a rubber ball, bounced around from partner to partner for six months. This unstable work condition somewhat stressed me, but at least I could observe how the other detectives functioned. Some guys worked very hard and bent the rules, some guys were straight arrows, but ruthless, and a few did no work at all. Where did I fit into this equation?

I still did not have a partner. Finally, the day came to hook up with someone steady. One of the old homicide dicks decided to go back to regular Homicide. I became his replacement. My new partner's name was Earl. We never worked together before, but met as police cadets. Earl was one hell of a detective.

Let me tell you a little about him. His nicknames were "Earl the Pearl," "Mr. GQ," "Starsky" (I was "Hutch"), and "Felix" (I was "Oscar"). We were like a bottle of oil and vinegar. When placed side by side, we tasted dreadful, but when blended, we were one hell of a salad dressing.

A married man in a two-income family, Earl had no children. The two incomes made life moderately comfortable. No one on the entire Chicago Police Department dressed as elegantly as Earl while at work. He styled better than the attorneys in court, and was often confused as one by numerous judges. He drove a Corvette, grew his hair long, was fanatically clean, and the word "wrinkle" did not exist in his vocabulary. I definitely felt inferior in the dress category, but my partner never rubbed it in my face, as the other guys did. I was never a messy person, nor looked dirty, but standing next to Earl, even a guy like the Pope looked dirty. So, that is how my nickname came about. I was "Oscar."

The first time we hit the streets, we worked together as well as a pair of brand new radials. He was a wiz on the typewriter, and a hell of a paper man. I was the talker, as well as the con man. We played the good guy bad guy routine hundreds of times, mostly successful.

We received an assignment from the office to assist the regular Homicide Division with a hot one. The thought of real police work excited me. Earl and I went upstairs and spoke with the dicks. They had some junkie who supposedly was kidnapped the night before by the same two offenders who appeared in the Daily Bulletin. They were wanted for a prior double murder and were at large for a month. Homicide made numerous attempts to apprehend them but failed. The junkie said he sat in a room alone with the two when they tried to blow his brains out, but the gun misfired. He did a Mark Spitz out the window and ran.

I spoke to the junkie for a short time and a gut feeling grew inside. I sensed he spoke the truth. He displayed a look of fear on his face and the sound of it in his voice. With all due respect to the other detectives, they thought his story stunk; besides, they had not eaten breakfast yet and were quite hungry. The dicks left the case to us and went for some chow.

Earl and I decided to check it out. We took the junkie downstairs and hooked him to the wall. He sent us to an address of a seven-room brick bungalow located on the south side of the city. It had been checked out previously numerous times with negative results. When we arrived, we banged on the door and rang the bell. No answer.

"Should we kick in the fucking door, Rich? What do ya think?" asked Earl.

We were hungry also. Was it time for breakfast? The house appeared empty and, normally, we would have kicked in the door without a warrant, but we hesitated. Earl and I decided to have breakfast instead and return to the office.

We spoke to the junkie and told him what happened. He informed us he might have been mistaken about the address but he could certainly show us the house. It appeared he seemed quite anxious to get unhooked from the wall and into the back of our police car for an opportunity to escape. Earl and I had no idea why. As long as he remained in police custody, he would be safe.

We denied his request and told him to describe the area in question. He indicated the cross streets of 105th and Peoria. We were supposed to look for a house next to an empty lot with a broken awning. Sounds pretty easy? WRONG! There are hundreds of houses with broken awnings in the ghetto, and there are four or five empty lots on many blocks created by abandonment and the wrecker's ball.

We returned to the station and picked up the informant. We needed him to show us exactly where the house sat. The junkie took us back to the original house Earl and I already checked out. He instructed us to check the side and look for the broken window he dove through the night before. We exited the car and

left him behind. Sure enough, broken glass on the walkway indicated the spot of his dive. How dumb were we, why didn't we
check out the walkway on our original visit?

Earl and I climbed through the window and yelled "police
officers" as loud as we could. Earl and his four hundred dollar
suit would not look as stylish with his head blown off. No one
responded to our shouts.

We peeked in the bedroom and there lay a man and a woman
either asleep or dead; we did not know which. They were the
murder suspects. Lying on the floor parallel with the bed was
a sawed-off shotgun. I picked it up and inserted the barrel in
the bad guy's mouth. His eyes opened. The woman next to him
snored away until she got a swift kick in the ass from Earl. We
made the arrest without any problems.

We took all concerned back to Homicide and you should
have seen the looks on the faces of the other two detectives.
They thought the junkie lied. We did not. It seemed, from this
point, these two detectives started to respect us much more. My
rationale for such a statement: these investigators requested our
personal assistance numerous times in the years to come.

The dicks separated both people and spoke to them individu-
ally concerning the double homicide. You never question one suspect in front of another. Interrogations are conducted in this manner so you could lie to one suspect in order to get the other to talk.
This technique worked occasionally; other times, it did not.

After forty minutes, one of the dicks approached Earl and
me and inquired if we visited the house earlier in the day seeking
the suspects. We responded in the affirmative.

"You guys should say a prayer right now you're still alive.
The bitch told me her boyfriend hid behind the door and intended to blow your heads off when you guys entered. She said she
couldn't believe her ears when you two choose breakfast over
kicking in the fucking door," he said.

"Yeah, that's something we picked up from you guys. You
didn't want to go to the house either because of breakfast. You
learn something new everyday," I said.

A good pinch makes you feel special inside, especially if the guy was about to blow off your head. It appears luck intervened on this arrest. First, we did not get our heads blown off. Secondly, it was a hunch Earl and I believed the junkie's story. If the guy upstairs gives you that lucky break, run with it. When the bad guy has the luck, you can forget about an unproblematic capture. Here is a good example.

Thomas Park is located on the south side of Chicago in a predominantly Mexican area. Where you have a Mexican culture, you have close-knit families. Along with the families come the teenagers. The next step in the equation, a lot of the teenagers form street gangs. It is like pie and coffee; do not ask me why, the gangs just form. These guys do not screw around. If you do not reside in the gang's area, they will shoot your ass just for strolling through their neighborhood.

It was a beautiful summer day with the temperature at ninety degrees. The park overflowed with kids and their families. Across the street and from out of a gangway surfaced three local gang-bangers. Two held handguns and the other a rifle. They fired into a group of teens, trying to hit specifically one, the leader of a rival Latin gang. After the shooting spree, a gang-banger lay wounded and two other bystanders were dead. The gang-banger had a .38 slug in the right cheek of his buttocks. Ironically, we were only able to find two witnesses to the murder. Both possessed long arrest records and were known gang members. What a dreadful combination as far as witnesses were concerned. We brought them into Area #3 for questioning and a statement. The press pounced all over this one. Earl notified the State's Attorney's Office to assist in the investigation and approve any charges that were to be levied.

Accordingly, many of these attorneys were two or three years out of law school. They do not possess much street knowledge, but are pretty sharp with the books. The only problem with this kind of system is the attorney plays judge and jury and adjudicates the case in the police station. If it sounds like a loser, you will not get an approval and they will demand more evidence, even though none exists. These attorneys must maintain a favorable conviction rate, especially come election time.

One way to solve the problem of denied charges is to tell the attorney the victim's family will be informed his office is playing politics with the case. Another approach: get a meddlesome reporter to the scene by placing an anonymous call to the newspapers. Funny, most of our charges always seemed to get approved on the first request at the threat of this unprofessional tactic.

The attorneys who arrived at the station dealt with Earl and me on numerous occasions. They knew we never aimed to hustle them on the facts of the case. The charges were not denied, but the attorneys did want a powerful case to assure a conviction. Our witnesses had long police records and they hesitated on the approval. We hit the streets for more tips and clues.

"Hey, Earl, I guarantee you if the two eyeballs were a nun and a priest or an attorney and his wife, those two castrated State's Attorneys would've approved the charges."

"Well, Rich, at least we know who did it. Now we just have to go out and get more evidence to prove it," said Earl.

One fact we were aware of from working in a Mexican area of Chicago was that gang members do not tell the police anything unless it benefits them personally. Community members also are reluctant to verbalize with the police for fear of reprisal. We spoke to probably forty people during our investigation. Everyone knew what happened and who did it, but no one would bear witness in court.

Our stomachs growled, reminding us it was dinnertime. We were dedicated investigators, but not that dedicated. A good cop never gets hungry and never gets wet. My thoughts jumped to the past and reminded me of Jimmy enjoying his retirement. Lady Luck must have also been hungry. She dined at the same restaurant as Earl and I. We could have eaten at any of over fifty establishments in the area, but we wanted pizza. Conveniently, an Italian restaurant sat in the vicinity of the homicide crime scene. We plopped in our booth and ordered. Slightly to our right sat an elderly Mexican man, his wife, and two children.

"Hey, Officer, you guys gonna catch the killer of those kids in the park?" he asked.

"I hope so, but we have shitty witnesses," said Earl.

The Mexican turned from side to side and looked over each shoulder. He leaned forward towards us.

"Try talking to Lisa. She lives down the street, next to the candy store," he whispered.

"Why should we talk to her?" I asked. (Even though we knew Lisa was the girlfriend of Tony Martinez, our prime suspect.)

We spoke to her yesterday, but she had an alibi, although unverifiable.

Still crouched over his table, he related that, on the day of the murder, Lisa walked into the restaurant and made a quick phone call. Her girlfriend, Tina, accompanied her. All they ordered were two cokes and they sat themselves in a booth. His suspicion grew because no food was ordered and both girls tipped the scale at over two hundred pounds. Thirty minutes later, all patrons of the restaurant heard the shots. He leaned back to join his family and continued to eat.

"I thought it funny they jumped up and left right after the shots. You'd think two women would want to stay inside where they'd be safe," he said.

Earl and I looked at each other and smiled. Could this be the lucky break of the case?

Now, we had to con the girls and unseal those painted red lips we knew would be locked up nice and tight. We finished our pizza and left.

We located Lisa's house and both girls were inside. Who was the weaker of the two? We began the interview and put the girls in separate rooms. Unfortunately, Lisa, the one we needed to talk, seemed to be the slickest of the duo. Earl and I always discussed our interrogation methods beforehand, and never went in cold. That is why we were so good at it. It is difficult for a suspect to out think you, if prepared. When they know you are bluffing, they will not tell you a thing and the interrogation will fail.

As soon as we informed the girls we wanted to speak to them again about the park murders, both their mouths dropped open. Our goal: get Lisa to admit she was in the restaurant before and during the shooting. The knowledge of the phone conversation was kept out of the interrogation, leaving Lisa to believe we knew nothing of the call. Her tone of voice and body language could only be described as cockiness. She told us zilch. She had won the first round of the interrogation. Time to talk to Tina.

"Okay, Tina, Lisa just spilled her guts. All I want to know is who you called on the phone from the pizzeria," said Earl.

"I didn't call anyone. It was Lisa who called," snapped Tina.

We now verified Lisa made a phone call and that statement backed up the witness' account of the incident. We returned to Lisa and told her Tina told us all about the phone call. Somewhat startled, she yelled, "I didn't make any fucking phone call, asshole!"

Why would somebody lie about a measly phone call if it did not have anything to do with the murder? We needed a sting to get more answers.

"Listen, you little cunt, we're going downtown right now, and on the way, we're stopping at Ma Bell. I'm gonna yank the records for that pay phone in the restaurant. You know computers do everything nowadays. If the list of numbers has a certain Mr. Martinez on it prior to the murder, you're in big fucking trouble, bitch. Now let's go. Get in the fuckin' car!" I said.

The first part of the con completed, we drove to Ma Bell. Earl pulled up in front of the building and I exited the vehicle. The girls assumed my mission was to examine phone records. Instead, I ended up in the cafeteria with a sweet roll and a cup of coffee. I returned to the car.

"This bitch is gonna need a good lawyer. The payphone tapes showed a call to that little wetback's apartment twenty minutes prior to the shooting," I said.

Lisa leaned on the back portion of the front seat.

"Anyone could have made that call. My boyfriend knows a lot of people," yelled Lisa.

"Yeah, but we have a witness who told us you made a call from the restaurant pay phone and were only on for thirty seconds or so. That would be just enough time to tell Tony the Kings were in the park, and exactly where they were," Earl told her.

"Bitch, your fucking taco is cooked and you're going down with Tony unless you fess up, right now," I said.

From this witness, Earl and I gathered enough information for approval of charges, the arrest, and even a conviction. This murder was solved and closed. It was not great police work that broke the case; it was where we chose to eat our dinner, then came the great police work. One tip for all new investigators: always try to eat in the area of the crime. You never know who will be seated next to you.

As time went on, I became very close to guys in the Gang Unit and very good friends with Earl. Our wives did not socialize, but then again, we did not socialize with our wives. Both of our marriages were on the rocks. Often, Earl and I would go out and party heavy. The women used to hang all over us, mostly cop freaks. My marriage eventually faded, but through no fault of my wife and children. The investigator's lifestyle was to blame. During my career, I knew many officers and supervisors who cheated on their wives. The schedule of a detective, and all the free time during investigations, added to the temptation. It was not uncommon to cover for a buddy while he snuck off to meet his mistress. Many of the guys used to joke about getting a quickie at work, and getting paid for the pleasure at the taxpayer's expense. Not all of the members of my unit took part in this practice, but many did.

Earl and I separated from our wives about the same time, and who would be more perfect for a roommate than him? The only problem that existed was our financial situation. Two kids in private school and Earl's clothing bill kept our pockets empty. Bet you snoops from Internal Affairs think I am about to confess we stole to survive? You could not be further from the truth. We both got lucky, found rich girlfriends, and our money problems vanished. We lived in a $900 a month luxury high-rise apartment on

Lake Shore Drive. The furnishings were right out of a magazine. I am quite sure a lot of our brother cops judged us to be thieves by our lavish lifestyles. Cops tend to think this way whenever someone does well and enjoys life at home and at work.

We continued to carouse, but it took its toll and affected our work. Our boss actually told us to slow down. The way it affected our work was obvious. We could not keep our eyes open while at the office, especially with the poor air conditioning in the summer. This condition existed from a lack of sleep and one tremendous hangover after another.

"Earl, I think the boss is full of shit. We're still one of the top teams in the unit, figures don't lie," I said.

"What he really means, Rich, is our work isn't bad, it's us coming in two hours late every other day. He might be concerned we're not giving the city a full eight. After all, he's the boss," said Earl.

I snarled at Earl and grabbed my crotch.

"I got your full eight right here. Why doesn't the boss tell the other teams, who get here on time everyday, to give their full eight? They give two and take six for personal use. So they arrive on time, big deal. We're late once in awhile, but the city gets a full six from us. The math doesn't add up."

One of the other gang detectives overheard my conversation with Earl.

"So, I take too much time to do personal shit, do I? I conduct my personal business on my lunch hour," he said.

"Your lunch hour shouldn't start at the beginning of your tour. Spread your crap around somewhere else," said Earl.

"Don't speak so fast, partner. Remember the time we took our lunch the instant we arrived at work? It put us on the front page of every newspaper in the city. We were heroes," I said.

I referred to the morning when I arrived at work pissed off and embarrassed. I neglected to pay our electric bill and the Common Wealth Edison people threatened a turnoff in two days.

"I don't care if the Mayor just got shot, I gotta go downtown and pay the electric bill before they shut it off," I said.

Earl got pissed because it was my turn to pay the bill. We jumped in the car and headed downtown, after steak and eggs, of course. I paid the bill and I returned to the squad car. We heard an all call broadcast of a robbery in progress that involved an armored car. We were ready to act if needed, but the location of the crime was actually ten miles to our north. It would have taken fifteen minutes to respond. We decided to forget it.

Just then, a flash message blasted out of the radio. The suspect hijacked a yellow cab and was last seen headed in a southerly direction.

"Hey, Earl, sounds like a real pro. He steals a yellow car for his get away," I said.

We had a hunch the suspect lived on the south side. The only two routes he could have possibly traveled for a speedy getaway were the Dan Ryan Expressway and Lake Shore Drive. At first, we thought he would have to be a real dumbbell to take Lake Shore Drive. The police would spot him in a minute. But then again, we were not dealing with Einstein; he did steal a yellow car to flee the crime scene.

We played our hunch and headed for Lake Shore Drive. Downtown traffic was heavy, but with sirens blaring and lights flashing, we arrived at Randolph Street and LSD very quickly. Our light turned red, so the southbound traffic started to move. The third car to pass in front of us was the suspect. He drove Yellow Cab #793. We could not believe it and immediately notified the zone operator.

We noticed the barrel of a shotgun laying out the open passenger window. It was time to stop playing around. Earl and I knew help would soon arrive, so we attempted to stay a couple of car lengths behind him. The radio blared with chatter, so much so that we could not understand a word that was being said. We hoped the squad got our original request for assistance.

We had one problem. The city had a reputation for not keeping their cars in top running condition. Our vehicle was okay, but it would not go over fifty miles per hour. Funny enough, cab companies had the same reputation, but Cab #793 would go over fifty miles per hour. I wondered if Lady Luck rode in his cab or our police car.

Brink's holdup foiled by guards

By Jon Ziomek

A nervous would-be robber failed in his attempt to hold up a Brink's Security truck Monday and then was captured by police after trying to escape in a stolen taxi.

In custody was Melvin Gilchrist, 25, of 8001 S. Loomis, charged with armed robbery and attempted armed robbery. He is a former cabdriver, according to Area 6 Robbery Comdr. August Locallo.

Police and witnesses gave this chronology of events:

A Brink's truck driven by Fred Kuhrmeier, with partner Richard Proppogio in back, arrived around 10 a.m. at the Belmont Hotel, 3172 N. Sheridan, for a regular pickup. The truck parked around the corner, on Belmont, as it always does, according to the hotel manager, L. E. Sineski.

Just as Proppogio climbed out of the back and shut the door, police said, a man wearing a green jumpsuit, a nylon-stocking cap and a construction helmet dashed out of a nearby alley and shouted, "Freeze!"

The man pulled a shotgun out of a sack he was carrying and held it at Proppogio's abdomen, demanding that he open the door, police said.

"I thought it was all over," Proppogio later told police. The gunman took his .38-caliber revolver, he said.

Proppogio had no keys to the back door, though, so he stood on the street while Kuhrmeier, sizing up the situation, threw the truck in gear, gunned the engine and started to pull away, which is Brink's policy in holdup situations.

The gunman then apparently panicked, Locallo said, and dashed back into the alley without ever getting into the truck. A witness told police that the man then climbed into a Yellow Cab with the clearly marked numbers "793" and drove off.

Passing policemen broadcast the cab number and it was spotted southbound on Lake Shore-Dr. by Gang Crimes Investigators Earl Zuelkhe and Richard Solita, who gave chase.

Shots were fired between the two vehicles near McCormick Place, but no one was injured. The two officers curbed the cab at the entrance ramp to the Stevenson Expressway, just off Lake Shore, Locallo said.

A green jumpsuit, Proppogio's handgun and a construction hat were found in the back of the cab, Locallo said. He said the cab had been stolen earlier Monday from a cab garage at 681 N. Green.

Gilchrist was to appear Tuesday in Felony Court.

Yellow cab 793—getaway car for suspect

LEFT: Police check the cab used as a getaway car by a suspect in the robbery of a Brink's armored truck at Belmont and Sheridan Monday. The suspect, Melvin Gilchrist, 25, was captured on the ramp leading from Lake Shore Dr. to the Stevenson Expressway after a chase along the lakefront. **RIGHT:** Gilchrist is taken into custody after the cab was curbed. During the chase south along the drive, gunfire was exchanged, but no one was injured. (Sun-Times Photos by Jerry Tomaselli and Carmen Reporto)

I looked to the rear down Lake Shore Drive. A sea of blue lights lifted my spirits. They were about a mile behind us, but if I could see the lights, so could the bad guy. We maintained our distance, but the culprit suddenly punched it and a cloud of black smoke burst from his tail pipe. Earl floored our pedal. Nothing happened, just a lot of noise. It sounded like we blew a rod. Not surprised, we chuckled as backfire sounds exploded from our exhaust pipe. The suspect's car sped on and the distance between us increased. The cab grew smaller and smaller from our view through the front windshield.

"He's getting away, Earl. What the fuck should I do, shoot the motherfucker?" I asked.

"No, don't shoot this prick. Think of the paperwork and those assholes from IAD trying to second-guess your kill. I'd rather let him get away than have them prosecute us for shooting someone in the back," said Earl.

"Fuck it, Earl. Gimmie your big gun, maybe the shots will give this jagoff something to think about," I said.

I leaned half of my body out the passenger's window and took aim. Earl's cannon pointed a good twenty feet above the cab's rear window. The robber's eyes peered at me through his rear view mirror. The highway was clear and time to fire. I let a round go from Earl's .44 mag and it sounded like a sonic boom. Not only did the bad guy pull over, but he also indicated his intention with his turning signal.

Earl and I approached the cab and ordered the offender to put both hands out of the driver's window. We grabbed him by the arms and yanked his body right out. He landed horizontal on the pavement. We cuffed him and completed the arrest with little effort.

By now, the troops arrived and it seemed the situation had been neutralized. We just forgot one small detail. When we jerked the offender from the car, we forgot to check the gearshift. As we cuffed and scuffled with the bad guy, the unattended cab drove down Lake Shore Drive. It traveled about two hundred yards and crashed into a side guardrail.

Picture a crowd of policemen chasing an empty cab down the freeway. The address of arrest had to be changed to cover our ass. Nothing was mentioned about our participation of the runaway cab; we were heroes on the front page of the Chicago newspapers. This all happened due to an unpaid electric bill. It appeared the cab had not picked up Lady Luck for a fare that morning.

Time went on and Earl and I were soon divorced men. Down and out and busted, my rich lady split. Two kids in private schools did not help my financial situation, but I realized education was important for my children and I would do anything to keep them in superior schools. The temptations on the job became more and more lucrative, but so far, honesty prevailed. I never lost any sleep worrying about something I stole the day before.

Then, one Sunday afternoon, I was eating brunch on Rush Street and met the second love of my life. It was clear from the moment our eyes met. She was a cocky woman, but possessed a heart of gold, a great combination. A classy lady, Susan and I became best of friends and lovers. She had a fantastic family and they accepted me immediately. Susan heralded from the east and displayed a very definite attitude about policemen. Basically, she looked down on them. I found this attitude prevalent among many people from her circle of friends. She used to call me Redneck or Hillbilly, and told me a police profession was not a very respectable one where she came from. College and professional people seemed to impress her.

As my love grew for Susan, she began to change my life. She wanted me to become a better person. She suggested I broaden my circle of friends to include other professional people who were not in law enforcement. I complied with her wishes. There really is another world out there besides this police crap.

She wanted me to return to college and complete my four-year degree. I agreed, and with her support, accomplished the feat. I became the first of my brothers and sisters to attain a four-year degree. But, a degree on the Chicago Police Department did not mean anything without clout. I finished for my own self-satisfaction. I have always felt one should have a college degree before taking the sergeant's promotional exam. This would keep all the dumbbells with clout out of the supervisory positions.

After the graduation ceremony, Susan was so proud of me. She immediately called her family and told them of my success. She continued to push me to better myself. She is the type of woman you would find behind every successful man. Susan would not care if you succeeded; all she wanted you to do was try. A real sweetheart, I owe her in part for any of my success.

Soon after graduation, I submitted an application for law school. My ambition was to become a hotshot defense attorney. What the hell, the blue bloods are not the only ones who had the market cornered. I studied my ass off the first semester and my clout got me one of those soft desk jobs for a while. I knew the laws inside and out. With finals just around the corner, I prepared myself as humanly possible.

The morning of the exams, I woke up very nervous. I imagined where my career in law might take me. After years of hard work to put people in prison, it would now be my job to keep them out. I was excellent in court and rarely could a lawyer confuse me. Even some of the best attorneys in Chicago took shots at me on the stand, but somehow, I manage to survive their questions without appearing to be an idiot.

The secret is to tell the truth. Lawyers expect you to lie, and when they uncover the lie, they strive to paint a picture of you as unreliable to the jury. When you tell the truth, you can never look bad. It is all a matter of matching wits with the attorney. The minute a lawyer determines you are not lying and you know your stuff, he will remove you from the stand as fast as possible. It felt great when you survived an attorney's attack unscathed.

Defense attorneys tend to judge anyone wearing a monkey suit as an idiot. So, you must wait for the right moment and steal his role when you are on the stand. Make the attorney look like the idiot. By this, I mean wait for a long-winded question from the attorney. It is usually accompanied by awkward arm waves and screams thrown right into your face. When counsel has finished the longwinded question, look very calmly into his eyes and say, "I'm sorry, sir, I did not understand your question, can you repeat it, please?"

Most of the time, they will ask the court reporter to repeat the question. The reason being, he has already forgotten the query himself. This form of cross-examination is taught in every law school in the country to confuse the witness.

I arrived for the test and it waited on my desk. Sweat dripped from my forehead, but soon stopped. The exam seemed to be trouble-free. I was confident I would pass with ease. I believed so because I thought law schools were on the up and up, but it boils down to what makes a law school run. All need tuitions paid and must have huge amounts of money from alumni donations come in on a regular basis to survive.

To be accepted, I needed a little extra help, due to my slightly above average entrance exam. A call was made to the dean of the law school. This means, if a call was made to assure my acceptance, others were made for people in the similar situation. It boiled down to seating space and clout.

The special summer session consisted of 450 students at $1,000 a pop. This semester would determine if I could hack the law school environment. Upon successfully completing these special classes, I would be accepted into the school. The institution knew exactly how many empty seats were available for the upcoming semester. I guarantee that it was less than 450 seats or all enrolled in the session would have been accepted in the first place. They informed me that if I successfully completed the session, admittance would be assured. But, that was impossible because there were only so many seats available. So, with my hopes high and the school $450,000 richer, I entered the program. Oh yes, I did flunk the exam. But, I have no complaints. I gave it my best shot and lost. Losing is part of life. There were many intelligent people in my class who also failed. I felt sorry for them, for, unlike me, they did not have a nine-year police career to fall back on.

The system was a stranger to them; they actually thought they had a legitimate chance for admittance. When you are told ahead of time that if you pass the session you will be accepted, and the school knows full well this is impossible, this means school officials had prior knowledge of how many students would be allowed to pass. This is easily accomplished by evaluating the tests a certain way. Instead of implementing the A.B.C. system of grading, the values of the essay answers are determined by the professor's interpretation. This type of grading is almost impossible to challenge.

Some who oddly passed the class were not the bright ones. Many of their fathers were alumnae. Students informed me on numerous occasions that their fathers' donated large sums of money to the school. It was now the school's obligation to return the favor. Some students were related to judges and some to politicians. It was the same old shit. The entire experience reminded me of City Hall and back room politics.

I realized my law career had ended before it even began. Once again, I returned to my passion, real police work. Earl and I teamed up again and still produced one big pinch after another. Things fell into place routinely and Lady Luck still slept in our beds.

Homicides were sluggish this particular week, so we decided to work on some armed robberies. There had been a rash of Ma & Pa grocery stores hit in our area. The same offender committed all of the robberies. The dicks knew his identity, but thus far, the offender avoided arrest. Our investigation led us to Mama's house and we immediately determined the bad guy only visited on occasion. Earl and I did not want to sit on the house, so we left with the intention to give it another try later in the evening. Who knows when he would show up again? Unknown to us, two robbery dicks went to our boss behind our backs and asked for our assistance in the case. Needless to say, the boss ordered us to watch the house and help out the dicks. They sort of made a joke of it, and sometimes drove by and waved at us. We were bored as hell.

"Hey, Earl, fuck these two old Irish pricks. I'm tired of making these guys look good. Let's blow this bullshit stakeout and go into the station and talk to the lieutenant," I said.

"Oh no, what are you gonna do? Don't fuck around," said Earl.

"Remember Charlie, our friend at the Welfare Department? He's gonna help us catch this guy," I said.

"Rich, he won't give us any information without a subpoena."

"When I get finished with him, he's gonna give us his damn office computer," I said.

We walked into the lieutenant's office with a proposition. I requested the boss pull us from the house sitting detail and promised Earl and I would have the pinch in seven days.

Earl's eyeballs bulged from his head when he heard my proposal.

"What's on your mind, Rich?" asked the lieutenant.

"Boss, you don't want to know. Just trust us on this one," I said.

"Okay, today is Tuesday. I want this guy in my office in one week, handcuffed and under arrest. Is that understood?" asked the lieutenant.

"Ten-four," I said.

Earl looked angry and worried both at the same time.

"Are you crazy? The robbery dicks have been after this prick for three months and we're going to catch him in one week?" asked Earl.

"Have I ever let you down, buddy? Let's go see Charlie," I said with a mischievous look on my face.

We walked into Charlie's office and were greeted with a friendly handshake. Charlie was somewhat nerdy, but certainly a concerned citizen when it came to crime.

"What can I do for you today?" asked Charlie.

"Charlie, we gotta problem. There's this pervert grabbing little girls on their way home from school and sexually assaulting them. Before he leaves, he gives them a beating. We're at a dead end with this one, Charlie, and I know you'll help us. We're dealing with kids here," I said.

Charlie agreed, and asked for the pervert's name. He left the room and ran our friend through his computer system. For those of you who wonder what kind of info one could get from Charlie, let me explain. It is as valuable to a policeman as his gun. The computer will tell us if the bad guy receives welfare checks. If he does, we can ascertain the name of currency exchange where he picks up the check and on which day. All we have to do is stakeout the building on payday and wait for the rat to snatch up his cheese.

Charlie approached with a computer printout in hand as he shook his head from side to side. He informed us the bad guy was dropped from the rolls about ten months ago.

Charlie supplied us with the print out and excused himself from the room to take a phone call.

"Hey, Earl, watch the door and let me know when Charlie is coming," I said.

"Oh please, Rich, what the fuck are you gonna do?" asked Earl.

"Don't worry about it. All I'm gonna do is borrow a couple pieces of paper," I said.

I stuffed the papers in my sport coat before Charlie returned. Earl and I shook his hand and I lauded him for being an outstanding citizen. A quick wink at Earl and we both split. Earl wondered how my antics were going to catch the bad guy. The lieutenant would have our ass if we did not keep our word.

We headed back to the office and I immediately went to my desk. I removed the "borrowed" stationary from my coat. I stole two envelopes and two pieces of paper. But these were not two ordinary pieces of paper. The letterheads indicated they were correspondences from the U.S. Department of Welfare.

"Partner, what in the fuck you gonna to do with those letters?" asked Earl.

"Look, our man is a junkie and everything he steals goes into his arm. He needs all the money he can get his hands on. This letter from the Welfare Department will show a mistake on all the checks issued for the previous year. I'll make it $10 per check. Since he gets twelve checks a year, that means Uncle

Sam owes our friend $120. I'll tell him he can pick up the money at his regular currency exchange and give him a few days to get the letter. You know all we've gotta do is send it to Mama's house. Trust me, he'll get it."

"It will never work, partner. Our guy is just too slick," said Earl.

"He's a junkie, Earl, it's $120, and he doesn't have to put a gun to anybody's head to get it. He'll be there," I said.

The next night, we drove to Mama's house and put our letter in her mailbox. We even put a stamp on it. Odds are, it will not take Mama long to notify her son. Mothers always know where their sons are, criminals or not.

The following shift, we informed the boss we were hot on the bad guy's trail. I told him we had a tip the offender might be headed to a downtown movie with his girlfriend. We wanted to check it out. The true reason we gave the boss the info was to catch a movie on company time ourselves. This covered our ass in case a field inspector caught us in the theater. We entered the show free with a simple flip of our badges and enjoyed the movie. I like this job.

The end of the shift came quickly. Before we left, the boss reminded us of our commitment. He walked out of his office and I yelled at him, "We'll have that dog junkie in the office tomorrow as promised. Make sure you have some coffee and doughnuts for him."

We left and walked down the stairs. Earl disgustedly shook his head from side to side. It worried him what would happen on the seventh day if we came in empty handed. I told him to have faith in the junkie. My statement made him even more nervous. We stopped for a cocktail to ease the tension created by the up-coming situation.

The seventh day arrived and it was up to our junkie friend to do his part. Earl's complaints erupted again in regards to the letter. I got tired of listening to him bitch and grabbed another piece of paper. I jammed it into the typewriter. Earl glanced over my shoulder and the keys hammered the ink ribbon. I ripped out the paper and handed it to Earl.

"We'll put this letter in an envelope and have the clerk at the exchange give it to our friend when he comes in for his money," I said.

The letter simply read:

"You're one stupid asshole. Put your hands in the air. You're under arrest. Don't move or we'll blow your fucking head off. Your days of robbing your brothers and sisters have come to an end. Yours Truly, Officer friendly."

Earl nervously ran both hands through his hair.

"You're fucking nuts. It'll never work," he said.

"Let's go get our man, partner, it won't be long now," I said.

We arrived at the currency exchange thirty minutes prior to the business day and spoke to the manager. He was very cooperative. Earl remained outside in an undercover van, with me inside behind the bulletproof glass. I posed as another employee. Before the exchange opened, I gave the letter to the clerk and instructed her to give it to the bad guy when he requested his check.

At 9:00 a.m., the clerk unlocked the door and we waited for the suspect. Earl joked back and forth on the walkie-talkie and most of the conversation consisted of what we would tell the boss if we came in empty handed. He finally changed the subject when some black broad showed up to catch a bus with watermelons under her shirt for tits. All of a sudden, Earl stopped right in the middle of a sentence and changed his thought pattern. He squinted through the peephole of the van.

"I don't fucking believe it. I'm thinking our man just pulled up," he yelled into the walkie-talkie.

The bad guy's arrival renewed my faith in how predictable a junkie could be.

"Hey, Earl, I'll bet you lunch this prick has the letter we left at Mama's house in his hand," I said.

Earl laughed out loud.

"You got a bet," he said.

A few seconds went by.

"Aw shit, where do ya wanna eat? He just pulled out a white envelope from his pocket," said Earl.

Now, I laughed out loud, but time to stop screwing around. It was important to take this guy by surprise to eliminate any chance of injury. I told the clerk to get ready for the bad guy. He entered and handed her the letter I sent him. The clerk read it and handed him the envelope that contained the second letter. He accepted the envelope, turned, and started to open it.

I instructed Earl to move in because we did not want to accost him on the street. Earl entered the front door and I covered the rear. We watched as he read, and waited for him to lift his head. He exhibited a look of surprise on his face as he turned back towards the clerk.

"Hey, asshole, put your hands in the air. You're under arrest!" Earl yelled with his weapon drawn and pointed at his head.

"Ah shit, I knew it, I knew it," he said.

The bad guy looked to the heavens to make sure this was not a dream. I cuffed the offender and said, "Yeah, you knew it, fuckhead, and you're on the way to the police station to turn yourself in."

Earl and I turned toward the clerk to say thank you. She leaned back in her chair and laughed so hard that she could not even wave good-bye. She signaled our departure with a simple nod.

En route to the station, we messed with his mind the entire time.

"I never knew anyone so stupid, man. You fell for it hook, line, and sinker. You're one dumb motherfucker," I said.

The poor guy was so humiliated. But, as far as I was concerned, the police verbal abuse was all part of his sentence, plus the seven to ten he got for the robberies.

He sat back in his seat and never uttered a word. After our arrival at the office, we hooked him to the wall and spread the story through the entire building. One after another, various policemen strolled through our office just to laugh at the guy and once again insult him. We notified all the Ma & Pa victims in the African American community and received nothing but praise and thanks. This community was rid of a vicious felon and the case was closed.

This pinch put us on top. We slowly established ourselves as one of the lead investigative teams in the Gang Unit. We had the respect of the lieutenant, as well as all the sergeants. Their evaluations verified this fact. We also led the division many times in penitentiary convictions, a very prestigious accomplishment.

The ultimate compliment occurred when a black supervisor asked us to assist him in a very important investigation already underway in the black community. He could have chosen any one of ten black investigators in the unit, but he opted for us. Our hard work and dedication to duty started to payoff and our self-esteem as an effective investigative team grew rapidly.

The men in the Gang Unit were a pretty tight-knit bunch of guys and all were very cautious whenever a new policeman transferred into the unit. It boiled down to a matter of trust. The transfer order brought in a new officer from patrol. We will just call him Cans.

Cans was a hell of a policeman, but an inexperienced investigator. A great street cop at the time, he lacked essential investigative skills to be an effective investigator. But Cans wanted very much to learn because the supervisors would not give him any difficult investigations due to his street cop antics. I guess you could say Earl and I took him under our wings as a rookie investigator. Cans caught on very fast and today is probably one of Chicago's top investigators. But, his education did not come easy, primarily due to his tough guy attitude.

Out of the blue, Cans arrived at work and joked with the guys that he was not only the best shot on the Chicago Police Department, but the best wheel man on the job. He enjoyed teasing the troops, but it became apparent to all he may have started to believe his own flippancy. Some of the guys used to get upset when he used to draw his gun in the office and twirl it around his trigger finger like Billy the Kid to prove how well he could handle a weapon.

Earl and I sometimes would find a problem with the manner in which Cans drove to assignments. Fast, very fast. We used to bust his balls, and arrived at work early to snatch the squad car keys so he could not drive. Our efforts would place him in the back seat for the entire tour, and antsy Cans would be upset for hours.

One day, the three of us, along with another officer, got stuck on a detail guarding Nazi demonstrators who wanted to show their muscle in the Jewish community of Skokie, Illinois. Cans arrived at work an hour early and grabbed the car keys. We were stuck with him behind the wheel. We sped around for hours and broke all sorts of traffic laws until I asked to take a piss. Cans pulled into a Clark Oil Company gas station, but believed my urge to relieve myself was a ploy to remove him from behind the wheel. He was correct, so he never left the driver's seat. When I returned, Earl suggested a switch in drivers.

"Hey, don't you think it's about time someone else drives?" asked Earl.

"Why would you guys want another driver when the best on the department is at the wheel right now?" asked Cans.

We buckled up. Cans dropped the transmission into reverse and slammed the pedal to the floor. We slid and skidded on the oily gas station driveway and he lost control of the vehicle. In our path was a fifty-five gallon drum filled with empty oilcans and garbage. It silently screamed, "stop". Painted bright orange with a white stripe around its center, only a blind man would have missed it. The contents of the can spilled out and rolled toward the street. It covered the entire area with debris. The three of us watched and did not assist as Cans sanitized the driveway. He was totally humiliated, but it was all in fun.

The next day at roll call, the entire shift had a little surprise to Cans. When the supervisor called his name, he requested Cans to rise. The boss reached under his desk and removed a trophy constructed from a plastic container that formally contained a cleaning fluid known as Janitor in a Drum. One of the guys painted it orange with white stripes and mounted it on a wooden plaque. The sergeant presented the award to Cans for being the best driver on the Chicago Police Department. Thus, the nickname was born.

Cans became skilled very fast and an awesome investigator. Before long, he hooked up with his own partner and both were assigned some really tough cases. Their effort and hard work paid off. They became experts on the subject of motorcycle gangs throughout the city and state.

But the day soon came when Earl and I needed a third man on the car for a special assignment. The boss gave us Cans. On this particular day, he appeared quite upset teamed with Earl and me. We were all good friends, on and off duty, and Earl and I wondered about the cold shoulder.

"Hey, Rich, when we leave roll call, I've gotta stop at a gas station to fix a flat tire on my personal car," said Cans.

"No problem, partner. Earl and I will take you and we'll wait. I know a freebie joint," I said.

"Naw, you guys can just drop the tire and me and go eat," said Cans.

Earl and I knew something was not copasetic because it only takes ten minutes to fix a flat and gas station people never make the police wait, plus the fact that Cans loved breakfast. Why didn't he want us to hang around for the completion of the job?

We arrived at the gas station and Cans walked in carrying his flat tire. He gave it to the attendant and I observed some small talk between them. Earl and I proceeded to the bay area of the garage and suddenly Cans stopped us. He wanted to show us some tires on sale in another section of the gas station. We complied with his request and moseyed out of the bay area. Cans kept us busy for the next ten minutes by bullshitting over the price of the tires, but we knew something did not jive.

A hand signal by the attendant indicated the tire had been repaired. Cans could not wait to leave and his nervousness further aroused our suspicion.

"Here ya go, Officer, she's all fixed," said the attendant.

"Thanks a lot, big guy," said Cans.

He darted toward the exit while Earl and I lagged a short distance behind.

"Yeah, funny thing about this flat tire," said the attendant.

"What's that?" asked Earl.

"Well, I found this hunk of metal in the tire. It's not a sharp piece, but it made a hole on the inner side of the tire instead of from the bottom side," said the attendant.

"Let me take a look at that, buddy," I said.

I grabbed the mystery metal from the grease monkey's hand and examined it. At first, I had no idea what it could be. Flabbergasted, I tossed the slug in my hand as I solved the mystery.

"Earl, it's a fucking bullet. It's a .38 cal. bullet. He had to be fiddling with his snub nose on the way to work and twirling it just like he does in the office. The gun discharged. That explains the hole on the wrong side of the tire. The best shot on the Chicago Police Department killed his fucking front tire," I said.

By now, Cans plopped himself in the backseat of the squad and waited for us to return. Not a word said about the incident, the slug remained in my pocket. Cans rested quietly and thought he beat the rap. But, the next day at roll call, the best shot on the department received another award. It was an antique manually-operated air bicycle pump and scotch taped to the base was Can's spent bullet. Cans tilted his chin toward his chest and chuckled. The best shot on the department was crowned.

The next shift, the Robbery Commander asked our boss for some assistance in a cold case robbery pattern. This stick-up man was really sharp. He had seventeen jobs under his belt in thirty-six months. The crime spree netted him over $85,000 in cash. His MO consisted of robberies of a large chain of grocery stores. He would hit the joint at closing when only four or five employees remained. Concealed under the produce counter until the right moment, his surprised appearance announced the stick-up. His face masked with a nylon stocking, he never raised his voice, panicked, or hurt anyone. We had a strange feeling about this one; he did not depict the normal stickup man. The unique thing about this case, the robbery section did not have a clue on the identity of the offender. Total height of only five feet and six inches tall, the guys in our unit gave him the nickname "Shorty."

When you have a case like this, you start from scratch. The proper procedure is to gather every piece of paper on Shorty's jobs and seek out a common denominator. We sat around and brainstormed for hours, but the denominator eluded us. Our group resembled a college basketball team in the locker room discussing strategy at halftime, blackboard and all.

Since we had zero to go on, one of the bosses suggested a simultaneous search of all the grocery stores in the pattern prior to closing. This search took in a five-mile radius. None of us could have imagined the number of grocery stores situated in a five-mile sector of the city. We Chicagoans sure do eat a lot of damn food. This tactic went on for a week, and we still came up empty handed. The only accomplishment from this portion of the investigation was a five-pound weight gain from the snacks, which were "borrowed" from the store's shelves. We were back at the chalkboard and square one.

The team focused on a new approach. Puzzled, we sat in the office and tried to figure out why a stickup man needed so much money at one time, and then vacation from robbing again for months. He had a good thing going. Why wait all that time before he pulled off another job?

Someone suggested he or a family member could be ill and needed money for medical bills. The majority threw that idea to the wayside because Illinois's welfare system provided ample medical assistance to the needy. Earl sat at his desk, rolled up his sleeve, and pointed at the main vein in his arm, saying, "Maybe this guy is a junkie?"

"Nobody puts that much shit in his arm. Besides, how would you explain the long gap between stick-ups? He's doesn't use his Visa to score," said one of the sergeants.

We sat in a circle baffled, elbows on the desk and fists pressed against our cheeks. I glanced down at the sports section of the local paper. The article stunned me.

"Hey, Earl, check it out. The track had a Trifecta that paid $14,000 yesterday," I said.

I slowly rose from the table and jammed my chair back against the wall.

"At the track, at the track, that's it, Earl, our man's a degenerate gambler. He's hooked. I'm telling you, he's hooked on gambling and that explains the gap. Sometimes, this prick wins, so he doesn't have to steal to stay afloat," I said.

Earl and I tossed out the idea to the sergeant. He looked at us as if we were crazy. He chuckled and spoke in the direction of the other officers.

"Okay, you two super sleuths go check out all the race tracks in the city," he said.

We were pissed. He did not even give us the courtesy to look us in the eyes. He accepted the idea, but only to appease us. We were somewhat disgusted with his attitude because he thought we were full of shit on this one. But, many have thought Earl and I were full of shit before, but somehow, we managed to find an enema.

Before we hit the street for the track, another supervisor entered the room with some very important info. He investigated the three big grocery chains and completed a background check on past employees who fit the description of our bad guy. He was quite thorough in his investigation. He went back five years and eliminated all but eight people from a list of possible suspects. Of the eight who remained, five were previously arrested and photos were on file at Police Headquarters. It was a shot in the dark, but that is all we had to go on.

We mulled over all the reports again, but we could not find one person capable of identifying the suspect by face. Remember, all his jobs were perpetrated while masked. We were about to proceed to the racetrack, and I asked Earl to get copies of all the suspected photos. He retrieved the pictures and returned to the office.

"What the hell do we need photos for? Not one person can ID this prick," said Earl.

"Yeah, Earl, but the jagoff doesn't wear his mask when he bets at the fifty-dollar window. Come on, we'll give it a whirl and make a few bets ourselves. Who knows, we might get lucky twice," I said.

We entered track and went directly to the big betting window. The teller made us immediately. A look of disgust appeared on his face, as he reluctantly agreed to glance through the photos. At a snail's pace, he pulled one out of the pile and said, "Yeah, I know this guy, big better, 500-600 a race. He's what we call a chalk better and he wins most of the time."

The teller described our better as a little man, about five feet six, and one hundred thirty pounds. The key word here is "LITTLE." Earl and I snapped our heads towards each other and smiled. I looked up to the heavens with such a feeling of contentment. He informed us our offender bet at his window about a month ago. We had no choice but to leave our card and a copy of the photo with the teller. I instructed him to give us a call if Shorty reappeared and Earl and I proceeded to the cocktail lounge. Maybe we would find Shorty there; if not, we could have a drink ourselves.

We did enough work for the night, but five hours still remained in our tour. We rousted up a few ladies and asked them to meet us for a pizza and a beer. We spent the rest of the night bullshitting, trying to figure out how to keep our newly found info from the sergeant who thought we were on a wild goose chase. Should he be told of our golden egg of info? We also wanted to notify the Robbery Unit, but hesitated. We feared they would try to steal our pinch. This technique went on for years, one unit trying to cutthroat the other. It puzzled me why the different sections of the department must compete for pinches. It should not matter who got the bad guy off the street, but in reality, it did.

We decided to tell only our crew and bring no other unit in on the investigation. We wanted this pinch ourselves because of all the man-hours our unit devoted thus far in the investigation. The Gang Unit deserved the credit for the arrest and the cleared case. In the Detective Division, it is a priority how many arrests are made; in the Patrol Division, it is how many tickets are written. The imaginary marquee above all police stations reads "quantity not quality." It probably still does today.

The next day, there were plenty of loose ends to connect. Primarily, we still did not have Shorty connected to any of the stick-ups. We had no current address and all the leads turned up negative. Shorty's characteristics defined a drifter.

Another brainstorm session commenced and the sergeant informed the troops he wanted every racetrack covered "like flies on shit." Mimicking a school child sitting in the back of the classroom, I raised my hand and said, "I'm sorry, I thought you wanted Earl and me to handle the racetrack detail. Remember you told us last week?"

The sergeant knew we owned the racetrack lead from its conception to the teller's photo ID. There are two words that can describe what Earl and I were doing to our sergeant,

"BALL BUSTING." He deserved it.

On the way to the racetrack, we received a radio assignment to call our office. Shorty struck again. The funny thing about this stick-up, he did not wait for the store to close. This robbery did not fit his MO. Could Shorty be out of money? People do what people always do. We are all creatures of habit. Shorty probably got a hot tip on a horse and needed quick money to make the wager. No matter how or why, he broke his pattern. There is always a reason when something like this occurs. Shorty will be at the track tonight. I was sure of it.

Full emergency equipment activated, we proceeded to the grocery store. Police were all over the place. I verified the modus operandi, but like all the other stick-ups, no one could ID the offender. I felt a little tug on my sleeve from one of the cashiers and she wished to speak to me alone. We snuck down the frozen food aisle and I started to question her. I did not expect to get much info for my effort and asked if she noticed anything out of the ordinary about Shorty. She rolled her eyes and gave me a funny look.

"Naw, not really, he looked like any ordinary guy," she said.

"Yeah, any ordinary guy wearing a nylon mask," I said.

The girl chuckled at my comment.

"I could see right through the mask. You'd almost call it a veil. The nylon just hung over his face, you know, really limp. I saw right through it," she said.

"Do you mean to tell me you can identify this man's face?" I asked.

"Yeah, I even saw it with the stocking off. Before he came up to the front, he snuck up on me in the rear of the store and told me to put my hands up. I thought he was one of the stock boys fooling around with a toy gun. Stupid me, I pulled off the stocking. He stared at me for about a second or two and ripped it out of my hand. He immediately put the nylon back on his head. We walked to the front of the store; he robbed us, and left," she said.

I signaled for Earl and gave him one of my looks. He knew something was up.

"Earl, stand in front of us as a shield. Let's get an ID on this guy, hopefully unnoticed, and we'll blow this fucking pop stand," I said.

Earl blocked everyone's view and you could see the enthusiasm build in his body at the thought of an ID of Shorty.

I grabbed the girl by the arm and said, "Step into my office."

We scooted behind a canned goods display and I handed her seven pictures. The cashier glanced through them and stopped right at Shorty. Bingo!

"That's the little asshole, I mean, that's the guy who stuck the gun in my face and robbed the store," she said.

She deserved a kiss right there, but, instead, got a little hug. I instructed the clerk not to tell anyone of the picture ID. I told her this investigation is a confidential matter. Earl and I quickly rounded up our gang crew and headed for the track.

"You think she bought the 'confidential investigation' bullshit, Rich?" asked Earl.

"She's only nineteen and blonde. What the fuck does she know? I could've told her we were Starsky and Hutch and she would've believed me," I said.

On the way to the track, I tried to borrow some money from Earl to make a few bets. He hesitated for some time, but forked it over when I told him I would pay him back as soon as they straightened out Grand Avenue. (Grand Avenue is an angle street.)

Our whole team arrived at the racetrack simultaneously. We had forty minutes until post time, so we chugged a few drinks to set the stage. All rehearsed our acting skills and contemplated which characters to portray in order to avoid detection.

Under the law, we had him. Probable cause existed after the photo ID, but a problem haunted us. We were under strict orders from our supervisors not to make an arrest. Our bosses did not know we attained an ID from the last grocery store holdup. They wanted to find Shorty, follow him for a couple days, and catch him right in the act of a robbery. They wanted to blow his head off. The difficulty with this scenario was that Shorty could return the favor. The good guy wins and the bad guy loses is crap you see on TV. The instructors at the academy persistently preached to the cadets that the first person you take care of is yourself, then your partner, and whoever the hell is left. This would be a difficult task to achieve while Shorty threw rounds at us.

We decided to contact both sergeants and inform them of the grocery store photo ID. Many times, their radios were off when in a bar, uh, coffee shop. Earl attempted numerous times to raise either supervisor on the air, but his efforts failed. We hung around the fifty-dollar window like a bunch of day-labor guys waiting to be picked up by a potential employer. Suddenly, Shorty appeared out of nowhere.

Two minutes to post rang out over the loud speaker. The curtain rose on our stage and the team attempted to blend into the crowd as betters instead of typical looking cops. This is a tricky thing to do with a couple officers wearing black, shiny, round-toed shoes, polyester pants, collared dress shirts, a wristwatch, and a U.S Marine tattoo on your forearm.

We watched Shorty bet hundreds and hundreds, race after race, and ironically, he won. I positioned myself behind him in line many times and even threw $10 on one of his horses. I won dinner money.

The last race finished. We wanted to follow Shorty to his vehicle to get a make on it and tail him to his residence. Our efforts failed. We did not plan on such a disorderly exit from the parking lot and we wound up losing the little shit. There were five cars on the tail and not one of us could stay with him. Shorty disappeared.

Ten minutes later, a call came over the radio from car #3480. The call number designated one of our sergeants. I answered up and he wanted to know what the hell was going on with all the radio confusion. I told him we were at the track, located Shorty, and lost him. The entire conversation pissed him off, probably because it took ten of his men to finally locate this elusive stick-up man and he vanished within two minutes. Many other officers heard the radio chatter and knew we were in hot water. Silence covered the airwaves until the boss wanted to know what additional info we had on Shorty.

I gave the sergeant a description of Shorty, his vehicle, and the license plate number. Here is where Lady Luck appeared yet again. Approximately five thousand cars left the parking lot and most headed for the expressways. Shorty happened to be driving in front of one of the sergeants who had command of the investigation. He was on a very special and important assignment. He had tickets to watch the White Sox and was on his way back to the office when Shorty appeared in front of him on the highway. The sergeant relayed his location and we scrambled from the track to assist him.

By now, a caravan of cars followed Shorty. The sergeant wanted things done his way, so he took command. We constantly switched cars on Shorty and he never picked up the tail. He finally stopped in a restaurant and sat down at the coffee counter. A cup of java and a pastry appeared in front of him. The sergeant sent Earl in to babysit and he ordered some pie and coffee and sat right next to Shorty. The rest of us gathered in the parking lot and tried to figure out what to do. About twenty minutes elapsed and the boss decided to take Shorty down during his exit.

We stooped behind a couple of parked cars in the lot and waited for Shorty to walk out. None of us knew what to expect. He burst through the glass door and strutted down the sidewalk. Before he knew it, ten pistols were pointed at his head.

"POLICE! POLICE!" cracked through the air and pierced my ears.

I thought the words came from one of the officers identifying our actions. Instead, it was Shorty yelling for help. Can you imagine, a professional stick-up man who thought he was the victim of a robbery yelled for the police to aid him? Well, he got his "POLICE." A couple of revolvers were now pressed up against his temple. We placed him under arrest. Before leaving, Shorty's trunk mysteriously opened. Inside, in plain view, laid evidence from his last robbery. The sergeant closed the trunk and we would take a second look after we procured a search warrant for the vehicle.

We took Shorty in and the Robbery Commander looked amazed when he saw us. We had cleared this ancient crime pattern. Was the Robbery Commander upset because his men were not involved and kept in the dark? Surprisingly, the commander thought we arrested the wrong man. He just smirked and figured we stepped on our dicks and would soon realize the error.

The team began the process of conducting seven different line-ups, which netted one positive ID and six voice IDs. We neglected to tell the Robbery Commander Shorty's pockets were filled with $4,000 cash at the time of his arrest. Possibly, if he knew this, he would have conceded we apprehended the right man.

We obtained a search warrant for Shorty's car and found a weapon, nylon stockings, and bank bags. The cases against Shorty looked better and better with time. I spent many hours with him that day and had an opportunity to get to know him as a person instead of a criminal. Shorty did not fit the norm of a stick-up man. Ironically, he was considerate and soft-spoken, and even spoke kindly about his captors. He even paid for the pizza the guys ordered, probably with the stick-up money. We shipped him downtown and completed the paperwork.

Shorty appeared in court the following day for a bond hearing. The team instructed the victims they need not appear at this hearing, but for some strange reason, Shorty's last victim showed up. The victim's appearance disturbed the judge. He wanted to claim the money taken in Shorty's last robbery. He could not wait one day for the cash to be processed as evidence.

I read over the report Earl wrote concerning Shorty's arrest and came to the part that discussed the $4,000. It read, "In the right front pocket of the alleged offender was $4,000 U.S. currency. All bills were of various denominations." No wording in our report connected the cash to the grocery store robbery.

The clerk called Shorty's case and the bailiff brought him into the courtroom from a back cell. Standing mute, his charges were read aloud. The judge set the bond at $50,000 and gave Shorty a future court date.

"Your Honor, he took my money, that's my money!" yelled the grocery store owner.

The judge glared at the man with a look of disgust, raised his brows, and briskly removed his glasses.

"Sir, this man is not guilty until proven so," snapped the judge.

"I just want the $4,000 he had in his pocket when he was arrested. The officers told me he had it," said the storeowner.

We verified to the judge the store owner's claim.

"Sir, how do you know this particular $4,000 is your $4,000? Is it marked in any way?" asked the judge.

Before he could answer, Shorty blurted out.

"Judge, that's my money. I won it at the racetrack and those officers can tell you that."

Shorty pointed in our direction. I did not know what the judge wanted me to say, so I just told the truth.

"Well, Your Honor, I did witness him pick some winners and watched him wager large amounts of currency," I said, smiling.

"If we can't connect the money to the robbery, by law, it is the defendant's money. Next case," said the judge.

The storeowner stormed out. Obliviously, all he cared about was his cash. Within three hours, Shorty made bond and was a free man. I found out later the storeowner returned to the courtroom and the judge jailed him for contempt over the disputed money.

A stick-up man is freed in three hours, and a legitimate businessman comes to court, loses his temper, and sits in jail for a day. JUSTICE CHICAGO STYLE.

Shorty later pleaded guilty to the charges and saved the state huge sums of money and a lengthy trial. He received a six-year sentence, but was only required to do three before he would be eligible for parole. He netted $85,000 cash, all tax-free, which is about $30,000 per year for a three-year sentence. Living in Chicago, this type of sentence sort of makes the profession of "stick-up man" worth its while and quite profitable.

Things were really going our way now as far as the big pinches were concerned. Earl and I had now earned the complete and total trust of our bosses. We were assigned to some of the top cases, or, as the newspaper would call them, "VIP Cases." Not all VIP Cases involve high profile celebrities. VIP Cases also means a story the press jumps on and blows out of proportion. Such newspaper headlines cause public outcry and unrest. This upsets City Hall. When this happens, the police brass has to kiss political ass and do whatever it takes to keep the community calm or their cushy jobs could be at risk.

The patrolman at the bottom typically takes the heat when there is a police screw-up. The only thing that saves a street level cop from unjust politically made decisions is the Federal Court System. At least they are good for something.

One case in particular involved a police shooting. The suspect took one in the back during his escape and the State's Attorney's Office said it could not file any charges because the officer did not violate any Illinois laws. He shot a fleeing felon, totally legal at that time. An abundance of public outcry erupted and the patsies at City Hall put the word out to the press the officer would be fired. The political windstorm caused the politicians and the police brass to bend.

Only the court could save the officer and retrieve his job. A federal court did and he received all back pay for the unjustified firing. At the time of the incident, the officer's weapon contained non-regulation ammunition. This rationalized the dismissal. The politicians overlooked the fact that police inspectors wrote up officers daily for the same rule infraction. The most severe punishment ever administered was a mere a two-day suspension. But the brass had to keep their cushy jobs, kiss some ass, and follow the orders to fire him. Unsurprisingly, when he got his job back, it tarnished some stars of high-ranking officers for allowing themselves to be used as puppets of the political machine. Most of the men referred to the people involved in the incident as ball-less, people who would do anything just to protect their high-paying jobs. They could care less about the morale of the men or the feelings of their families. The community wrongly condemned this officer for a legal action. But, to keep everyone happy, the politicians threw him to the wolves.

Time rolled on and my age started to show. If you do not take care of yourself on this job, it can make you feel and appear a lot older than you really are. With nine years under my belt, police work came easily. But, stress and sore muscles started to take over my body. I attempted to build my strength and stamina and began to visit the gym. Most of the time, I would work out while at work along with many other officers. It made the training a lot easier when one gets paid to sweat while building up your muscle tone. I ran as the tool to accomplish my goal.

When you work in the ghetto, one thing you have to be is a speedy runner. You would be astonished how swiftly these little shits can run with a portable TV in one hand and a hubcap in the other. Sometimes, you have to even out the odds and play a little dirty.

A call of a burglary in progress hit the airwaves. Only two blocks away, Earl and I arrived at the door of the apartment in about a minute and a half. We could see the thieves through the front window as they ransacked the premises. We tried to figure out where they entered because this is usually the same route in which they leave.

Time is an element when answering a burglary in progress call. This is so because there are two types of officers who respond to a crime of this nature, the officer who wants to catch the thief, and the one who does not. This particular day, we wanted to catch the offenders.

This situation could have the other type of officer who responds to the scene, the one who suffers from the pounding hangover and does not want to do any police work that day. He pulls up to the premises with his lights and sirens screaming and slams on his breaks. The bad guys are alerted. The burglars know it is a matter of seconds before the police enter. They usually flee out of an open door or window. The hungover policeman avoids an arrest, paperwork, and any chance of physical confrontation.

The echo of sirens pounded our ears. Promptly, four blue and whites were on the scene and the whole damn block knew the police had arrived. The reason why everyone activated their sirens that day was that most all attended a shift change party the night before. There is an enormous amount of alcohol consumed and hangovers are in the abundance the following day of the watch change party.

My partner and I entered the apartment. Earl spotted one of the offenders and the kid dove out an open window. He followed and chased him down the street. I entered the basement to seek out the second offender.

Darkness filled the room and, to make things worse, I forgot my flashlight in the office. Just then, a wooden rocking chair clobbered me in the back and the punk took off out the basement door. I sprinted down the alley after him, but the thief was too fast. I huffed and puffed the entire chase, and the offender widened his lead. I could have sent him to meet his maker, but he was just a kid, fourteen, maybe fifteen years old. He turned and entered an empty lot. A twelve-foot cyclone fence enclosed the property at the other end, so I slowed to a trot. By the time he tried to climb over the fence, he would be in my grasp. I was exhausted. Two packs of cigarettes and JB Scotch daily made Rich a tired boy.

He scrambled to the top of the fence. I grabbed one of his legs with a bear hug grip. He could not climb any higher without me. He attempted to pull his body over the top, but I still kept one leg on my side. While he hung upside-down, he looked at me eye to eye through the fence. We even spoke.

"Let go of me, you fuckin' pig," said the sprinter.

"Fat chance, shithead. You're all mine," I said.

He tried to bite my arms that wrapped his leg, but they were just out of his reach. I shouted for Earl.

The little rug rat became heavier and heavier and my grip slipped. By now, I only clutched his ankle. All of a sudden, my sixth sense kicked in. I sunk my teeth into the kid's right calf and could taste his blood. He screamed. I dropped him and he limped off. He turned around only to give me the finger.

I stood there stunned and really upset at myself. He had out-slicked me. Both my arms throbbed and cramps set in. Thank God the kid was not a fat ass or he would have given me a hernia. Earl finally arrived with the other half of the sprinters in handcuffs.

"Okay, you little nappy headed motherfucker, where the does your friend live?" I asked.

"Hey, ya better leave me alone, I'm a juvenile, I'll tell my dad," he said.

"That's a switch, this kid knows his father," said Earl.

"Fuck you and your father; you're not going to tell Daddy anything. Only pussies tell their mommy and daddy about the police, and one thing you're not is a little pussy," I said.

This reverse psychology tactic works almost every time on teenagers. When you tell teens stool pigeons are pussies, which they are, it usually avoids a complaint to the parents about the abusive verbal or physical treatment received from the police. It really did not matter to me if he told us where his friend's crib was or not. Black gang-bangers hang together and frequently live in a four or five block radius of each other. We would spot him eventually, but we were low on heads for the month and we wanted the kid now. A plan had to be formulated to accomplish this goal and I already had one in mind.

We took the punk in for processing and hit the street again. Earl and I were famished, so we went to dine. I knew our plan to catch the burglar would work, and it would work the very same day of its implementation. Later on during the tour, Earl asked if I recognized the punk I grappled with on the fence.

"Naw, I never saw him before, but he'll have my teeth marks on him for the next few days," I said.

"What the fuck you talkin' about, Rich?" asked Earl.

I looked at Earl and licked my teeth. He got the impression I had a full stomach.

"You didn't?" asked Earl.

"I sure did, right in the middle of his calf. I bet he looks for medical treatment from that Chink doctor at 63rd Street and Green," I said.

"He's not a chink. He's Filipino," said Earl.

"What's the difference, his eyes are still slanted," I replied.

"Yeah, but..." said Earl.

"But your ass, that's like saying he's not a shine if he's Jamaican. Look, Earl, if he's Italian, he's a Dago and weighed down with gold chains. If he's Pollack, he's stupid with short pants. If he's a Jew, he's cheap with a big nose. I could go on and on," I said.

I burst into laughter.

"Partner, I'm just fuckin' with you. Don't you know by now when I'm goofin' around? I can't believe you thought I was serious. Let's go see the Filipino doctor," I said.

Odds are an infection from my bite would materialize rapidly and the kid would have to seek some kind of medical treatment as soon as the next day. It is difficult to get an address from a doctor, so a con job would be needed.

The next day, we pulled in front of the medical clinic, and suddenly, another scheme popped into my head. Earl waited in the car as I ran into a shoe store next to the clinic. I requested to see the manager. I inquired about a pair of All-Star basketball gym shoes, bright red in color, and asked to see them. The manager met the terms of my request.

Instead of paying for the shoes, I asked if I could borrow them for ten minutes. He looked bewildered, but I identified myself as the police and he gave me the gym shoes. Most police are treated especially well in the ghetto, due to the fact that they might respond slowly to a call that involved a person who did not treat the police with respect.

We walked toward the clinic and I left one shoe in the car and took the other one inside. The price tag, still on the shoe, read $32.95, a relatively a large amount of money for a pair of gym shoes in the early '80s.

We crossed the threshold of the office and the receptionist greeted us. She did not speak or understand English very well, a good sign. I informed her we were here to investigate a gang fight. We showed her the shoe and told her it belonged to the offender and it fell off his foot during his flight from the crime scene. We told her the cost of the shoe and explained the family probably could not afford to buy their son a new pair. A gloomy look appeared on her face. I also told to her, my victim stated during the fight he bit the boy who beat him somewhere on his calf.

She instantly smiled and went to the filing cabinet. Before we knew it, she handed us a card with our bad guy's name and address printed on it. The offender visited the office that morning and claimed his brother bit him on the leg while they clowned around. I jotted the info down and glanced up at Earl.

"Dum-de-dum-dum, just the facts, ma'am, just the facts. Another flawless con," I said.

Earl laughed and shook his head in disbelief. We brought the shoes back to the store and thanked the manager. We drove to the offender's home and Earl politely knocked on the door.

"Who is it?" asked a man from the other side.

The answer came from an elderly male with a deep voice that sounded very aggravated.

"Poll-ece, we'd like to speak to you sir," said Earl.

"Get the door, Malcolm. I's got to put my pants on," said the identical voice from beyond the door.

The door opened slowly and there stood Malcolm with his head shamefully tilted down, unable to look us in the eye. We were invited in and walked over to the couch and sat. Malcolm limped a few yards behind us. I looked at him and smirked. Daddy had not entered the room yet.

"Did ya beef to Daddy, ya little pussy, and tell him that the badass policeman bit you?" I asked.

"No, man, I didn't," he said in a cool voice.

I knew he did not tell his father; he reminded me of a stand up kid. Shortly, Earl and I would know why.

Daddy appeared. He was enormous. He stood 6 feet, 8 inches and weighed 270 pounds. One punch from this guy could break a jaw. We could see the fear in the kid's face.

"What can I's do for you two?" asked the father.

Earl started to explain about the burglary as Malcolm slumped in his chair. The mere presence of the police in his home angered the father. I interrupted the conversation.

"What we're trying to say is we believe Malcolm witnessed a burglary. We're afraid one of the local gang-bangers might try to take action against your son," I said.

Earl glared at me and, being the first-class partner he was, followed my lead at once. He knew I was up to something and he always gave me his trust. On occasion, we did not agree and he would end up calling me a "fucking idiot." I must admit, sometimes he was right.

We did not arrest Malcolm and left the house. I contemplated, as much as I disliked this kid, he would have been in for the beating of his life if arrested. You should have seen the look on his face when we gave him a pass. We already caught the other offender and returned the property. As far as we were concerned, the case was closed.

Earl seemed confused as to why I let the kid go. Something about this kid sat funny in my stomach. I thought of the future and realized we could go to Malcolm if we needed a favor. He owed us big time and the kid knew it. Earl agreed with my rationale and came to the same conclusion.

A couple of weeks later, the boss handed us a gang-banger homicide of some poor junkie left in the middle of the street with six rounds embedded in his body. Two full days of work and we still did not have a lead.

"Well, Earl, this is as good a time as any to call in our marker with Malcolm," I said.

"We might as well, partner. We're not getting anywhere on this one," said Earl.

We tracked Malcolm down at the neighborhood pool hall. When detectives enter a poolroom, silence always seems to follow. Then, some loudmouth starts to throw out insulting police cracks. To save face in the ghetto, you have to return fire with a remark and put the smart ass immediately back in his place. Something like "Say, jagoff, how'd you like that pool stick shoved up your ass."

We walked up to Malcolm and I grabbed him around the throat.

"You think you could hide forever, you little prick? You're coming with us," I screamed.

During our sluggish exit, our eyes ricocheted off everyone who tracked our retreat. You have to be careful in a pool hall because you never know when someone wants to be acclaimed as a cop hater and use your head for a cue ball with the wrong end of the pool stick. Earl looked back at the crowd and yelled, "You punks might as well finish Malcolm's game. He's on his way to the shit house."

Malcolm did not know it, but the entire scene we created was for his benefit. I must admit Earl and I performed well. Our theatrics avoided the possibility of Malcolm being labeled a trick for the police. You constantly have to do things this way in the ghetto, even if you just want to have a word with someone.

Once inside the car, we explained everything to Malcolm and asked him for help. Our performance was so good; Malcolm actually thought he had jail time in his future.

"Word around the hood, the cappers you're looking for are Iceman and his rat partner, Jabo. They both deal and this one went bad. They had to take him down," said Malcolm.

"Did you see this, Malcolm, or is this just street talk? I asked.

He claimed he did not witness the shooting.

All we had was street talk, or so we thought. We lied to Malcolm and told him the victim was hit in the head with a shotgun blast. We wanted to test his reliability. Malcolm enlightened us that no shotgun was involved and both offenders used handguns. How did he know this important fact?

"Don't misinterpret my kindness for stupidity, but if you did not see the shooting, how did you know they both were shot with handguns?" asked Earl.

"Okay, okay, you're cool, they both had handguns office', but I ain't testifying."

Earl looked at Malcolm and gave him a nod of approval with reference to a pass on his court testimony, but he wanted to make sure both offenders were the shooters. These gang-bangers were killers and Malcolm was as good as dead if forced to testify. We understood Malcolm's situation, but still questioned him as to what he saw.

He informed us Iceman shot first and put four into the victim's chest. He believed it was a .45 automatic. Within seconds, Jabo shot twice with what appeared to be a snub nosed .38. Malcolm really knew his shit; the coroner advised us the bullets were indeed from .45 and .38 caliber weapons.

We gave him a ride home and I browsed through Earl's little black book of nicknames to find out the offender's proper identity. Earl possessed a complete file on both gang-bangers. We called for more troops. Earl and I wanted to hit both cribs at the same time. It is always best when you have two suspects at different locations to raid both places simultaneously. It did not matter if the homes were five miles apart, the first suspect will somehow get word to the second suspect that the police are on the way. Sometimes, I think these little gang-bangers sneak up to the roof and actually send smoke signals. Phones even get yanked out of walls and the message still gets through.

Two different teams hit both residences right on schedule. Earl and I were at Iceman's apartment and placed him under arrest for the murder. The other team went to Jabo's crib where he also met the long arm of the law.

I put the cuffs on Iceman and he spit right in my face. I wiped the saliva from my eyes and Iceman found his head stuck between the refrigerator door and its frame. A few good whacks to the skull changed his attitude. Maybe the temperature within the fridge caused the attitude adjustment? The other team at Jabo's crib met no such resistance. Both bad guys were transported to the station, and along with the regular homicide dicks, we tried to formulate a plan of action.

At this point, an informant's word was our only lead, but Earl and I believed in his reliability. With no other witnesses, only a confession would make our day. We were at a dead end. Earl shook his head and looked up to the heavens for guidance.

"Well, we can forget about Iceman talking, that's how he got his name. He's as cold a witch's tit," said Earl.

We tried to con Iceman to confess. But Earl was right. Iceman was one slick killer. We needed Jabo to talk about the murder. To accomplish this, we needed another con. Even though it is legal for officers to use deception in an interrogation, we knew there would be only one chance to turn Jabo against Iceman or confess on himself.

I headed for my typewriter and grabbed a blank police report on the way. The heading on the report simply read, "Coroner's Medical Report." I then typed in capital letters, "CONFIDEN-TIAL- EVIDENCE ONLY." I made the report very official and typed in the victim's name and address. I started the narrative with the words, "Coroner's Findings." It read something like this:

Examined, one male Negro; deceased, 27 years of age, six bullet hole entries, and three exit holes. .45 caliber bullets and .38 caliber bullets were used in this homicide. Victim killed "IN-STANTLY" when a .45 caliber bullet struck and burst the heart chamber. All other bullets appear to be secondary wounds.

I showed the document to Earl. He told me to go for it. I walked into Jabo's interrogation room to shoot the shit with him. I held the report in my hand as if it was just any other piece of paper. Earl gave me about five minutes and called me out. Before I left, I set the report in front of Jabo.

"Well, it's up to Jabo now. Sure hope the prick can read," I said to Earl.

"Aw shit, we never thought of that," said Earl.

We gave him about ten minutes and walked back into the room. The report was disturbed, so we assumed Jabo read it. Earl and I now could put the con into action. For those of you who are in the dark on the con, it goes something like this: Malcolm gave us the key; we knew what types of weapons each used, how many shots both offenders fired, and who shot first. What to do with this knowledge is the question.

"Well, Jabo, it looks like you are really up shit's creek," I said.

"What the fuck you talking about, man? You pigs ain't got shit on me."

"We don't need any shit, asshole; Iceman put the rap on you. He said you shot the motherfucker when he wouldn't pay up for the drugs," said Earl.

"You're talking out your ass, office'," said Jabo.

"The only ass you better watch out for is yours. It's pretty cute and those guys in Joliet would love to lay it out and throw it a real nice butt fuck," I said.

We left the room and let Jabo ponder his thoughts for a while. The wheels in his brain churned as he wondered if we lied or told the truth.

"Did Iceman really trick on me?" yelled Jabo.

We were ready for part two of the con. Earl brought Iceman out of his interrogation room so Jabo could witness he was no longer handcuffed.

"Okay, Iceman, you're free to go, take a fucking walk," said Earl.

At the end of the hallway stood four other detectives ready to take Iceman back to his interrogation room from another direction.

"Say, motherfucker, what about me?" yelled Jabo.

I looked at him and slammed the door in his face, still handcuffed to the steel ring bolted to the wall.

In a short time, we would have to let Iceman go. Earl and I had no evidence against him except for Malcolm's ID, and we were the only ones who possessed that exclusive knowledge. The Supreme Court previously ruled one defendant in custody for murder cannot testify against another defendant who committed the same murder. So, as far as we were concerned, Iceman could walk right out of the police station in a few hours.

I entered Jabo's room and beads of sweat sat on his temples and forehead. Could this be an indication he would talk to us about the murder?

"Listen, fuckface, your friend left you holding your prick in your hand. He's a real stand up guy, isn't he?" asked Earl.

"Man, let me think about what happened," said Jabo.

"No, I already know what happened. Iceman told me," remarked Earl.

"Iceman's a mothafuckin' liar," said Jabo.

"Look, Jabo, will you put in writing what happened the night of the murder?" I asked.

"Yeah, if he did, I'll do it too," said Jabo.

"Somebody up in the heavens must really like you, you're getting a real big break," said Earl.

"What do ya mean?" asked Jabo.

"Well, you read the medical report, the one my partner left on the desk. The report said the first bullet that hit the victim was a .45 caliber and it struck him in the heart. It killed him instantly. You know Iceman used the .45 and you the .38. You also know Iceman shot first and you shot a couple of seconds later. Think about it, the report concluded the victim died instantly. This means by the time you shot the victim, he was already dead. You can't murder a man who's already dead," said Earl.

Jabo took a split second to ponder Earl's words with his scanty brain. This is our last chance. If he bought what he read and heard, he would confess. All we can do now is wait. We were finished with our final performance in the con. Earl and I hoped he would bite the hook we placed inside his mouth.

"Okay, man, this is how it went down. This guy owed Iceman $75 for a score. He didn't want to pay, and we couldn't let him fuck us. It looks bad in the hood to play us like chumps. We both pulled out roscoe. He put four in him; it happened really fast, man. The next thing I knew, I capped him, too," said Jabo.

For some strange reason, we felt sorry for this guy. He was scared and trembled during his entire confession. He thought his words would allow him to beat the rap; instead, they helped us put him behind bars.

The lab matched the bullets in the body to the murder weapon found in Jabo's apartment. Not only did Jabo take the hook, but he also swallowed the line and sinker. If he had only kept quiet for two or three more hours, he would have been released. He copped a plea in court and received a lengthy prison sentence. Oh, and Iceman, he still walks the streets and spits towards Earl and me whenever our paths cross. Bottom line, Malcolm remained alive and a murderer went to prison. Case closed!

The outcome of the murder investigation made the boss quite happy. We could now screw around for a few days and he couldn't care less. Basically, it is kind of a compensation for solving a mystery and getting our unit credit for the pinch.

We put police investigation aside for the next couple of days and Earl and I did nothing but back-up work for the other gang teams. We enjoyed observing the way the other detectives worked. Their styles of investigation always interested us. You learn something new everyday, even from other investigator's mistakes.

On one of those days, John and Mark requested our assistance in the execution of a search warrant for some smoke. We had a few dealings with the both of them in the past, but Earl and I disagreed with some of their methods and police tactics.

"Hey, Rich, we need a hand with a warrant. Can you and Earl handle it," said John.

"Maybe, all depends. Who's the sergeant in charge?" I asked.

"Fuckhead," replied John, referring to the same sergeant who sent us to the racetrack in the Shorty case.

"I don't feel like working with him. He turns every little job into a disaster," said Earl.

Reluctantly, we agreed to join them in their endeavor.

A team of six hit a PR's house located on 25th Street and California Avenue, which is a low-income housing project. The building consisted of single story units with only front and rear entrances. This made the execution of the warrant quite simple and no one got hurt upon implementation. Once inside, the premises were secured. Pretty routine job; that is, until "Fuckhead" started his crap.

To show his authority, he flung out orders that indicated to the occupants he was the individual in charge. The rest of us were the pieces of shit beneath his authority. All of us were grown men, although we sometimes acted like kids, but we did our job suitably. Unfortunately, he was in charge so we followed his instructions not to make him look foolish in front of the prisoners. But his bellowing got a little out of hand and we tired from hearing his authoritative intonation.

The straw that broke the camel's back occurred when he told an elderly woman, with a six–month-old infant in her arms, we were going to snatch her baby if she did not tell us where the dope could be found.

My personal theory of this profession called "policeman" is you mess with the bad guys, not some old woman who does not understand why six grown men with guns on their hips were tearing her home apart. She was petrified and damn near hysterical. We calmed her down, behind the sergeant's back, and assured her we were not going to take her baby.

Earl and I glanced at John and he gave us a wink. He reached into his pocket and displayed a pack of exploding cigarette loads. As soon as the sergeant turned away, I removed his smokes from his coat pocket and tossed them to John. He stuck five or six loads into one cigarette, replaced the smoke in the pack, and tossed it back to me. I slipped the pack into the sergeant's coat pocket without him being the wiser.

We were done with our work and headed for the station with five prisoners. I rode with the sergeant, and as he put a Marlboro to his mouth, he flicked his Bic. I squirmed in my seat but nothing happened. The dud cigarette gradually burned.

Once inside the office, we hooked the prisoners to the wall and retreated to the back room for a cup of java. While in the rear, we could hear the sergeant loudly chucking out orders again. Why he wanted to impress these pork chops hooked to the wall puzzled everyone. The only conclusion we came up with was he wanted all to know he commanded.

Coffee in hand, we exited the back room and watched the sergeant reach into his shirt pocket. Our anticipation filled the office. We prayed he removed the loaded smoke from the pack. He did. The cigarette dangled from his mouth as he barked out more orders. The whole scene disgusted us because it resembled a nerd attempting to act cool in a room full of people who were already cool, prisoners included. This sergeant could not be cool; he did not have it in him. He tried and tried but failed to impress anyone in the room. He yelled and screamed more orders at us, but now his lighter illustrated a flame. If the butt blew up at this moment, it would be the perfect time.

He touched the flame to the tip of the cigarette, and without even a breath, it exploded. The noise echoed through the room as the sergeant covered both ears with his palms. Only a few seconds elapsed when he overcame the initial shock of the blast. He stood there with pieces of the cigarette paper embedded in his thick eyebrows. His untrimmed moustache sported bits of tobacco and all that remained in his mouth was the Marlboro filter. We accomplished our mission and he finally shut that big mouth of his.

We ran back to the coffee room and laughed our asses off. Disorientated, the sergeant stood alone in the room with the six gang-bangers while he picked tobacco bits out of this mustache. The prisoners were all in hysterics as they looked at the spectacle in front of them. I must admit his response was not what I expected. All he said to us was "I don't get mad, but I get even."

Out of the six investigators involved, he singled me out as the culprit. From that moment on, I had to be cautiously alert for his counter-attack. I knew it would come almost immediately.

About a month later, I began to receive an unusual amount of unsolicited mail. Every type of book and magazine ended up stuffed into my mailbox two or three times a week. A few weeks after the merchandise arrived came all the bills. I wrote the companies and told them I did not place the orders for the books and I did not want my credit ruined. I spent a fortune on stamps and phone calls in an attempt to straighten out the mess. I knew that "Fuckhead" had something to do with my problem. Should I fight fire with fire?

His personal locker stood approximately one foot above eye level and contained his coffee mug. Every morning, he reached up high and removed the cup. So, one of the guys picked open the locker and filled his coffee cup with maple syrup, right to the top. The next day, he reached into his locker and grabbed the cup. Instantly, the sticky syrup spilled out all over his immaculately clean white shirt. He started to swear loudly and leaped up and down in place. The guys thought he lost it, but I guess that is how he lets out steam when he is pissed off. He calmed himself down and left the station to go home to shower and change. But my book problem still existed.

The books kept coming and coming and all were from out of state companies. This made it very difficult to check the handwriting samples from the order forms the companies possessed. I could not prove the sergeant committed the forgery, but my gut feelings told me otherwise. So, two days before the next holiday, the electric company received a phone call to shut the power off at a certain address. They sent a man out the next day to complete the job at the sergeant's house. I thought no power the day before a holiday should keep the sergeant from pulling any more stunts with the books and magazines. But this inconvenience did not curtail the determined sergeant.

Finally, a magazine arrived with a home office in downtown Chicago. At last he made a mistake. Earl and I played detective and went downtown to retrieve a copy of the order form. If he took the time to type it, we were screwed.

The secretary furnished me with the order form and a grin blossomed on my face. The sergeant printed out the request. All criminals get sloppy and lazy, policemen included. There were numbers as well as letters to compare. We immediately returned to the office and pulled out one of the sergeant's time due request forms, which were normally printed. It was a perfect match. We had the sergeant by his Irish balls.

Time went on and I continued to complain about the books at the office in order to convince the sergeant my dilemma still existed. He had no knowledge I owned the upper hand and could wait any length of time for my moment to strike back.

That moment appeared in a few days at roll call. All the guys sat and complained about a bullshit order from downtown; this sergeant's answer to any of our complaints, "If you don't like this job, you can always sell shoes." He would chuckle in our face, and to be honest, his detestable quote drove us nuts. That day, a quarrel ensued between the sergeant and some of the men. It got a little out of control and quite loud.

"Hey, Sarge, you better be careful. There are eight of us in this room and only one of you. All we would have to do is blow your fucking head off, and when the I.A.D. asks what happened, we'll just say you lost it and pulled out your weapon. Who will they believe? Plus, dead men don't talk. They'll just chalk you up as another cop who fell prey to the stress of the job," said one of the detectives.

Without delay, the sergeant calmed down and shut his mouth, but not before he gave everyone a wicked stare. After all left the room, the sergeant asked to speak to me alone. We did not get along, so I had no idea why he wanted to talk. But if it pertained to the books, the ace in the hole was on my side of the table.

He started to chew me out, all this crap about respect, do the right thing, and follow orders without complaints. He yelled on and on. I could see Earl laughing in the other room at my expense. I peeped at him and slid my middle finger up the side of my nose as if I had an itch. The sergeant's ass chewing continued.

"You got a lot of fucking nerve preaching to me," I said.

With that remark, I took the handwritten order form from my pocket and chucked it on his desk. He glanced at it and did not say a word. He sat confused and stared at me for a moment. The sergeant realized I just placed him behind an eight ball.

"Now, it's your turn to listen. You committed fraud in my name. I notified every company and they'll sign a complaint if I discover the thief. So, the books will stop coming to my apartment, right, Sarge? You'll also stop fucking with Earl and me. You got it, Sarge?" I asked.

He snarled at me and walked out of the room. He did not say another word because he had enough brains to know when to keep his mouth shut. Neither of us ever brought up the incident again. The book and magazines stopped coming.

Not all sergeants acted in this manner. Two of three on days were really sharp. A couple of tactical officers transferred in from patrol and they wanted to quickly make their rep in the unit. Day after day, these two guys would bring in guns off the streets like no other team in the past. At first, it seemed amazing. Earl and I were in the unit for years and in three months these guys confiscated more weapons than us and four other teams combined. Something did not jive.

A couple of the sergeants became very suspicious at their instant success at retrieving illegal weapons. Suddenly, the officers started to bring in sawed-off shotguns off the streets, one a week for weeks. Their stupidity and eagerness to make a name for themselves backfired.

One of the sergeants checked the court convictions for all of their arrestees. In many of the cases, the court released the offender on the weapon charges, even without a fine. More peculiar, all the weapons but the sawed off shotguns were returned to the defendants.

After a little more digging, the sergeants figured out the officer's little scam to appear superior to everyone else in the unit concerning recovered weapons. These guys went to City Hall and checked gun registration cards of newly migrated Mexicans to find out who owned large amounts of legal weapons. They would con the uneducated Mexican to let them search his home or apartment and then arrest him when he could not produce gun registration forms needed to prove the weapons were legally owned. They assured the offender all would be straightened out in court and, in most cases, the bad guy agreed to let the criminal justice system handle the matter.

Secondly, the edges of their recovered sawed-off shotguns all seemed to be very sharp and still notched as if from a fresh cut. The sergeants did not pursue their suspicions on the matter and informed the officer their tactics better change immediately. Weeks went by before the two brought in another illegal weapon from the street, and this one did not even have a firing pin.

Many times during our careers as gang investigators, Earl and I received calls from personal friends who loved to play policeman. They would supply us with the info to play out their cop fantasies through the real police.

Patty, a friend of ours, asked to see Earl and me at her place of employment. She is a girl who I attempted to date for a long time without much success. You know the type, just out of a bad relationship and sworn off men. We set out for her office. She informed us for the past five months a tenant in the high-rise apartment building she managed paid his rent in cash. The amount was in excess of $1,000 per month.

She deemed it peculiar because he was an older man who lived with a very young stewardess. Her job took her overseas on many occasions. She told us she did not believe the man earned an income and no way could a stewardess live in this particular building on her salary alone. Both drove very expensive autos.

"Let's see, Earl, he's an older guy and he doesn't work. He can't be living in this apartment on social security. He lives with a young broad and she flies. Let's check him out. If he gets a lot of five minute visitors on Friday and Saturday nights, he's dealing," I said.

Earl chuckled and he concurred with the theory. What swayed us to believe we were on the right track was the fact that the gentleman paid his rent in small bills, tens and twenties. We advised Patty we would investigate, but needed some assistance from the doorman. She told us this would not be a problem and instructed him to cooperate in any way possible. We went back to the office and ran the alleged dope dealer for any priors. He came back clean, very unusual.

The next weekend, we set up surveillance in an undercover van. We instructed the doorman to approach the window and take off his hat whenever our buddy got a visitor. It turned out; the doorman practically wore out his hat from the large number of visitors.

We took the license plate number of every car involved. Not one guest remained longer than fifteen minutes. We ran the vehicle registrations to determine if the registered owners had any prior narcotics involvement. All of them turned out positive with priors for narcotics and other felonies, but one particular sports car caught our attention. The registration came back to the government.

This means the "G" had an inside man. Sure enough, we got a phone call from "Big Brother" after the computer alerted the F.B.I. the Chicago Police Department was checking on one of their confidential plates. The "G" wanted to meet us at the Federal Building. I had an uneasy feeling about these red necks with their CPA degrees. Nonetheless, we went to their office and oddly received the VIP treatment.

Many of the F.B.I. men who worked in the Chicago area were implants from the southern part of the country. The guided principle of the government was to assign men from different locations of the country to major cities for the sole purpose of maintaining the integrity of the agent. Southerners were assigned to the north and easterners were assigned to the west and visa versa. The rationale, if their agents were not familiar with residents of the city, the likelihood of corruption lessened significantly.

The government's kindness and hospitality did not fool Earl or me for a second. These country bumpkins attempted to out slick the city boys. Between us, we possessed over thirty years of street experience. Our five counterparts netted a grand total of approximately twenty years. We let them speak and it seemed all they wanted was the information we accumulated, which, by the way, consisted of nothing but license plate numbers and names. After about ten minutes of their bullshit, I told Earl I would wait outside in the truck. Earl knew we did not drive downtown in a truck, but he anticipated a method to my madness.

"Did you all drive downtown in a truck?" asked one of the southern agents.

"Not really, but isn't that what you think?" I asked.

"What do you all mean by that?" he asked.

"The way you're talking to us Yankees, it appears you believe we just drove up to the big city in a fucking pumpkin truck," said Earl.

They did not comprehend the wisecrack at first, but suddenly, they seemed displeased with our attitude. We got up to leave and one agent demanded we return. You would have thought the guy was General Lee spitting out orders at his troops.

"Who in the hell do ya think you're talking to?" I said.

None of the agents answered. We left the office and the elevator arrived. As the door closed, two of the hillbillies stood and stared at us from a distance. All appearances indicated we would hear from them again.

All that crap with the "G" stirred up our appetites. Earl and I headed for a restaurant near our office for a freebie meal.

"4801, 4801, go into your station immediately, I repeat immediately," said the zone.

We gave the squad a 10-4 and drove to the office.

"Well that's it, we're in for another fuckin' ass chewing," said Earl.

"Take it easy, partner, it's not the first time, and it won't be the last. Why don't we let the boss say what he has to say, and we'll play it by ear," I said.

We walked into the office and Bob glanced at us while he shook his head from side to side in disbelief. We did not know why, but we could make an educated guess it had something to do with those redneck F.B.I. men. In the background, our boss conversed on the telephone.

"I can't understand why they would say something like that. They are two...Yes, I know they are good detectives...Yes, I am really sorry about this... Yes, I'll take care of this; they'll cooperate with your investigation."

We recognized we were in for it when our easygoing boss slammed the phone on its base.

"Hey, Bob, are them two motherfuckers here yet?" yelled the lieutenant.

We looked at each other in amazement. The boss rarely, and I mean rarely, used foul language. We slowly walked towards his office. I must admit I was a little troubled at first, but then I looked at Earl and snickered.

"No, Rich, please don't do it. I know that laugh," begged Earl.

"Have I ever let you down before, partner?" I asked.

We entered the boss's office. He rose from his desk to push the door shut as he yelled and pointed his finger in both our faces. It reminded me of my high school days when Father O'Malley caught me smoking in the bathroom as a freshman.

"Who do you two think you are? I can't believe…" he yelled.

"Boss, I heard someone refer to you as a dumb nigger," I said.

The boss acted as if he did not hear the words that just came out of my mouth.

"I can't believe two of my best investigators…"

"I heard it, Lieutenant," I said.

With that second remark, the boss stopped bellowing in mid-sentence.

"What did you say, Rich?" he asked.

Earl ran with the con.

"You heard him right," said Earl.

As Earl spoke, he stood taut and pointed at the ceiling and concurred with my earlier statement. To my surprise, he went along with the stunt. He looked like the Haymarket Statue, which sits on Randolph Boulevard commemorating the death of policemen who died in the riot.

"Why, that fucking hillbilly asshole!" the boss yelled.

"Exactly, boss," said Earl

"We didn't have to sit there and listen to those glorified door-knob shakers talk shit about you. You know they love putting cops in the joint," I said.

"Fuck them. I'll straighten this mess up downtown with the deputy. You know, you guys have to cooperate. You've no choice in the matter. Go get some lunch and be back here in an hour," he said smiling.

We walked out of the office and passed the deskman. His face displayed a gigantic grin plastered all over it. Bob grabbed my arm and raised it to his noise. He inhaled and sniffed my wrist and then slid his nostrils up to my elbow area.

"I don't know how you two do it. You guys shit all over yourselves and come out smelling like roses," he said.

He reached into his pocket and slipped me two bucks.

"The coffee is on me. That's one for the record books," said Bob.

He knew the rednecks never referred to the lieutenant as a dumb nigger.

The next day, we returned to see the G-Men. The cocky attitude still existed, sort of like the little schoolboy who just squealed to the teacher concerning the culprit that pulled Mary's pigtails. We gave them the information they requested, but they were quite upset due to its vagueness. They still wanted to bust the dope dealer and would share the pinch with us in exchange for more information. We agreed, but lacked more information at the time. Earl and I knew something was not right. Why would the government consent to share a big pinch with the local police? This is normally not done. Why did they need us? Could it be they could not tell us to back off the investigation so they were just stuck with us? Earl and I would soon find out.

The investigation entered the third week. By now, we gathered much more info about the bad guy and turned all over to the government. The way the "G" wanted the arrest to go down appeared simple. The man on the inside would make a four-ounce buy of heroin. We would be allowed to serve a state search warrant and seize all the illegal narcotics located in the offender's apartment. They were satisfied with the pinch from the buy.

Earl and I, collectively with our G-Men partners, were huddled in an office at the Federal Building and planned the raid. There was a scent in the air that somehow or some way the "G" planned to screw us. They acted so oddly. By odd, I mean nice. We recognized they were up to something and we could not help but feel like a cow in a bullring. Our curiosity demanded we figure out what they intended to do with us.

That night, Earl and I went out to party, but we could not get our minds off the rednecks. We brainstormed many ideas, none of which made any sense. One thing came to mind. At the last minute, they would appear with a federal search warrant for the apartment. The G-Men would turn over the pinch from the buy to us and steal the credit for the arrest pertaining to the narcotics found in the apartment. They surely know there will be a large amount of drugs on the premises, compared to the measly four ounces that would be confiscated from the under-cover buy. That must be it.

Earl and I knew a state search warrant could be obtained much easier than a federal one. Federal judges are real sticklers when it came to someone's constitutional rights and demanded specific details with each warrant. The state judges would sign a warrant no questions asked, as long as they could make their tee time. We did not need the info from the Fed's dope buy to es-tablish probable cause. We had our surveillance and much more, our credibility with the judge who we would ask to sign the war-rant. That night, Earl typed out the warrant and it was superior. He was one the best warrant men on the entire Chicago Police Department.

Our strategy was to go along with everything the "G" planned for the arrest. If they deviated at the last minute, our options were open. The buy went down and we recovered the marked money, but to our surprise, it was only a half-ounce of heroin instead of the four we were promised. This was a very small amount of heroin for the "G." Any Chicago policeman could travel down to south Halsted Street and find a half-ounce of heroin in any number of dealer's pockets.

As expected, the government supervisor made the switch and told Earl and me to take the buy arrest and they would hit the apartment later that night with a search warrant.

Obviously, all the G-Men were in on the scam. The expres-sion on their faces verified this fact. Admittedly, a couple of them seemed to feel sorry for us. They knew we got the shaft for all our hard work.

Earl and I began to have second thoughts on whether to act on our plan. It did not take long before we decided to screw the "G" in the same manner they screwed us. We sped into the station with the bad guy, booked him, and got our central booking number to get credit for the pinch. We assembled our troops and headed right back to the apartment with our search warrant.

On the way to the apartment, I asked Earl to stop at the drugstore so I could make a quick purchase. I ran in and grabbed the articles I wanted and we were on our way again. We arrived at the residence and it was empty. This made our surprised entrance moot. The drugs were easily located; the stash lay on top of the bed, one kilo of Mexican mud, brown heroin. Now, we knew why the "G" wanted to change plans. I ran back to the car and got the items I purchased from the drug store. Magic Marker in hand, I wrote the following letter:

"Dear Edgar and Company, Earl and I always kiss someone before we fuck. We also lubricate dried up pussies like you guys. So the items on this table are for all of you. ENJOY!"

Perched on the table with the note was a bag of Hershey's Kisses, a small tube of K-Y Jelly, and our calling card from the CPD. We removed the all the heroin and left.

Earl and I returned to the office and the bosses were quite pleased with results of the arrest. We wanted to conclude our paperwork and leave before the "G" got our note. There were only twenty minutes of loose ends to tighten when suddenly the telephone in the boss's office rang.

Earl and I rolled into a corner atop our swivel chairs and tried to avoid eye contact with the lieutenant. The call was from Deputy Superintendent Dramowski. The lieutenant's face appeared flabbergasted, probably due to the lateness of the call. Our faces just turned insipid.

It seemed the worst happened and the boss came out and ordered us to report downtown immediately. He just looked at us and said, "Only the good Lord knows what the fuck you guys did now." Once again, our lieutenant was swearing. That scared us.

"Hey, Earl, do you think the G-Men called the deputy? I thought they'd only call our boss again to bitch," I said.

"I don't know, partner, I've never met this deputy, but we will shortly," said Earl.

We sped downtown and entered the deputy's office. We felt like Christians entering the Coliseum for the slaughter. His secretary announced us and we entered a second room.

"You guys made a pretty good pinch tonight, I hope you feel good," said the deputy.

Did he just congratulate us? Suddenly, his face became flushed and the veins protruded from his neck.

"Who do you two think you are to pull this shit on a government agency? This will cost you a suspension," he said.

"But, deputy, you don't understand. I overheard their boss refer to me as a stupid fucking Pollack. Even though only half my blood is Polish, I felt insulted. Who are they to be throwin' ethnic slurs at anyone? That's why we did it, Deputy Dram-ow-SKI," I said.

The blood that ran through this man's veins was one hundred percent Polish. They are a people who are very proud of their ethnicity. The deputy took a deep breath while his hands covered his face. He appeared to be praying. He glanced at the door and dismissed us. We hurried out of his office without a suspension. High fives were in order. Earl and I stepped into the elevator and once again the air reeked of roses.

The next couple of weeks went by pretty routinely. That is, if you want to call the crazy shit that goes on routine. We fell into one good pinch after another. Our bosses were astounded at our success. But, we never failed to remember, Lady Luck slept in our bed.

Back in the ghetto again, we stopped for a soda at one of the local liquor stores. In the Chicago ghetto, you come across a liquor store on just about every block in the local business area of a neighborhood. While inside, we started to rap with some of the resident punks.

I could get along with the ghetto kids a little better than Earl due to my upbringing. On many occasions, I told Earl to stand in silence and shut his mouth rather than try to jive with this type of street person. Earl would always seem to step in shit every now and then. I got the biggest kick out of it. Like the time he rubbed the tummy of a gang-banger's mother and asked when the bundle of joy was due. Only problem, she was not pregnant, just really fat.

"Say, office', I hear the poll-lece grabbed one of the dudes who booked from the County Jail. I read the papers," said Slim.

"That's right, Slim, one down two to go," I responded.

"You guys just missed the other two about ten minutes ago. They came in, bought a six pack of malt liquor, and booked," said Slim.

Earl and I pondered the same thought. Was our friend shooting his mouth off to look good in front of the brothers, or did he speak the truth? We left and drove up and down the streets in search of the two bad guys. We had their pictures with us because they appeared on that day's Daily Bulletin.

"So what do ya think, Stanley? Should we play our gut feeling and really start to hunt for these guys? He could be telling the truth," I said.

"You're absolutely right, Ollie. It won't hurt to check out his story," said Earl.

In about an hour, we spotted a drunk sitting on a porch guzzling malt liquor and quite intoxicated. Could this be one of the escapees?

"Hey, my man, c'mere," yelled Earl.

He staggered off the porch and headed for our vehicle. He balanced himself by clutching the galvanized pipes of a make-shift ghetto fence that ran adjacent to the sidewalk. He appeared to swing from side to side in his effort to reach us. We watched and laughed as he tried to remain upright.

"Hey, partner, is that where that name came from?" I asked.

"Shut the fuck up. You're unbelievable," said Earl.

"I thought I'd add a little levity to the situation. I'm only fuckin' with you. Don't be so uptight. Is it that time of the month, or what? I asked.

Earl rolled down the passenger side window. I giggled while he tried to avoid the spit that launched from the drunk's mouth as he answered Earl's questions. We did not ask him about the escapees, because he would probably lie anyway. Obviously, he was not one of them. The escapees were both dark skin and our intoxicated friend was three shades lighter. Earl ordered him to get in the car and he complied.

Intentionally, Earl laid the day's bulletin next to him with the pictures of the wanted clearly visible. In a short time, he spilled his guts and told us he knew the people in the pictures. He had just seen the pair on Green Street about twenty minutes earlier. We questioned the drunk thoroughly and threw his ass out of the car.

"This would definitely be a front page headline if we caught these guys," I said.

"You're right, partner. There's no question about that," said Earl.

The jail escape balanced on the fence of a political controversy. At the time, the current warden of Cook County Jail dodged attacks from his political adversaries for his incompetence pertaining to prior escapes. On the other hand, the warden alleged the prisoners were aided with their escape from allies of the warden's political foes. If we capture these guys before the county people did, the public would know the truth, as opposed to the lies the politicians would force-feed the press.

Without delay, Earl called the lieutenant and informed him we needed to work some overtime on earlier gathered info from a top-notch informant concerning the recent escape. He approved our overtime.

"Partner, what did you tell the boss in order to get the overtime approved? I asked.

"I told him we had info from a drunken porch monkey on where the escapees could be found," said Earl.

"You what, are you fuckin' nuts? You know you can't play around with the lieutenant like that, I said.

"Well, the guy was sitting on a porch when we found him, wasn't he?" asked Earl.

I sat silent for a brief moment. Was Earl attempting to pull a fast on me?

Cops snare 2 jail escapers who fled during kitchen duty

By Philip Wattley
and William Juneau

CHICAGO POLICE Thursday night recaptured two Cook County Jail inmates who escaped last week by riding out of the jail yards on a delivery truck they had just loaded with food.

Acting on a tip, Investigators Earl Zuelke and Richard Solita, of the Gang Crimes West Unit, saw James Williams, 18, and Benny Dolls, 23, in front of an apartment building at 6420 S. Eggleston Av.

Williams, of 2640 W. Jackson Blvd., was grabbed immediately but Dolls fled thru the building. He was found a short time later hiding in the attic of a house at 5725 S. Shields Av.

BOTH WERE turned over to sheriff's police who were questioning them to determine if they had any accomplices in their Sept. 3 breakout.

Williams and Dolls, of 5017 S. Shields Av., escaped from the jail shortly before dawn by hiding inside or underneath a van truck they helped load with breakfast food for delivery to inmates at the nearby House of Correction.

Both men had been awaiting trial on armed robbery charges.

A Cook County grand jury is investigating reports that it would have been impossible for guards on duty at the time not to notice the two as they boldly made their getaway.

ONCE THE VAN left the jail, the two reportedly jumped off and got into a red car driven by a woman.

Their escape added more fuel to the controversy surrounding Winston Moore, embattled executive director of the Cook County Corrections Department.

Moore is expected to face tough questioning Friday when he appears before a meeting of the Cook County Corrections Board. Besides last wee's jailbreak, Moore has come under fire for:

● What Sheriff Richard Elrod called the "preferential" treatment given by Moore to Norman Swenson, jailed president of the striking Cook County College Teachers Union.

● The escape of a federal prisoner that went unreported until the prisoner arranged to surrender three days later.

● The competence of jail guards.

PLANS CALL for this meeting to be open to reporters, unlike others in the last two months that were closed while the board considered demands that Moore be fired.

Moore finally was placed on probation for 180 days and warned to tighten jail administration and stop trying to operate independently of Elrod, his superior.

Elrod had asked that the board fire Moore.

Board members noted Thursday that Moore opened a newly built dormitory at the jail to provide comfortable living quarters for Swenson, tho Elrod had ordered that Swenson be given no preferential treatment. Swenson is serving a five-month jail for contempt of court in connection with the college teachers strike.

PRIVATELY, SOME board members are furious that Moore opened the center in advance of a special dedication ceremony planned for Oct. 1.

Moore was expected to be questioned in detail about the Aug. 24 escape of Raoul Uribe, an illegal immigrant held as a federal prisoner until he could be deported to Mexico.

Tho Moore was under orders to notify Elrod immediately of all escapes, Elrod was not informed of Uribe's escape until Aug. 27, the day the prisoner arranged to surrender to a Elrod aide.

In all, 35 inmates have escaped from the corrections complex this year, raising questions about the competence of guards. Investigators have told the board that Uribe strolled from a work-release area thru a door that had been left open for 12 hours.

"Take it easy, partner. I'm fuckin' with you the same way you always fuck with me, said Earl.

"You had me going for a second, you cocksucker. Let's go find these two pricks," I said laughing.

At the end of the shift, we returned to the station empty handed, but not discouraged. The next tour came quickly and we prepared to stake out the area haunted by the escapees. We could not patrol in the ghetto because, if seen three or four times on the same couple of blocks, the local criminals would know Earl and I were on the hunt. Our objective was not to spook the escapees or any of their contacts.

We located our drunken friend for a second time on the same porch. He did not appear as drunk as the day before. Just then, we were instructed by the C.C. Room to call our boss. After careful consideration, he did not wish to get involved with this political hot potato. He alerted Cook County authorities and, within minutes, they flooded the area with their deputies. This certainly cut down the odds for us to make the pinch and, most of all, would spook everyone off the streets.

Suddenly, the radio loudly broadcasted a call of shots fired. We drove down the street, and at the end of the next block, we observed a scuffle. It was the County Police brawling with a man who they believed to be an escapee. They were beating the hell out of him until we pulled up.

This character was a close friend of the convicts, and odds are, he held info as to their whereabouts. The county people established that he did. Armed with this newfound information, the deputies made the pinch of the escapees within hours. Earl and I were out of luck on this one and two day's work went down the drain.

Later, we spoke to one of the supervisors from the County and requested if we could be put on the paper of the deputy's arrest report since the arrest dealt with two detached police departments. We could make a duplicate arrest slip and actually get credit for the pinch for our unit. The county supervisor did not mind, so we completed an arrest form without an actual body.

The very next day, the warden conducted a news conference and declared his men alone were responsible for the arrest and the investigation that lead up to it. These two deputies could not get lucky in a women's prison with a handful of pardons, let alone conduct an in-depth investigation. At that time, most county sheriffs were politically appointed and were trained very little in investigative procedures.

A major Chicago newspaper ran a second page story that credited Earl and me with the arrest. We caught heat from downtown about the duplicated arrest slip, but our boss backed us. After all, we were the gang investigators who tipped the lieutenant who, in turn, tipped the county on the escapees. Once again, the air was rose-scented.

A couple of days later, the sergeant called us in his office and threw a crime pattern in our faces.

"Some asshole is sticking up all the Fannie May Candy stores. He thinks he's a real slick motherfucker and I want this guy caught," he said.

The sergeant acted noticeably displeased. These particular candy stores were the targets of our robber for one reason. All the victims were young teenaged girls or female senior citizens. Even if he got caught, an ID would be difficult due to vision problems suffered by many elderly women and the reluctance of a teenager's parents to allow their daughters to testify in a court of law. In a way, Earl and I did not fault the parents for their unwillingness to have their child testify. At the time, our court system treated its victims just as bad as the criminals and showed little concern for their safety or needs.

The boss wanted this guy off the street. He told Earl and me he did not care in what manner we accomplished our goal. Whenever we get a green light of this nature, we would make our own rules on how to conduct the investigation. This was a difficult case to solve. We got lucky with some earlier mysteries, but now the boss expected us to solve every one placed upon his desk. This guy already had seventeen robberies to his credit, and thus far, able to elude arrest.

"You know, Earl, this shit gotta stop. The boss has us working five or six hours a day," I said.

Earl shook his head and laughed.

We headed downtown to pull the paper on the crime pattern with intentions to brainstorm over a cold one. It took us a couple of shifts to get our facts together and figure out what made this guy tick. He robbed every Fannie May store in the city twice, except one. There was no geographical pattern to his crimes, so we came to the conclusion to stakeout the only Fanny May that avoided a second robbery.

This day in September began hot and sticky, the kind of heat that causes your shirt to stick to your body from a mere stroll. The high temperatures soared well above ninety degrees for a week straight during the stake out. The candy store ran their air conditioner at full speed the entire business day. We froze our asses off for five days straight. Earl and I decided, if the robber entered, after forcing us sit around and freeze for a week, we would blow his head off and ask questions later. We were frustrated, and all we accomplished for our lengthy investigation was a weight gain from all the free candy.

Thus far, we failed, so we decided to take a day off. I dozed in and out at my pool and occasionally sipped on a scotch and water when the phone rang. The caller was Earl and his voice declared a dilemma.

"The asshole robbed our Fanny May today. How fucking lucky is he?" asked Earl.

I guzzled my cocktail, got dressed, and drove to the office. Earl anxiously awaited my arrival. We possessed some tips and clues as to the identity of the bad guy, but nothing concrete. Earl located an address of the stepbrother of our robber by making a few phone calls to informants. We had to locate the stepbrother and conduct one of our extraordinary interviews.

We pulled up in front of the stepbrother's apartment building as quietly as possible. He lived in a typical two-story ghetto structure. By typical, I mean cracked sidewalks, busted steps, nameless mailboxes, no doorbells, and burglar bars on all the windows. We were clueless to the exact apartment number, so I went into the car and got my Commonwealth Edison Company hardhat and an old toolbox we frequently used when we needed this type of performance.

Earl hid in the hallway and I started to pound on doors. The first person that answered was very uncooperative, but he changed his tune when he observed Earl slithering along the wall with his .44 mag drawn as my back up. We wanted to get into the basement and shut off the electricity a couple of apartments at a time. We would then wait outside the apartment doors for the curiosity seekers to exit. It works every time.

The tenant, now eager to help, led us to the basement. He wanted his power to remain on to keep his malt liquor ice cold. In a short time, the stepbrother appeared in the hall to inquire about the power outage. We immediately grabbed and cuffed him.

Earl and I entered and searched, with permission, of course. The apartment was empty. Upon the dresser, in plain view, were seven wallets that contained identification of people who lived in Chicago's Gold Coast area. This is a very ritzy part of town and a large number of the residents are fairly wealthy. Of course, our friend claimed he found all seven wallets. Armed with his airtight alibi, all of us went to the office. Earl began to run victim file checks seeking out crimes connected to the stolen wallets. The search puzzled him. Not one victim reported their crime to the local police district. How did the stepbrother get all these wallets? We began to contact each victim for our answer.

All seven people were robbed, the weapon of choice a sawed-off shotgun. Our Fanny May man used the identical type of weapon and his physical description, to some extent, matched. Shockingly, every victim seemed uninterested in our investigation and all only cared about the return of his or her property. Some of the crimes took place weeks ago, which would account for the victim's lackadaisical attitude. You cannot report an armed robbery to the police weeks after it occurred and expect police cooperation, let alone a court conviction. We reached another dead end.

We were desperate and decided to use up a special favor from an informant. It was a long shot, but we wanted to know if the informer could get any street info on our robber. We got lucky. The informant told us he knew the bad guy and he would be purchasing some smoke from a gang-banger named Black Jack that very evening. Black Jack was known quite well by the CPD. Earl and I also criminally dealt with him in our many years of fighting gang crime. He was one bad character.

We located Black Jack and offered him a deal. We would allow him to push his dope, for a short time anyway, for a flip on our stick-up man. Our only interest, get the location where we could locate the offender and apprehend him. He accepted our proposal and told us all he knew about the suspect.

We watched Black Jack for about two hours. Five or six customers walked up to him, shook his hand, and strolled away. We took no police action. These people were not hassled because they were small time compared to our stick up man. We made an agreement with Black Jack and planned to keep our word. The minute you double cross these people on a pact, word spreads through the streets. It would be very unlikely to ever obtain information again from prior informants once they become aware of any double crosses. Our suspect never showed up to purchase the dope from Black Jack. We only had nominal info in our bag of tricks to act on.

We squandered the next week looking for the stick-up man and absolutely nothing panned out. Then, one day, we were stopped at a red light during our tour. Leaning on a pole in the bus stop was an individual who resembled our robber. We did not stop at first because it seemed too coincidental for the Fanny May suspect to be standing on a corner awaiting arrest. We decided to go around the block and take a second look. I pulled to the curb and we stared at him for a few seconds. He looked back and waved hello. Earl and I exited the squad.

"Hey, partner, what's your name?" I asked.

"Tommy Watkins," he said.

"So where do you lay your bones at night, Tommy?" asked Earl.

"67th Street and Green." he responded.

"Look, asshole, do ya live on the streetlight? Give us some fucking numbers," said Earl.

He complied with the request but none of the info matched our offender.

"What's your birthday, man?" I asked.

"It's the 27th of September, 1965," said Tommy.

For some strange reason his response went in one ear and right out the other.

Something appeared wrong with this guy; we could feel it. We scrutinized a mug shot, in color, and still could not determine his identity. We reluctantly showed Tommy the photo. He told us he was stopped numerous times in the past week by many detectives who mistakenly took him for the stick-up man in the picture. He suggested all of us drive around the corner and question his auntie to verify his identity. So, instead of taking him into the station to thoroughly check him out the proper way, we got lazy. We ran with the easiest and quickest way to get to a conclusion. We decided to speak to Tommy's auntie, a regretful decision.

Lacking an ID in his pocket, which is not uncommon in the ghetto, we accepted his word for his name, address, and date of birth. I drove up to the auntie's house, exited the car, and rang the doorbell. As usual, it did not work. I banged on the door and an elderly woman opened it. She crept out onto the front porch. I asked her if she knew the identity of the man seated in the back seat of our squad. She gave me the exact name and address Tommy furnished to us earlier. With nothing else to go on, we released him. Tommy quickly walked away and out of our sight.

A minute later, we were back to work. We turned the corner and there stood Black Jack. Earl and I cruised by and he gave us the thumbs-up sign, which was very unusual. Dope dealers do not say hello to the police. Suddenly, a radio check erupted from the speaker and announced the date and time. I yelled at Earl to return to the aunt's house immediately.

En route, Earl yelled back, "What the fuck's the matter with you?"

"I'll tell you what the fucking matter is; we blew it like a couple of stupid rookies. Do you remember when I asked that jagoff his birthday?" I asked.

"Yeah, he said it was the 27th."

"Do you know what day today is, partner?" I asked.

"Yeah, it's...holy fuck. I can't believe it, we blew it," said Earl.

You see, we must ask the birthday question ten to fifteen times a day to suspects on the streets of the ghetto. Every time we stop and ask someone when they were born, they always say, and I mean always say, "Hey office', today's my birthday," and tell us their correct date of birth. Maybe they expect less of a hassle from the police if the officer knows it is their birthday. Our stick-up man did not say it was his birthday, although the date was the 27th of September. According to the logic of the ghetto, his DOB was fabricated. People rarely break their pattern. Earl and I could not remember the last time we inquired about a birth date from a gang-banger and this phenomenon did not hold true. PEOPLE DO WHAT PEOPLE ALWAYS DO! If stopped by the police, and it is their birthday, they want the officers to be aware of that fact. I do not know why, they just do.

We searched the entire area over again. We were extremely mad at ourselves for being so lazy and stupid. You see, in the eight years of working together, he was the only gang-banger who completely conned the both of us. We might have gotten conned one at a time, but the other half of the partnership always caught the con and put us back on track. We were good, but certainly not on September 27th, it is day I will never forget. On that day, the people who usually did the conning got conned. The stick-up man was free and our stupidity now enabled him to rob again. Thirty days went by and four more robberies went down before his capture by a couple of beat guys in an unrelated incident. Plus, we lost another front-page pinch.

Not all our time in the gang unit was spent playing cops and robbers. Earl and I were asked on many occasions to act as public relation officers. We spoke well during question and answer sessions, and, if necessary, could fill a room with enough bullshit to fertilize a cornfield.

One time, the lieutenant sent us to speak at a district roll call. The station, located in one of the worst gang areas of the city, sat on the west side of Chicago. He wanted us to speak to the officers about gang problems in their area. Most of these guys were quite knowledgeable about gangs anyway and did not feel our assistance would aid them with their district's problems. They should have been working right along side us; only they lacked the political clout to get transferred into our heavyweight unit.

We stood in the roll call room and waited for our turn to speak. Many officers entered the room and most displayed a wretched attitude. They dreaded coming to work in this crime-ridden area of the city, but they had no choice. It was so bad in this district that the bosses were elated if the troops showed up for work, let alone did any. The working conditions were deplorable.

What really upsets a shift sporting an attitude of this nature is a new supervisor who thinks everything is on the up and up. He is a guy who elevates himself above the troops just because his shirtsleeve displays three stripes. This is a recipe for trouble.

Well, one of these supervisors attended roll call. He positioned all the troops in a straight line and, during the inspection, asked the veteran officers questions face to face. He was a quota sergeant, young and with an attitude.

He stood with his nose adjacent to the officers' mouths and hunted for the odor of alcohol on their breath. This method of inspection quickly stopped when one of the old-timers sneezed in the sergeant's face. The inspection continued and he resembled Patton browsing over his troops. But, like the general he made a fatal mistake. The sergeant asked a 6'4", 250-pound Irish officer a question. He grabbed the officer's shirtsleeve and rubbed it between his thumb and trigger finger.

"What asshole ironed this shirt? It looks terrible," said the sergeant.

The officer's posture went from attention to the stance of a prizefighter. A quick jab to the nose, and before he knew it, the

sergeant lay on his back. His eyes filled with tears from the impact and blood tricked from his nose.

"My wife, sir, is the asshole who ironed this shirt. Do ya
gotta problem with that?" asked the officer.

The officer towered over the sergeant for a second and then
walked away. The other officers were stunned, but did not act.
The sergeant got up, brushed himself off, and exited. Earl and
I gave our speech and got the hell out of there. Thirty minutes
later, we were in search of a coffee stop and heard a radio broadcast that caught our undivided attention.

"Beat #1530," yelled a male voice.

"Go ahead, Beat #1530," said the dispatcher.

"I's got a hot car," said the sergeant.

It was the quota sergeant who previously received the right
cross reprimand in the roll call room.

"I's got a hot car and need some help," repeated the sergeant.

Now, any policeman in the country would decipher the sergeant's radio transmission to mean he is presently observing or
following a stolen vehicle.

Quickly, the dispatcher said, "Does your vehicle have occupants, and if so, how many?"

"Ahh, that's a 10-4, squad, one occupant," said the sergeant.

"Give me your location, Sergeant, so I can send back-up,"
said the dispatcher.

He informed the radio dispatcher the location of the alleged stop. Immediately, other units began to assist the sergeant with his felon. Cars scrambled toward the scene with
lights activated and sirens that ruptured the normal sounds
of the streets. Everyone gave their beat numbers to the dispatcher, indicating mostly rookies were en route. You never
put yourself down on tape unless you have to. One never
knows what will happen at the scene, and depending upon
the situation, you can save yourself a lot of headaches if the
shit hits the fan. If someone from the IAD tried to screw
you, just for being there, you can simply deny your presence
and they cannot prove a thing.

Earl and I arrived at the scene along with the other assist cars. Uncertainty filled the street intersection. The next thing Earl and I witnessed amazed us. No other words could describe it. The sergeant sat in his car actually dozing. His hood in the raised position, you could see the engine spitting out white clouds of steam. He had a hot car, all right; it was his own, and nothing more than a busted radiator hose. We looked at the situation, shrugged our shoulders at the other officers, and drove away unsurprised. It was par for the course.

Later that evening, the boss called Earl and me into the office. He wanted us to break in a new gang investigator. For the time being, we had no problem with the extra company, so we left the office and hit the street. We decided to coast for the rest of the night and get rid of the new guy by the next shift.

Earl and I were at a crossroad in our careers where a problem existed concerning the trust of unknown police officers. It was a time in the political arena where the "G" implemented undercover stings monthly in an attempt to catch policemen off base and dirty. When you make the police look bad, it gives the perception the city is loaded with corruption. Perception then becomes reality. This crap usually went on in an election year when Republicans occupied the White House.

Chicago has historically voted democratic for the past sixty years and Illinois is a must-win state in the presidential race. Many jokes surface at police stations come election time. They went from people who voted twice, to dead registered voters participating in an election, and lastly, purchasing a drunk's vote with two bucks and a bottle of Ripple wine. I often wondered on an election day why hundreds of skid row residents never showed up for their day labor jobs and all carried bottles of Ripple in their rear pocket. Ask a Kennedy how important Chicago's vote is.

When a new man comes into a unit like ours, you must always be cautious. The way the government operates, he could be a planted mole looking for some "G" brownie points. All policemen should realize their worst enemy is another policeman. Every hard working officer knows it is sometimes necessary to break a law to catch the big law-breaker. Accordingly, I would not think twice about lifting a document off someone's desk, if it would help me catch a bad guy at a later date. Any energetic officer who tells you he has never broken a law, violated someone's civil rights, or broken a major rule during his course of employment is a damn liar. It is for the above reasons most policemen prefer to work with the same partner, someone you can trust at all times.

During our cruise, we passed the area of 67th Street and Union. A few weeks earlier, we unsuccessfully sought after a stick-up man who haunts this section of the city. We sat on a corner for about an hour and accomplished nothing more than killing time.

"Hey, Earl, hit the alley. I gotta tap a kidney," I said.

Earl drove to the mouth of an alley and leisurely proceeded to look for a rat-free area to pull over. Halfway into the alleyway, he stopped. The three of us exited to urinate.

At the other mouth of the alley, a man entered. He carried what appeared to be a bat or a large stick. This was not an unusual sight in the ghetto. These gang-bangers would walk around with a bazooka in their hands if the law would allow it. I remember thinking, here is a man walking down a dark alley at 11:00 p.m., fact. Here is a man, who sees three other men pissing in an alley, yet he approached fearlessly, fact. Here is a man who had an opportunity to take another route but he did not, fact. Top-notch detective conclusion, he is packing.

He got closer, and what appeared to be a stick or a bat now resembled a rifle. When our eyes finally focused on the object, it became apparent that it was indeed a rifle. We drew our weapons and ordered the punk to halt. He was just a kid, only in his teens. The sight of three weapons pointed at his face frightened him and he dropped the weapon.

This was no ordinary rifle. The weapon was beautiful, hand engraved, monogrammed, and in mint condition. It must be hot. Immediately, we put the fear of God in the kid before he got a chance to gather his thoughts.

"Where did you get the gun, kid?" I asked.

Still shaky, he answered, "My uncle, he gave it to me to see if I could sell it."

"Where's your uncle now?" asked Earl.

"He's at home and he's got a lot more guns like this one," he said.

The teenager continued to talk, and when he told us there were at least ten or fifteen more rifles on his uncle's kitchen table, Earl and I just shook our heads in disbelief. Lady Luck must have been pissing in the alley alongside us.

"Hey, Rich, aren't you glad I picked this alley for a piss stop?" asked Earl.

"You're driving the car. You get all the credit for this one, partner," I said.

I threw the kid in the backseat and we immediately proceeded to the uncle's house. He told us his uncle, along with three companions, burglarized a home in Naperville, Illinois. Naperville is a very affluent suburb adjacent to Chicago.

Before we arrived, Earl pulled over to use a pay phone and called the Naperville Police. When he returned, he rattled off a long list of the stolen items. The burglary in question became reclassified to a home invasion/robbery.

Earl's effort obtained serial numbers of other stolen weapons and the rifle in the car matched the Naperville job. Our little friend told us the house was loaded with stolen goods taken during a crime spree. He said his uncle and others were in the process of moving everything to a garage, but he did not know its location.

I heard enough. Probable cause existed to justify a search. There are only a few occasions when you can search a home without a court order, and one of them concerns the element of time. If we waited for a warrant, all the stolen goods would be relocated. We called for some additional manpower from the local tactical team and hit the house. Our entrance was unproblematic and half of the stolen property still remained in the house in clear view. The other half of the property had already been loaded into a van parked in the garage. We coordinated serial numbers of various items and everything checked out stolen. While in the house, Earl notified adjacent suburbs of Naperville and spoke to their Robbery Division detectives. He informed them of our arrest and MO. Crimes popped up all over the 'burbs committed by this home invasion team. These dumbbells never changed their method of operation. All other robberies were matched with little effort.

When it was all over, we cleared six armed robberies/home invasions, recovered thousands of dollars of stolen property and weapons, and put four dogs in prison for a long time. This all happened because three coppers were too lazy to look for an open gas station to take a leak.

Months went by and the high-quality arrests kept falling into place. Pinch after pinch and all Part Ones, which means felonies. It seemed Earl and I never wanted to work on any thing but felonies. We felt misdemeanor crimes were a waste of our time, plus the big bosses did not care much for bullshit arrest. Most of the guys who worked on nothing but misdemeanors were really heavy politically, so the brass could not move them out of the Gang Unit anyway. The unit was broken up into teams that worked on felonies, and teams that handled the bullshit misdemeanor arrest. The change did not upset either Earl or me because we loved to work on felonies anyway.

The antics of two Latin gangs in the southern portion of our gang sector troubled the city. The boss wanted a little extra manpower to keep the boys in the Ivory Tower at 11th Street happy. Earl and I were taken from the area we normally worked, and used as fill-ins to help out the guys with the Latino punks. We were only familiar with one of the local Latin gang leaders from a past experience, a cocky punk that Earl and I just could not stand. The mere sight of him pissed us off.

His name was Danny the Nail. He got his nickname when one of the local gang-bangers turned trick and bought a nickel bag for the police to get an insignificant marijuana dealer off the street.

Well, Danny found out who tricked, and administered his own form of street justice. The kid ended up in an abandoned garage, dead and nailed to the door in a crucifixion-like execution.

Before the fastening, the stool pigeon took an intense beating from someone. The family showed the victim in a closed casket. We figured Danny did it, but no proof existed. I must admit, other gang dicks hassled him weekly because of the murder, but he took it like a man and kept his mouth shut.

One day, during our harassment session with Danny, he looked at us with a cold expression on his face and said, "If I could cut both your throats and beat the rap, I'd do it tomorrow."

It took a lot of balls to make a comment of that nature to a couple of cops. That said, Earl and I decided to have a little fun with this so-called fearless gang leader. We grabbed him by the hair and dragged him in the backseat of the squad. Earl got behind the wheel and we sped off.

"Where we going with this prick, partner?" whispered Earl.

"Fuck this little asshole. He ain't as bad as he thinks, and we're gonna prove it," I said.

I informed Earl of my plan of action and he gave me the nod of approval. It's about time Danny got a peek at the Angel of Death. En route, I peered at Danny's face in the mirror and observed many different expressions. First, the cool look, very common among criminals, followed by the thinking look as he pondered our destination. Then, his face displayed the final and third look. Foes of the police have given it many names; it's the

"Hey, are you fucking guys crazy?" look, or "Hey, we ain't going into the station" look.

Suddenly, Danny figured out our destination and begged us to turn around.

"Hey, man, this ain't funny, chu gonna get me killed. Please," he said.

Simultaneously, Earl and I gave Danny a "fuck you."

We drove across Danny's gang boundaries and were now in Latin Kings's turf. Danny would not walk through this neighborhood for a free year supply of tamales. We pulled up just short of the corner about twenty-five yards from a bunch of King gangbangers. (What the hell, Danny needed a head start.) Danny slid his torso down the rear of the backseat and hid from the group.

The gang-bangers knew Earl and me by sight, so they just stared as I exited the squad. I approached the collection of scumbags and told them I carried a personal message from Danny the Nail.

"Danny says you're a bunch of pussy motherfuckers, and he enjoyed fucking all of your girlfriends last week."

A voice from the crowd yelled, "Chu can tell him to go fuck himself."

"I'll do better than that, you asshole, tell him yourself," I said.

Earl threw open the back door and dragged Danny out. I jumped in the passenger's seat and we took off. At first, everyone froze and Danny started to run towards our fleeing vehicle. The entire gang trailed a short distance behind. Danny ran for his life. We let him continue his jaunt almost an entire block until he began to lose ground between himself and his pursuers. Earl slowed the vehicle and Danny gained precious ground.

"That's enough, Earl, don't ya think?" I said.

"Yeah, partner, party's over," said Earl.

By now, Danny ran parallel to our back door. He dove through the open window just in the nick of time. Once we had our cargo inside, we sped away.

I turned and asked, "You aren't so bad now, are you, motherfucker?"

There was no response.

"Just remember, we can get you killed anytime we want and get away with it. Don't you ever threaten us again. Do you understand, asshole?" asked Earl.

"What a fun day, don't cha think, partner?" I said.

Every now and then, the boss would take Earl and me off of homicide and robbery and have us assist other detectives with various crimes. One time, we were to assist investigators with an arsonist who loved to burn down condemned garages in the ghetto.

The local newspapers tried to blame the occurrences on the firemen's strike, but that stretched a hunch a bit too far.

At first, Earl and I thought gang members were the perpetrators, portraying the arsons as a form of intimidation toward the neighborhood people. But, this also was not the case. After days of investigation, we had nothing. Earl and I could not put forth the effort needed to solve the crime. This type of investigation bored us to no end and we convinced the boss the mystery appeared unsolvable.

We completed our activity report for the shift when an idea popped into my head. Somehow, we had to cover all the man-hours wasted on the arson investigation. Earl and I decided to have a little fun with the boys downtown. The finished report stated, "We have a suspect concerning the arsons and we are in hot pursuit. Arrest is imminent."

I ripped the report from the typewriter and brought into the bathroom. We used a cigarette lighter and burned all four corners of the document. We left ashes at each of the right angles. I sent the report downtown and, as expected, we got a pretty good ass chewing from the deputy about the prank. A couple of days later, the big boss admitted to the lieutenant his office personnel got a big kick out of the burned arson report. He instructed the lieutenant to have us slow down on the hilarity. Back to real police work.

It was near the end of the month, so crime was slow in the ghetto. If you wonder why police business is sluggish at this time, it is because welfare checks come out at the beginning of the month and it makes no sense to rob anyone with no cash or food stamps in his pocket. The boss requested our assistance in a Mexican gang area of the city, around 18th Street and Ashland Avenue.

The night before produced a gang-bang murder. It was your typical 18th Street killing. A bunch of punks drive through a waring neighborhood, find a couple of gang-bangers hanging on a corner, and unload their weapons. This type of shooting usually succeeds because the shots are fired into a crowd. In this case, one of the punks on the corner caught one right in the head. He checked out twenty minutes later in the hospital, and naturally, there were no witnesses at the time.

In reality, there were plenty of witnesses, but the Mexican gang members like to take the law into their own hands, the logic being that if the culprit is in police custody, no revenge can be taken.

After a couple of hours of legwork, we identified the shooter and the other occupants of the auto. Our strategy: pressure must be exerted on the weakest member of the group. After two more hours of pure bullshit and cons, we managed to persuade the occupants of the vehicle to trick on the shooter for their own freedom. We now had probable cause established to apprehend Snake, our killer.

We knew where he lived, but, of course, he was not home. His mother did not speak English, another snag. The next person you must speak with is the girlfriend of the suspect. Sooner or later, her man will make contact.

We pulled up to Juanita's house and she sat on the front porch. At first, she made a move toward the door, but changed her mind and decided to sit and look as if she was cool with our arrival. The weird look on her face already gave her away. Obviously, she knew something. We cautiously approached the porch, because there was a good chance Snake hid inside.

"Hi, Juanita, how are you?" I asked.

"Chu know you don't care, so why ask?"

I spoke and Earl kept his eyes glued to the front windows.

"Is anyone in the house, Juanita, or are you alone?" I asked.

"The only one home is my grandmother and she is upstairs sleeping," she said.

That is what we wanted to hear. We knew if the curtain moved it must be the curiosity of Snake. Juanita told us she had not seen Snake for about a week. She reluctantly gave us that bit of information only when I grabbed her forearm and squeezed.

Suddenly, the curtain moved and one eyeball peeped through the crack of the separated material. Earl leaped off the front porch and immediately ran to the rear via the next-door neighbor's yard. I tried to pull the screen door open as the little bitch climbed up my back. We heard the sound of glass breaking from the opposite side of the house. I jumped off the porch and entered the gangway. Snake ran at full stride toward the alley and I drew my. 9mm. I took aim. My sights focused directly to the middle of his back. Snake had nowhere to run but straight because the buildings wedged him in. No way could I miss my target with a twelve round clip and one in the chamber.

What seemed like a few minutes took a few seconds. My finger tensed on the trigger and my brain instructed it to squeeze. Just then, for an unknown reason, my finger went limp. I questioned my right to put a bullet in this kid's back. Why? I would have saved the state a lot of money and I knew Snake committed the homicide. He did not deserve to live.

My hesitation gave Snake enough time to make the turn and hit the alley. I followed down the gangway after him and collided with Earl as he flew over the fence from the neighbor's backyard. Snake escaped. We holstered our weapons and walked back to the car.

"I could've killed him, Earl. It would've been real easy," I said.

"Yeah, I know, partner. I could've killed him, too, but it's not worth it in these bullshit times," he said.

Our true reason for the hesitation stemmed from the hassle that lay ahead from a police kill. If the press does not destroy you, the politicians will. A controversial police kill is a sure vote getter if you are a politician and on the side of the public's view of the issue. If the matter is a racial political controversy, white police officers kills a young Hispanic teen, those brown noses from IAD jump on it and try to pin a medal on their chest and screw a brother officer. They make a friend at City Hall if their actions serves a politician's needs, and the community involved is now satisfied their unjustified complaint of police brutality has been resolved.

Many officers commonly refer to these IAD guy as "empty holsters." "Most of them have their retirement parties in a phone booth" was a very common phrase used to describe their departure from the force by the troops. Many racial police shootings in our country cause civil unrest and property damage. Politicians do what is needed to avoid such a catastrophe, even if it means destroying a policeman's family and life. Police and politics is a dirty game.

We still had to find Snake and clues did not come easy as to his whereabouts. Mexican people are closed mouthed with the police; sort of like the Italians, they do not want to be labeled as stool pigeons. We finally got a break in the case when we discovered Snake, of all things, was hired part time at the University of Illinois. He worked for a government program that dealt with job training for street gang members. The purpose of the program was to keep kids off the street and find them something to do. Snake found his employees something to do, all right; he showed them the ins and outs of how to kill a rival gang member.

The following day, our investigation led us to the faculty building of the university. In a conference room, we could see Snake through the glass window of the entrance door. The room contained a long table where eight people sat. Snake and Juanita were two of the eight. The other six were men, all over sixty years old, very educated, and appeared to us as the liberal type. In those days, police described liberals as pipe smokers or guys who wore French tams on their heads indoors, as well as outdoors. One of the professors sported a French tam and a pipe was visible in his shirt pocket. We knew the professor would be trouble. We were right.

We could hear the conversation and these idiots were actually taking notes and advice from Snake, a twenty-one-year-old high school dropout and killer. We decided to enter casually to keep the situation calm. Snake had no other exit except through Earl and me.

"Let's nonchalantly walk in and just drag the asshole out of the meeting," whispered Earl.

"Sounds good to me, partner. I'm right behind you," I said.

When Juanita observed our entrance, she let out a scream. The educated six looked at us as if we were crazy, but then again, Juanita and Snake were the only ones who knew our intentions and identity. There was a lull after the shriek and we slowly walked up to Snake. We identified ourselves and I placed him under arrest for murder. His rights were read in the presence of the six witnesses, but before I could finish, I felt a hand on my shoulder. One of the liberal professors wanted to play defense attorney.

"Excuse me, Officer, you can't do that. What seems to be the problem? Are you aware that you're on university property?" asked the professor.

Snake and I glared at each other, and even a punk like him knows you do not lay your hands on a police officer when he is effecting an arrest. I glanced upward and then bowed my head. I looked up again and slowly exhaled into the professor's face. Luckily, my patience overcame the thought of delivering a right cross to his eye. I finished Miranda with Snake, but the professor still crammed me. From the table, someone yelled at Mr. Weinstein to give the officers some room. I agreed with the gentleman and gave Mr. Weinstein a little shove.

"Mr. Weinstein? Is that your name?" asked Earl.

Earl and I looked at each other and smiled quite noticeably.

"Do you find humor in my name, Officer?" asked the professor.

"No. I just want to make sure I have the correct spelling for my arrest report, the one that's gonna have your name on it if you keep fucking with my partner," said Earl.

"I think you owe us an explanation for your actions here," said the professor.

That was it. Earl and I had put up with enough of the professor's crap. Snake knew what was about to happen. He just backed up slowly, sat down in a chair, and shook his head in disbelief. It was as if he had his own crystal ball. Suddenly, the professor went to assist Snake in the chair. I grabbed the belt that held the rear of his pants up, knocked off his tame, and clutched the back of his hair. Earl and I pinned him against the conference room wall.

"Listen, you cocksucker, if you interfere with this arrest one more time, you're gonna get your ass beat," I said.

Snake chuckled and Earl snapped, "What the shit ya laughing at, you wetback motherfucker?"

"I resent that ethnic slur, Officer, and demand an apology to this gentleman right this second," said the nutty professor

I released the professor and pushed him away from Earl and me. I cupped my crotch with one of my hands.

"Fuck you and your apology," I said.

Snake was in our grasp and Earl and I started for the door. I turned and looked at the self-made hero.

"You all have a nice day, yeah here," I said.

My comment made the professor angry and he charged us. If it were not for one of the professor's colleagues, he would have joined Snake. Funny thing about the professor, he stunned us. He never beefed regarding our abusive verbal and physical altercation.

We arrived at the station and allowed Snake to call his lawyer. That was his right. Earl and I did not ask one question until his attorney arrived, but Snake refused to talk about the murder any way. All the witnesses were interviewed and the Felony Review Unit approved charges of murder. We finally put Snake behind bars and had the satisfaction of a job well done.

It was gratifying to personally hear from the family of the victim. They thanked us from the bottom of their hearts for the capture of their sons' murderer. That is what makes this job worthwhile, recognition from the victim's family, not so much the brass. Any veteran investigator knows the hand that pats you on the back one day is the same hand that slaps you on the ass the next. Screw up and make political waves, and the ass slapping occurs. It is the appreciation of the victim's family members that really is important.

Weeks later, it was time for the trial and the emotion that erupted from the incident subsided. As far as we were concerned, it was just another day in court. More interest developed when Earl and I learned we were up against one of the city's top defense attorneys. He had never been an adversary before and matching wits with him would be a challenge. I went into the trial and felt the odds were with the state because Earl and I believed the investigation was thorough and fair.

The prosecuting attorney decided to put me on the stand first. Earl would have his hour in the spotlight after mine. The pretrial conference was over and it ran rather smoothly. I entered the courtroom and took my place on the stand.

Oddly, my nerves built and I became somewhat jittery. The questions from the state were very basic and to the point. After all, it is the state's objective to make the police officer look honest, intelligent, and, most importantly, reliable. In contrast, the defense tries to portray the police as stupid and unreliable in the hopes of destroying all credibility. I have seen some cases where lawyers can accomplish this feat with no difficulty at all.

The questions from the state came to a close and now it was time for the cross-examination. Admittedly, this attorney's experience did intimidate me somewhat; that could account for my unexplained jitters. He started his dialogue very measured.

"What's your name?"

"Where do you work?"

"How long have you been a police officer?"

During the entire time, he paced up and down in front of the jury. It is a technique taught in law school to get them to focus on the defense attorney rather than the police officer. I had one advantage in my favor. I attended law school for a short period of time and was aware of some of the tricks in the defense's bag.

Abruptly, the door of the courtroom swung open and in walked another attorney. He bolted to the front table and sat down next to Snake. How ironic, we knew this man very well. Earl and I intertwined with him on numerous murder trials. His former job was a supervisor in the Gang Prosecution Unit. Presently, he sat on the other side of the fence, with his objective being to get the bad guy off instead of putting him away. This lawyer was good, but he also knew we were good. too.

"Detective, can you tell. . ." said the lawyer.

The attorney who just entered the courtroom signaled his partner right in the middle of a sentence.

"Strike that question," he snapped at the court reporter.

He swiftly proceeded to the defense table and asked the judge for a minute to confer with his legal partner. I used the spare time to chitchat with the court reporter.

The meeting of the minds concluded and the bombardment of questions resurfaced.

Suddenly, the defense attorney stared me down and slowly walked toward the witness stand. What did he have up his sleeve? My palms started to sweat. Face to face, he slapped the rail that surrounded the stand, and yelled, "I have no further questions for this investigator."

Totally confused, I thought, what a slick son of a bitch. I was off the stand and the rest of my testimony would be negated. I looked at his partner and he produced a mischievous grin on his face. It was all a mystery to me. The state called its next witness and I gave my friend, the defense attorney's colleague, a gesture to meet me in the corridor.

I entered the hallway where Earl still hung out and waited for his turn to testify. My attorney friend followed close behind. He extended his hand towards me. I grabbed it firmly.

"Well, if it isn't the famous Starsky and Hutch," he said.

"Yeah, it's us and I'd rather shake your hand than grab a hundred dollar bill," I said.

We all laughed.

"I didn't know you're representing Snake," said Earl.

"Yeah, just think, three years ago I tried to get him the chair in the Vasquez homicide. He beat us on that one. Think you guys can put him away with this one?"

"I don't know. It's a good bet," I said.

"I doubt you guys will win this one; it is even weaker than Vasquez. You can go home now, Rich," said the lawyer.

"So that's why the questions stopped so abruptly, it was you. What did you tell him?" I asked.

"Look, I've had a lot of trials with you two and the one thing I learned is you guys don't panic on the stand. Earl will be sent home next, and quite soon, I might add."

We thanked him for the compliment. He was right; our testimony concluded and we had no further input the rest of the trial. Snake was found not guilty due to the unreliability of the eyewitness and their long police record.

I would begin my furlough within the next couple of days, but I had made the decision months earlier that I would not be traveling. I hung around the house and completed the odd jobs that were weeks overdo in an effort to get my wife to stop complaining about the many eyesores on the property.

The phone rang one morning and it was a supervisor from the Internal Affairs Division. The super sleuths from the F.B.I. wanted to speak to me concerning parking tickets. This totally confused me because I had not written a ticket in over eight years. The sergeant ordered me to report downtown and cooperated with the "G" in any way possible. Yeah right!

I arrived at headquarters and went up to the 11th floor. Two agents awaited my arrival and were ready to arrest me for none other than fixing traffic tickets. With this knowledge in hand, I was thrilled, but also baffled. I have done a lot of thing in the past few years that could possibly warrant an arrest, but fixing parking tickets was not one of them. Boy, were these guys out to lunch.

A good investigator never shows his hand in an ongoing investigation before he completes all his homework. These guys not only forgot to do their homework; they did not even show up for school. They were two of many agents assigned to the famous undercover sting that nabbed numerous judges and lawyers for fixing tickets and drunken driving cases. The way the "G" became so successful in this investigation was not great investigative work, but wiretaps were used to gather all the info they needed for prosecution. The mouths of the individuals involved put themselves in the spotlight of the federal investigation. Once they deciphered the incriminating evidence on the tape, it was a breeze to get the stool pigeon lawyers to save their own asses and trick on the judges.

The arrest and prosecution of judges sells newspapers. Since this was a political prosecution, it was no big deal to prosecute some two-bit traffic lawyer as opposed to the chief judge and his cohorts. The lawyers squealed and got off the hook. The name of the undercover sting was "Operation Greylord."

Well, it seems the "G" men uncovered paperwork that I received approximately forty parking tickets during the prior year. All remained unpaid until about two months ago.

I contacted the State's Attorney's Office and requested a court date to plead my case concerning the tickets in front of a judge.

On many occasions, my work allowed me to use my personal vehicle for sensitive investigations. Most of the time during an investigation, Earl and I would take our lunch in the Rush Street area. To be honest, I parked my car wherever I felt. Legal parking was scarce. I was on official business and in an official undercover police vehicle.

Although my vehicle displays my union emblem, there are many disgruntled police officers that do not honor your status and refuse to give you a courtesy pass. They write police officers tickets like anyone else. After realizing I had so many citations accumulated, I requested a letter from the deputy that explained to the traffic court judge the circumstances of the citations. The deputy requested the judge to take the facts of the undercover investigations into consideration before rendering a decision. The judge did and instructed me to be more careful where I parked my car in the future. All the tickets were dismissed and no fines assessed. This shot up a red flag with the government.

They automatically assumed I fixed the case and paid off the judge or prosecutor. If they wanted the truth, all they should have done was ask the judge or the attorney, but they did not. They came to me thinking I was guilty and offered me a deal to stool pigeon on the both of them. The problem with their offer was that neither court officials violated any law. The "G" was head hunting. What could I tell them? They did not believe I ever possessed a letter from my deputy. When they realized how dim-witted they were, and how easy it would have been to resolve the entire issue without any accusations, they released me. But, to save face, they told me to expect a subpoena from the federal grand jury about the fixed tickets. The subpoena never arrived.

Weeks later, I was out with a lady partying on Rush Street. I stopped in a club called the BBC and already consumed quite a few cocktails. My date and I walked to the dance floor and passed the entrance of the bar. Snake appeared with five of his gang-banger friends and Juanita attached to his hip. At first, I thought we went undetected, but from the dance floor area, I noticed a friendly wave from Snake and a couple of his buddies.

I ran down the unusual circumstances to the girl, but she did not seem to realize the urgency of the situation. The packed bar would be a perfect place for one of the gang-bangers to walk up behind me and stick a blade right in my back. The joint was loud as hell and packed to the rafters. To make matters worse, I did not have my weapon. It was not unusual for policemen not to carry a gun when he knows a night of heavy drinking lay ahead.

I finally convinced her to leave and we made our way through the crowd for the exit. Snake and Juanita were also on the move and on a collision course. We crossed paths and Snake cockily introduced himself. I smiled and responded hello, but still worried something might happen. I started to leave when Snake grabbed my hand and placed it into Juanita's hand.

"Officer, go dance with Juanita, she likes you," he said.

He gave the both of us a slight shove toward the dance floor and followed with my date.

The four of us danced side by side, but my thoughts were on the location of his friends. I could not see any of them due to the crowd. The over-packed dance floor caused the four of us to move closer to each other. Snake whispered in my ear.

"I heard you scared the shit out of Danny the Nail a couple of months ago."

"I don't know what you're fuckin' talking about," I said.

"Oh, you and Earl know what I mean," said Snake.

An opening erupted through the crowded floor and I grabbed my date's hand. We started to leave when Snake clutched my arm.

"You see, asshole detective, I could've killed you anytime tonight and got away with murder for the third time, but I didn't. You remember that," said Snake.

"Fuck you. Are you threatening me?" I asked.

He did not answer. Quickly, my date and I left the bar. What could I do in that crowd and half drunk? I will just have to wait for another time and another place. Besides, I wanted to get laid anyway. At the end of the night, I called Earl and ran down the incident. He was drunker than me, so it was no big deal to him. He blew me off and wanted to return to bed. Earl begged me just to go to sleep and forget about it. I complied with his wish. Unexpectedly, I never saw Snake again. Word on the street was he moved to New York City. He's their problem now.

Time flew by in the Gang Unit, and instead of working conditions getting better, they got worse. A new commander transferred in, and as you well know, everyone has his own way to enforce the law. Some ways are good and some are stupid. The Gang Unit headed in the direction of stupidity. Sadly, the most productive police unit in the history of the Chicago Police Department appeared domed. The new philosophy of the gang units' brass was quantity not quality.

Headlines splashed across the front page of the newspapers daily concerning the gang problem of Chicago and the mayor made the decision to switch some of her command personnel. The news media periodically received bullshit press releases to minimize the gang problem and to keep the community activist away from City Hall. It worked for a short time, but while gang-bangers thought we were hot on their trails, instead, we were conducting massive sweeps and arresting nothing but fifteen, sixteen, and seventeen-year-olds for loitering on a public way. Was this police action legal? I think not.

The unit arrested hundreds of people a night. But, this type of police work does not come without concerns. Hundreds of man-hours kept officers inside stations completing police reports when they were needed on the streets. The Gang Unit's mere presence in a neighborhood deterred crime. Secondly, all the prisoners were sent to district stations that contained holding cells because the gang units had no personal detention facilities. The commanders of these districts frowned upon our presence because we tied up their manpower to process the prisoners. Thirdly, and most importantly, this police strategy devastated the morale of the troops. How do you think these officers felt, as they sat in a police station and wrote reports until their hands cramped, to watch these punks walk out before them with an I-Bond? To add insult to injury, they would wave good-bye to us while we still continued our paperwork. It was degrading to Earl and me, especially when compared to the quality of our past work.

We decided to speak to our boss who was always fair and understanding with us. We explained we could not compete with the other teams who were policing solely for the purpose of head hunting during sweeps. Quality was no longer propriety. Much to our surprise, the boss told us not to worry about anything. He wanted us to continue to work on nothing but felonies, which suited Earl and me just fine. What the hell, someone in our unit had to arrest the gang felons.

Four weeks later, the gang investigator rating sheet came out and, in one period, Earl and I pulled off four part one felony arrests, two misdemeanors, and no sweep disorderly conduct arrest. We were rated second from the bottom. Quite upset, we stormed into the boss's office. Before we could say a word, he informed us he was only following orders from downtown. He had no choice but to rate us on our numbers rather than quality of our arrests. We were forced to accept the boss's explanation.

The first thought on our mind was to transfer, but where could we go, not to mention the pay cut if we returned to patrol? When the boss got word of our impending transfer thoughts, he summoned us to his office. He said he would not approve any transfer because we knew too much. We informed him we would leave all our personal records and notes. But, what really interested him was implanted in our heads. He knew that information could not be left behind. Once again, we requested him to go to bat for us. Earl and I pleaded with him for the opportunity to continue our work on the problems that really plague the city, gang violence. We received the answer from the expression on his face, which made it obvious his hands were bound by the downtown brass.

"I know and you know this department can give two shits about the city's gang problem. What would you think if I called the papers and told them what the Gang Unit has become?" I asked.

"Don't make waves, Rich," said the boss.

He knew that would never happen. I could not stand stool pigeons. It was a life long pet peeve of mine. I turned and left the room.

My imminent transfer would soon be a reality. This was the first time a dime was dropped to get out of a unit everyone wanted to get into. We never did have a problem with the lieutenant; the problem lay with his superiors. But, we left him the files as promised.

Of course these files did not contain the street knowledge in our heads, which made them virtually useless to the new investigators who would try to analyze them. The information would have to coincide with an entire network of street informants created over the years to attain its potential value. It would take a long period of time for that phenomenon to occur.

I pondered my options of the transfer, but a return to a beat car sent chills up and down my spine. Seven years of that crap was enough. My clout limited, he did have an ace in the hole. He used to say, "I can't get you promoted, Rich, but I can get you transferred anywhere you want to go." I decided to call in my marker and requested the favor. To my astonishment, his response was "A transfer, that's a drop in the bucket. Just get back to me when you know where it is you want to go."

The very next morning, I called and informed my clout of my desired destination. He got the ball to roll in just two days. By the end of the week, I had an appointment with the Deputy Superintendent of Traffic.

"So, Officer, I understand you're very good friends with a relative of mine?" asked the deputy.

"Yes, deputy," I said.

"Well, if all my nephew wants is a transfer for his friend, then a transfer is what he'll get. You just pick your spot," he said.

"Okay, deputy, how about the Hit and Run Unit?" I asked.

Before another word came out of my mouth, he was on the phone with the Assistant Deputy of Traffic. My transfer was a done deal. I left his office, and there outside his door stood another police officer that waited to duplicate the process. It reminded me of the time my dad and I went to see the alderman in regards to trees in front of our home that needed trimming. Dad walked in his office, made his request, and if you are on good terms with the politicians in the area, the trees got cut.

My transferred confirmed, I told Earl of my intentions. Earl also had enough clout to move, but where? Maybe he still wanted to play policeman and remain in the gang unit. I knew I did not want to remain any longer. Well over a decade of this cop and robber shit had been enough for me. I paid my dues. Now let some rookie have a go at it and give me one of those gravy jobs.

If I possessed this knowledge twelve years ago, who knows where my career would have taken me. There are literally hundreds of do-nothing jobs on the Chicago Police Department. Most comprise of merely showing up for work and then you are on your own. Of course, all these jobs are what you call "Clout Jobs."

It is very easy to explain, so go the elections, so goes the clout. There are many officers who think they would never want a gravy job. But, after you put your time in and get screwed enough, trust me, you will seek out one of those gravy jobs very quickly. To you, crime fighters remember one thing, at the end of the pay period, your check and my check are exactly the same. You may have arrested twenty people, written twenty tickets, and been in two barroom brawls and possibly injured, the check is still the same. Now, who has the better job?

I used to laugh and, at the same time, feel sorry for the guys in patrol. Daily, they would work their butts off and put their lives in danger and rarely get any perks or recognition. Oh, there are honorable mention awards the department gives these officers, but they are meaningless. Maybe these same officers would grab a headline for a couple of days, for instance, if they were shot or seriously injured in the line of duty. But, they paid the price for that headline. To sum it up, with a handful of these commendations and a buck, you could take a CTA bus ride in Chicago.

These awards have nothing to do with furthering a career and as soon as the young officers realize this, the better off they will be. The only legitimate honorable mention awards are the ones prepared personally by your sergeant or lieutenant. I have

witnessed many officers create their own fantasy honorable
mention award for exceptional police work. They merely would
present it to a sergeant when he was extremely busy, and he
would sign it. The officer now possesses a department award.
Earl and I received approximately thirty awards in our gang careers. These accommodations, drafted by our supervisors, did
nothing to advance our careers. Clout did.

I arrived at work one morning and Bob informed me Earl decided not to check in for roll call due to an early court appearance.
I hit the street 10-99 with nothing urgent to do. I pulled the squad
into a convenient store parking lot, got a cup of java, and decided
to read a little while waiting for Earl to return to the office.

I got so wrapped up in the book, the needle on the gas gauge
went unnoticed as it slipped pass empty. After sitting about an
hour with the engine still running, it started to sputter. I ran out
of gas. Fortunately, the convenient store had pumps on the premises. I hand-pushed the squad to the pump and put in just enough
gas to get back to the office where the petrol was free.

Suddenly, members from the south side gang unit called in a
chase from right in front of the courthouse building. The fleeing
offender happened to be one of the biggest gang leaders in the
city accompanied by four bodyguards. Recently released from
prison, the offender was required to report to the court building
and tie up some loose ends concerning his parole. The chase
headed my way and I asked the squad operator the reason for
the pursuit. He did not know and the pursuing units would not
respond to my question.

Since this gang figure was so important, the CPD tailed on
him just about around the clock. It was general knowledge he
retained a high profile attorney who filed a federal lawsuit for
millions against the department and the city for harassment.

I stood in the store lot with the gas hose still in my hand. From
the opposite direction, I could see the wanted vehicle speeding
towards the intersection. The long black caddy whipped a sharp
right turn and slammed on the brakes. The rear door opened and
out jumped a large man dressed in a fluffy brown mink coat.

Oversized sunglasses partially shielded his facial features along with the wide brim of his hat. He slammed the door shut, the caddy took off, and the man casually strolled to the bus stop pole and leaned against it. The chasing units could not see the offender from their position due to the cement wall that sustained the steel viaduct suspended over the city street.

The two pursuing units were about a half block behind and traveled at a high rate of speed, maybe sixty to seventy miles per hour. They hit the intersection and took the turn on two wheels driving right past the pole leaner. He watched and laughed out loud as the police continued to chase the caddy with no one of importance inside.

I now recognized the person supporting the pole. Labeled as the most feared and notorious gang leader in the state, he controlled and headed the largest street gang in the City of Chicago. The Black P-Stone Nation Street Gang, later renamed EL Rukns, brought fear to the African America community at the mere mention of the gang's name. I guessed I had to do something. After all, I was a gang investigator. It took only an instant to create a con.

I stuck my radio in the back of my pants, shoved my snub nose in my rear pocket, and walked across the street. I approached the bad guy from his side. Luckily, he did not pay too much attention to my arrival and still stared in the direction of the chase. I stood five feet from him and gawked at the bus schedule posted on top of the sign.

"Hey, buddy, you got change for a five so I can get on this bus?" I asked.

"Sure, my man," he said.

He reached for his wallet beneath the bulky fur coat and came out holding it in his hand. He split the wallet and reached inside for the singles with the other hand. Now was the time to make my move. I slowly reached towards my rear pocket. He assumed I would be removing my billfold, but instead, my snub nose showed up for the occasion. I pointed at his face.

"What's up, Jeff? How ya doing?" I asked.

"Who da fuck are you, man?" he asked.

"Who da fuck are you?" I mocked back.

"Who the fuck do ya think I am, you fuckin' idiot. Police, you're under arrest," I said.

Jeff's head snapped back and forth from me to the direction of the chase.

"Where da fuck did you come from?" he asked.

I pointed across the street to the detective car parked at the pumps.

"Were ya sitting there the whole time and watched me jump outta the caddy? And what the fuck am I arrested for," he asked.

"How the fuck do I know? Just put your hands on your head and sit the fuck down on the curb," I said.

Jeff slid down the pole and sat at the curb. He offered no resistance. I started to radio the other gang dicks, but figured they would beat the shit out of the bodyguards to find out what happened to Jeff. Sure enough, I was right and they were on the way to assist me. They took the prisoner into custody, wrote down my name and star, and took off in a big hurry.

I went into the office and told Earl the whole story. He got a real big kick out of it. Thirty minutes later, the phone rang and a gang south investigator requested my presence downtown in one of the boss's offices. When we arrived, sitting on the lieutenant's desk was a completed arrest report, case report, and criminal complaint forms. The signature box at the bottom of these papers was blank. I read the paperwork and it contained a detailed account of Jeff's aggression prior to my arrest. I did not witness any of these events. Also contained in the reports were allegations of threats against me from the offender. I did not recall any such remarks. Earl and I were dumfounded because I just told him the whole story of the incident and the interpretation on the reports were quite different.

"Here ya go, Officer, just sign these reports on your arrest," said the lieutenant.

"Are you crazy or just plain stupid?" I asked.

Boy, did that remark piss him off.

"What's the problem? You made the arrest," he said.

"The problem is the reports are all fuckin' lies. I'm not signing it unless you order me to," I said.

He grabbed all the paper off the table and told me I had not heard the last of this. He left the room and we left his office. Before he could make his move, Earl and I went straight to the top and spoke to the deputy superintendent. We told him my story and he assured me he would handle the matter. He better, this was the man who Earl and I made look so good with all our big pinches. He knew us quite well. All I cared about on this one was my name be omitted from Jeff's big money lawsuit. That's what the shaky lieutenant feared or he would have signed all the reports himself. If I signed the papers, it would be a good bet I would be added to the lawsuit as an additional defendant.

A couple of hours left to the shift, Earl and I decided to check out the home of a kid we had been looking for in a shooting. I asked Earl if he wanted to go home and change the expensive light beige winter wool suit he wore for his court appearance. He said no. I had the strangest feeling that something would happen to his suit and asked again, but he insisted on wearing it the rest of the shift.

We knocked on the offender's door. Mama answered and invited us inside. What a ghetto looking apartment. It was one of the filthiest places I have ever seen. Leftover food discarded on the floors, piles of grimy clothing everywhere, torn up repulsive smelling carpets, and the entire wall in the living room lacked plaster. This particular wall was infested with roaches. I found out the hard way when my conversation with Mama got a little verbal. I pounded my fist on the lathes for effect and the entire wall appeared to be moving. I disturbed a nest of roaches and they poured from the wall. Half of the dining room floor was covered with insects. We walked to the kitchen with a nauseating crunch sound accompanying every stride.

Atop the kitchen table on a hot plate simmered a pot of ground beef and taco mix. Two small children waited for Mama to fix lunch. As Earl continued to question the suspect's mother, I noticed one of the kids climbing up a stool. He dipped a taco shell in the pot of meat and it emerged soaked in a greasy red sauce. The child approached Earl from the rear grasping the messy shell. Should I tell my partner to move? Or maybe I should teach him a lesson that very expensive suits should not be worn in the ghetto. Just then, the kid grabbed Earl's leg and threw a bear hug around it. After I heard the crunch of the shell, I yelled.

"Earl, get the fuck outta the way."

I believe my comment came a little late as Earl's beautiful suit turned into a tie-dye.

For the next four weeks, my job would be less stressful. Soon, I would depart from this grammar school unit. The guys tried to talk me into staying, but I could not take the bullshit any longer. The patrol officers found it amusing that the main function of the Gang Unit consisted of nothing more than arrest for loitering. In reality, a large majority of these arrestees should not have been arrested at all. They broke no laws. It made me feel like a fool when I followed orders from downtown concerning sweeps for the purpose of a head count. But the true fool was the one who came up with this unconstitutional solution to solve Chicago's gang problem. Just like the cockroach, the gang problem will be impossible to eliminate. In the months to come, the courts would rule the sweeps illegal and this tactic ceased to exist.

Earl and I were driving around the Rush Street area one day when we received a radio assignment to return to the office. We arrived as quickly as possible and the station was in pandemonium. Police officers and reporters were everywhere. Two gang officers just got blown away during a traffic stop and both offenders were still at large. In the past, gang investigators rarely made traffic stops unless it was absolutely necessary, but the guys needed heads to survive in this new unit and they would take any bullshit arrest they could get theirs hands on. Gang investigators normally worked strictly off case reports that pertained to gang-related crimes. That is what investigators do, or were suppose to do.

In order to understand this story, you must first absorb the emotional situation. Anger and rage were prevalent due to the police murder. It clouded the minds of the officers involved. Now add racial overtones. Two black suspects murdered two white gang investigators. Not all perceived this as a black/white incident, but some did. Quietness lingered over our unit and a halo of sadness blanketed the building. Lastly, the emotion of revenge, which was probably the most prevalent, interfered with police judgment. All the gang investigators wanted to do was go out and blow the murderer's heads off. Not only would this satisfy their bloodlust, but also they could now rationalize their intense feelings of hatred.

Regular homicide detectives oversee any murder investigation in the city. They were the trained experts. One little foul up could blow the entire case, and this explains why, at a crime scene, they have total control of the situation, even over the brass. The problem in this situation was two of our guys were murdered and some of our bosses thought they were more intelligent than the trained detectives. In my twenty years on the police force, I have never seen an investigation in such chaos. It took Earl and me awhile to break from the group, but as soon as we observed this circus-like atmosphere, that is exactly what occurred.

Approximately forty officers from the newly reorganized Gang Unit hit the streets. Their mission, locate any tips and clues to solve the murder. Thirty of the forty only had minimal investigative experience and possessed the cocky street cop mentality of "locate the suspect, beat him, arrest him, and find out everything else later." Of the ten left, a portion of them were too emotionally involved and should have been sent home. Their eagerness to help only hindered the investigation. We worked a solid twenty-four hours on this case and all we could come up with were maybes, could haves, and what ifs. None of the info accumulated checked out. There were bodies hooked to walls all over Homicide and the Gang Unit. They were all potential suspects. Their presence was based on mere innuendos. We were only looking for two shooters and there were twenty suspects in custody. The press had a field day on this one. Why are two cop killers still at large? The criticism from the newspapers and television media added more stress to an already dreadful situation.

Earl and I could not operate in our normal manner owing to the confusion and the fiasco of police officers that bumped into each other during every step of the investigation. We were about to say to hell with it, and let everyone else handle the job, when one more bit of info emerged.

An eighteen-year-old who lived in the area of the incident claimed he saw the shooting and knew the offenders. We decide to go along with the group and give it one more shot. Before we left, we ran a name check on our alleged suspect, adult and juvenile. Not one arrest. It is rare when you have a ghetto kid with no police contact as a youth or adult and he is now a murder suspect in a police shooting. The tip appeared to be another dead end.

A new group of gang investigators formed with the intentions of checking out this late tip. It consisted of twelve newly promoted gang specialists and a Deputy Superintendent for a supervisor. We arrived at the suspect's house and surrounded it. One officer began striking the front door. I could see one occupant inside through the front glass window. She was an elderly woman about sixty, tired, wrapped in a flannel robe, and her head was covered with a red hanky. It was not her we were after, but we wanted to talk to one of her sons.

She refused to open the door and walked out of everyone's view. We stood there, and before I knew it, the boss ordered an officer next to him to kick in the door. We did not have a warrant. Police anger and eagerness fueled the officer to obey this order. The next thing in my range of vision showed a suspect being dragged down the vestibule steps by his hair. This poor kid, dressed only in underwear, ended up wrapped in a blanket and handcuffed to the wall, waiting to be questioned in a police homicide. I took one look at this scared kid and knew we did not have our killer.

Every officer in the gang unit who worked on this homicide became extremely frustrated. All the man-hours and effort were for naught. Reluctantly, I sat in on some of the interrogations that were conducted by members of our unit. Even though these detectives tried to give off an air of experience, they were poorly playing the good cop/bad cop. The problem with this line of questioning is the kids never saw the good cop of the duo. They were all threatened with an ass whooping, and in order to avoid one, they would make up anything the police would accept. It appeared to me some of these kids were so scared that they would trick on anyone they knew who had a police record. At this moment, I realized how we acquired all the phony leads.

The investigation went nowhere. I grabbed Earl by the sleeve and we snuck out of the police station. We headed home and no one even realized we were gone. Both of us agreed the obvious problem was too many chiefs and not enough Indians. We made a decision to start fresh in the morning.

The next day, I awoke early and got dressed. Before I left, I turned on the television and the news reported the Chicago Police Department arrested the suspects in the police shooting. I immediately called the station and got the particulars of the case. The regular homicide dicks produced the arrest and also were able to get charges approved through the State's Attorney's Office. Not only was the Gang Unit in left field on this one; we were out of the ballpark. The arresting dicks purposely withheld information from our division concerning the case. To be honest, I did not blame them. The manner in which the new Gang Unit handled the case seemed somewhat unethical.

Change day finally came and my name appeared on the transfer order. I was really going to miss Earl. He was my best friend, on the job and off. I had some doubts as to whether I could perform without him. We were a team, and a damn good one, but now that was over. I said my goodbyes and left for my new unit, the Major Accident Investigation Section. In the old days, this unit was referred to as the Hit and Run Division and some still call it that today.

This unit's basic function consisted of investigations of traffic accident that involved fatalities, as well as near fatalities. I was now Joe New Guy again, but the pay remained the same. Everyone in the unit accepted me and I fit right in. This was probably because of my seniority on the job and the fact everyone in the office knew you must be politically heavy to get transferred into this type of unit.

I had not handled a traffic accident in over twelve years. It was now my duty to investigate fatal accidents and charge the offenders accordingly. But, just as in the gang unit, adjustment followed. After about fifty or sixty cases, everything came easily and I had the job down to a science. I still possessed my investigative techniques, but instead, they were to be applied differently.

Soon after my transfer, a group of traffic investigators were sent to the Police Academy to learn various new techniques of traffic accident investigation. A Northwestern University professor taught the subject matter. Uncle Sam paid for the program and that is the only reason we were all there. It did not cost the city a penny for the training.

We spent seven weeks at this school and gained an education on everything from traffic accidents to Newton's mathematical theories. The problem with the class was there were many old-time traffic guys from other divisions whose only skill consisted of writing traffic reports and tickets. This new form of investigation really did not matter to them; they were more interested in how they could evenly split a twenty-dollar bill three ways.

The group faced another problem. The instructional material and visual aides were antiques. Demonstrations took place on rural roads minus heavy traffic flows. If we tried to apply these theories on the Dan Ryan Expressway, a vehicle certainly would strike a police officer. But I did learn the proper way to investigate fatal accidents.

The one thing I will always remember about the Traffic Division was my observations at accidents. In my Gang Unit experience, I saw teens with gunshot wounds to the head, throats cut wide open, and guts that hung from bellies. What amazed me about this unit was that in a mere six months, I saw the same thing.

On occasion, I observed legs lying on highways. Monthly, I witnessed arms dangling from torsos and feet attached merely by hamstrings. Motorcycle accidents were largely to blame for these types of occurrences. In most cases, I had the responsibility to notify the family of the injuries or deaths. It never came easy to talk to a mother and inform her that her son just lost a leg in a motorcycle accident. Some guys were tacky and came right out and said it. I was somewhat tasteful, but the results were the same. Usually, someone would collapse right into my arms.

After about a year in the unit, everything fell into place. This was by far the best job I have ever had on the police force. At first, I wondered why I enjoyed this unit so much. Then, it hit me. Not one supervisor thought he or she was above you. Every one of the bosses was pleasant and that made it a joy to report for duty. No one was ever on your back. All were former Detective Division supervisors. It reminded me of the old Gang Unit and the treatment I received by most of the sergeants.

This type of assignment allowed a lot of free time, because we only worked when someone died in a traffic accident, or was about to die. We had our playtime, but one thing was for sure: if the bosses needed us, we were there performing our job.

During my brief stay in the unit, I met a lot of great people, offenders as well as victims. Probably due to the fact that most of the people I came in contact with were not criminals. They were people in accidents and victims of accidents. No rapists, no muggers, and no shooters. On the other hand, things seemed to have gotten monotonous investigating accident after accident. It has been a long eighteen years to this point. Was I burned out? My true feeling eluded me.

We just checked off the day shift and six of us stopped for a cold one at Ernie's, which was our unit's watering hole. We chugged down five or six beers and watched our favorite television game show of the time, "Family Feud." We continued to drink heavily and began to razz George, a fellow black police officer about the contestants on the show. A white family competed against a black family and we bet George a beer on the outcome. George, a very good friend, frequently traded taunts with me about the black and white crap. This was an issue on many police officers' minds at that time with the new affirmative action promotions and all. But, for the both of us, it was just a matter of jiving and teasing, nothing more.

"Come on, guys, stop fucking around with this black and white shit, you know I don't play that game. I only fuck around with Richie about that shit when we get bored at the office," said George.

Well, that was all the guys needed to hear. Never tell a bunch of drunken coppers not to tease you or let them know it bothers you. All could not wait to get on his case and razz George a bit more. The guys ordered another round of beer.

"Okay, guys, I'll take the black family and you guys can have the honkies. The loser buys a round of beer; 10-4?" asked George.

We accepted the bet. The game was close all the way to the wire. Finally, the last question was asked to take control of the board.

"Name a famous Rudolph," said the host of the show.

The white family buzzed in first and took control. We jumped to our feet. All George could say was "Take it easy, boys; it's not over 'til the fat mama sings.'"

The two obvious answers were thrown out immediately, Rudolph the Red Nosed Reindeer and Rudolph Valentino. The third of the four answers needed to win was a famous Rudolph Russian dancer. Who knows what the hell his thirteen letter last name is? The white family only needed one more correct and the beer was ours.

Suddenly, our team hit a snag, and to be quite frank, so did their cheering section. We could not think of another famous Rudolph. George licked his lips and chugged his beer when the white family ran out of time. The black family, who huddled at the other corner of the stage, appeared ready at the microphones. They all jumped up and down in place and were very excited. Obviously, they figured out the fourth Rudolph. I reached into my pocket and pulled out a sawbuck. I threw it on the bar. George looked at the bartender and laughed.

"I'll have the imported stuff as long as my honky friend Richie is buying," said George.

We all laughed and continued to watch the show. The fourth Rudolph still evaded us. We waited for the black family to produce the final answer. The host walked to the head of the family and put his elbow on the counter in front of her. He clutched the famous answer cards in both hands.

"Well, Francine, I need an answer," he said.

Francine continued to jump up and down and shook all over. She resembled an old Italian woman in the grape barrel.

"Richard," she said. "GET THE MONEY READY. . .RUDOLPH HITLER!"

Dead silence on the show, as well as in the bar, a look of disbelief covered our faces. The host looked at his audience, and with a slight flick of the wrist, threw his question cards up in the air. I put my hand on the bar, looking for my ten dollars. George buried his head in his arms and was chuckling. I quickly snatched my ten spot off the bar.

"Yeah, bartender, sir, we'll have that round of imported beer on my friend Rudolph, I mean George," I said.

George dug in his pocket, paid for the round, and we all laughed out loud.

In that short year, all of us in the unit became very close, especially George and I. A difference existed between the officers in the Gang Unit from those in the Hit and Run Unit. I noticed this fact soon after my transfer, but I did not want to make any snap judgments about my co-workers. The difference being, the guys in the Gang Unit loved to have fun on the job some of the time, whereas some of the guys in the Hit and Run Unit loved to have fun on the job most of the time.

We were all policemen, but there existed a vast difference in attitudes. The reason was twofold. First, every man in this unit had over fifteen years experience. They were fed up with the politics and the police work bullshit. Secondly, all of the men evolved from their John Wayne Syndrome years ago and knew police work and politics were one and the same. They also realized the police department could not change society. I heard the words many times during my stay in this unit, "You can't change the world, and it's too late." What made this unit even better was that most of the supervisors possessed the same attitude.

The four years spent in the unit were educational, both on the job and off. After mastering the skills needed to be a vehicle homicide detective, more time became available to play while working. Who am I kidding; most of the guys played on the job more than they did on their regular days off. That is how many kept their wives in the dark as far as their extra curricular activity. Their regular days off were spent with the family, and those who had girlfriends spent time with them at the expense of the taxpayer.

Like other jobs, once the learning process is mastered, months fly by routinely. You might even call the job boring. But a new problem developed within the unit. The supervisors seemed to have a difficult time making decisions about the function of our unit. They all had their own personal beliefs on what type of assignments should be investigated. And once again, as in the Gang Unit, we started to get rinky-dink jobs other than very serious accidents.

One day, my partner and I received a call from a patrol car to go to St. Peter's Hospital on a possible fatal accident. We asked if the victim died or not. The policeman who called had no idea if the man passed, so we simply instructed him to call later with the time of death. In reality, we hoped the guy would hold on until the next shift. Then, if he kicked the bucket, we would not be stuck with the job. Somehow, another boss got wind of the call and sent us anyway.

When we arrived, our victim sat in the emergency room with a turban on his head. It displayed spots of blood throughout. He resembled a snake charmer. As it turned out, the only injury incurred was a cut on his forehead that appeared circular in shape. Further investigation revealed that it belonged there and we later discovered the actual injured area of the skull. It was not as severe as originally reported. We had no business handling this accident because death was not imminent. My partner and I thought we would have some fun.

I asked the victim to explain his accident. During the conversation, he mentioned he knocked down a city streetlight.

"What's the name of your insurance company?" I asked.

"Ooooh no insurance," he responded.

The victim spoke in an exceptionally heavy Middle Eastern accent. I took out my pen and pad of paper and asked him to spell "Ooooh no". A puzzled look covered his blood-stained face.

"Please, sir, spell the name of that insurance company, 'Ooooh no.' I've never heard of that company," I said.

"You don't understand, Officer, I don't have any insurance," he said.

"Oh, you don't have any insurance at all," said my partner.

"That's right, Officer, none at all," he whispered.

Our friend was basically a hardworking, nice fellow, so we told him to forget about the street pole. No one knew of the damage anyway. He thanked us and said he would not tell another soul.

The truth of the matter was that the street pole was knocked down three days earlier in a different accident. This poor guy thought he toppled it when he woke up in the ambulance and saw the pole lying on the ground. He figured we let him slide on the damaged pole. We always took advantage of an opportunity to make the Chicago Police appear good-hearted toward the public. It was a simple matter of public relations. The victim left the hospital happy.

A short time later, we heard one of the other detective teams receive a job of a dead one on North Cicero Avenue. We were in the area and decided to stop by and see if we could give any assistance. We beat the team to the scene and were mistaken for the investigating detectives.

The beat man related the facts of the case, and instead of stopping him, we let him ramble on. It appeared to be a simple one. A car catapulted over the center lane cement dividers and struck a vehicle. The impact caused the second vehicle to lose its roof. Unfortunately, along with the removal of the roof from the body of the auto, the vehicle also removed the head from the body of the driver. For reasons unbeknownst to us, the entire body, minus the head, already waited in the wagon. The head remained in the backseat of the car.

The reporting officers assumed we would need photographs of this phenomenon. That not the case, I grabbed the head by its long, wavy, black hair, and ran for the wagon before it left for the hospital. My path blocked by rubbernecking traffic, I walked by one vehicle with a little old lady behind the wheel. She smiled and waved at me and I returned the smile. Being Italian and normally having to talk with my hands, I raised my right arm to return her greeting. I forgot about the disembodied head still in my hand. The look on her face surprised me at first and I had no idea why she let out a very loud scream. In any case, I ran to the wagon to deliver my package and the sweet little old lady called me a "fucking asshole" as she drove away. I just stood shocked. I could not respond as I usually did. Chalk one up for the little old lady and zero for the police.

The shift was almost over and we were about to call it a day. When working the early day shift, I was in no hurry to leave because all my friends were still at their jobs. Most guys despised the day shift because the bosses were always around and they usually found you some errand to run to make their job a little easier.

"Hey, Pete, have you seen Lieutenant O'Hara?" I asked.

"I haven't seen that pussy around for three or four days now," he replied.

Just then, another officer told us Lt. O'Hara checked himself into St. John's Hospital for his annual check-up. He would return to work in a couple of days. Pete got a smirk on his face and I knew he was up to no good. He picked up the phone and dialed the number to the hospital.

"Hello, may I please speak to Timothy O'Hara? You'll have to look up his room number, I don't have it with me," said Pete.

Pete sat up in his chair and gave me a stare. He began to chuckle.

"Hello. Is this Lieutenant Tim O'Hara?" asked Pete.

"Yes, it's the lieutenant. What can I do for you?" he asked

"I'm Dr. Valuko from the Police Medical Section. How are you feeling today, lieutenant?"

"I'm feeling just fine and should be back to work shortly, perhaps two or three days."

"Well, I don't see a problem, Lieutenant, except for the fact that we received a letter from your doctor that indicated a tipped uterus is located in the rear of your throat."

"I have what in my throat?" snapped the lieutenant.

"Yes, Lieutenant, your doctor said it's a tipped uterus in your throat. It's very common among a lot of bosses, especially the ones who are cunt heads!"

The lieutenant could hear the laughter from the other officers in the office and demanded to know the identity of the caller. Pete quickly hung up.

"Boy, is he fucking mad. I thought he could take a joke. I wouldn't have called if I knew he'd get so upset," said Pete.

All of us hung around about thirty more minutes when the phone rang. This time, a legitimate doctor from the Police Medical Section was on the line. He inquired the status of Lt. Tim O'Hara and wanted to verify his confinement at St. John's Hospital. Pete answered his questions and got the strangest request from the police doctor.

"Can you please call the lieutenant and tell him I've been trying to contact him? It seems every time I call, he answers the phone and I introduce myself as Dr. Weiss from the Police Medical Section. The response I receive from your lieutenant is quite disturbing. He simply tells me to go fuck myself and promptly hangs the phone up."

Pete just stood there in amazement at such a coincidence. The shift ended for the day and we went home.

I have been in the Major Accident Section for months now and finally landed a partner on a regular basis. His name was Frank. He was a great guy and we got along very well. I think I felt this way because he reminded me of Earl. Frank was a fantastic detective, a good paper man, very street smart and a clean freak. Every time I saw him cleaning something, I thought of my ex-partner.

Many funny things happened while Frank and I worked together, but this was the topper. Frank and I were assigned to a hit and run fatal accident investigation. It occurred in the northeastern section of the city. This neighborhood is well known for its large population of gays.

We arrived at the scene and interviewed two witnesses. Obviously, they were gay by their clothing and the tone of voice they used. They spoke freely about their sexual preference during the interview, so our observation was a moot point.

They related the victim, their gay friend, stepped out between two parked cars and an oncoming vehicle struck him. The poor guy got wedged in the undercarriage of the car and dragged one hundred yards before the driver brought the vehicle to a complete stop. The victim was immediately rushed to the closest hospital and pronounced dead on arrival. It was our job to respond to the emergency room and get the particulars on our victim and the accident.

We walked into the emergency room and saw the gay corpse lying on a dolly. Covered with a plain white sheet from head to toe, Frank and I found it peculiar that both emergency room doctors and a nurse chuckled a few feet from the body. They stood next to a makeshift desk that leaned up against the wall. On top of the desk was a small lamp. The nurse repeatedly turned the lamp switch on and off as the others stood by and laughed.

"Hey, Doc, we're the investigators from Major Accidents. Is there something funny about this case, or are you guys just on a break?" I asked.

"Gee, we're sorry, officers. We didn't mean to seem so insensitive, but we've never come across a case like this," said one of the doctors.

At present, the case did not seem irregular or weird in any way to Frank and me. Frank asked the trio what they found amusing about the death of a human being in an automobile accident.

"Oh, we're not laughing at his death, Officer. We're laughing at the circumstances surrounding his death. It's one for the books," said the other doctor.

It seemed that when our victim was plopped on the emergency room gurney, the medical staff noticed a very large bulge protruding from the crotch area. The trauma nurse unzipped the victim's pants and removed a 100-watt GE light bulb, still intact. All three went to the desk and exchanged the bulb in the lamp with the one removed from the victim's pants. Much to everyone's surprise, the bulb that was dragged one hundred yards under a moving vehicle survived. The human being did not.

"Boy, what a great idea for a commercial," said Frank.

"Don't even go there, buddy," I said.

Now, we understood their comical attitude and joined them in their laughter. Thus, another shift had ended.

That evening, I went out and got really drunk. The dollies in the bar seemed to look better around three in the morning and all my time and effort paid off. I ended up with a date and followed her home that night. I had no idea where we were headed, but I rode her bumper the entire trip. Horny as hell, I did not let her out of my sight.

One thing led to another and, after a little more scotch, we both ended up in the sack. After a brief wrestling match, we fell sound asleep. The next thing I recall hearing was the deafening roar of a bus engine. It zoomed right by her apartment window. From a distance, I could hear the voices of little children playing outside.

I sat up in bed and glanced at the nightstand. I could not believe my eyes. The clock read 2:30 p.m. I had exactly thirty minutes to get home, shower, put on a suit and tie, and report for duty.

An impossible feat, I decided to try my hand at conning one of my supervisors. I would just tell him I over slept. This had become a bad habit in the past six months. My late night binges, coupled with strange bimbos, began to interfere with my work again.

I dialed the office while she still slept. Luckily, one of the player sergeants happened to answer my call. He bought my excuse for tardiness and happened to ask my location. I panicked because I did not know. My silence aroused his suspicion.

"Rich, you don't know where the fuck you are, I can't fuckin' believe you," he said.

"Aaaaah, I really do, I know where I'm at," I said.

I jumped off the bed and ran to the window. The sergeant heard the sound of me fiddling with the blinds.

"You're looking out the goddamn window, Rich. You're looking for a goddamn street sign. You amaze me," said the sergeant.

"Okay, okay, I don't know where the fuck I'm at. The signs are blue and white, help me out here," I said.

Before he answered, I tiptoed back to the bed and looked for a clue on her nightstand. A picture frame sat in the corner. It became clear I was not with Marilyn Monroe. The bimbo never switched her personal photo with Marilyn's. I disturbed her sleep and asked for directions to my office. The sergeant still on the phone heard the entire conversation. When I got to work, I received the razzing of my life. Someone even taped a local map on my office wall and highlighted all the suburbs, including the major highways leading to and from the office. I took my lumps and just kept my mouth shut. The teasing stopped after a couple of days.

My time in this unit was a very interesting part of my career, but like all good things, it soon would come to an end. Boredom erupted. Finally, the worst that could have happened actually did. We got two new bosses. They were both young and from patrol division. Boy, they really thought they were slick. One had a grand total of five years experience on the job. If you added up the years of experience of the men in this unit, it far exceeded four hundred years.

One time, an argument ensued with the rookie supervisor and a twenty-eight-year veteran police investigator. The old timer, not too sharp with words, appeared to be losing the verbal duel. Abruptly, from the mouth of the old-timer came a statement I will never forgot.

"Listen, punk, I got more time waiting in line for gas than you got on the police force."

The men could not hold back their laughter. The sergeant was totally embarrassed and he retreated to his office.

It would not be too long after this incident that my hit and run days would come to an end. My partner and I were driving during our tour of duty when, out of nowhere, appeared a giant

Cadillac. It was right in front of us. I slammed on the brakes, but the Caddy could not be avoided. Our squad T-boned his vehicle. A "poof" sound preceded airborne glass and the heavy steel from the dash collapsed on my leg. A blanket of glass chips covered us and my leg was trapped under the crushed dashboard. I managed to wiggle free in a second or two, and Frank and I were able to exit the car.

We were shaken so much; we actually leaned on the remains of the squad for support. My first thought was the both of us cheated death. Quickly, the uninjured driver of the caddy leaped out of his vehicle and approached like a raging bull.

"You two fucking assholes, are you blind? Look what you did to my fuckin' Cadillac," he yelled.

We nonchalantly stared and a painful smile appeared on our faces. The driver noticed the police microphone that dangled out of the squad car door still intact with the dashboard. The radio was torn out of the glove box from the impact, but words still could be heard from the speaker.

"Hey, are you cops?" he asked.

Neither Frank nor I answered his question and, once again, he glanced at the radio. He noticed the weapons on our hips.

"Holy fuck, I'm screwed," he said with a sigh.

My pain was very severe. A bent stance seemed to be the only position that eased the throbbing.

"You're not screwed, you're really fucked," I said.

Frank and I ended up in the emergency room badly injured. My main concern after the accident was not the damn job, but my health. My leg was severely damaged, particularly the knee. I went under the knife three different times. Work absenteeism reached one year, although I was still being paid. There were times when the pain in my knee went unnoticed, usually when I held a glass of scotch in my hand. Since there was no police work for drunks or people high on pain pills, I thought my career was over. One year on the medical role and in the bars took its toll on my mind and body. To walk was difficult; running was out of the question. But I could sit up straight on a barstool.

I finally returned to work and was assigned to light duty. This meant my street time was over. My medical classification read no prolonged walking, standing, running, sitting, etc, etc, etc. I would probably get a nice cushy desk job downtown. I would not mind that at all, considering the female scenery that comes with the job. But instead, I ended back in Major Accidents. All the ass kissers had the downtown jobs locked up. The luck that seemed to follow me in my career disappeared.

A short time after my return to the Major Accident Section, the federal government began an investigation concerning police corruption in my unit. The investigation involved kickbacks from hit and run accidents. They had a few officers under investigation but the "G" decided to investigate anyone whose last name ended in a vowel. Word around the unit was that when the "G" dealt with Italian suspects in Chicago, their first thought was the Mafia could be involved. The fact that there were fourteen officers under investigation and ten were of Italian decent somewhat confirmed the rumor. They even went so far as to confiscate a group picture ten of us posed for while at dinner (nine guys were Italian) at the grand opening of a new Italian restaurant just around the corner from our office.

We just finished dining and the check arrived. All the guys went into their pockets for cash to split up the bill when the owner appeared with a life-size replica cardboard cutout of "Aldo." He was the representative of a wine company and the cutout display was used as a form of advertising. The owner requested a picture of the group and we surrounded the cardboard cutout. All of us stood around the table with Aldo in the middle. Since we were just about to pay the check, the group acted as if we were giving money to Aldo. The picture displayed all of us shoving the money in his face.

Days later, the photo hung on the restaurant wall. Weeks later, this same picture was used in court as evidence against one of the officers that depicted the arrogance of the police by flashing all our stolen money. This could not be further from the truth, but the "G" showed it to the jury anyway. They always depend on the "spaghetti theory," throw pasta on the wall and let's see what sticks. Of course, the defendant's attorney objected, but the jury still heard the tainted evidence. The officer was found guilty.

As a punishment until their investigation was complete, the "G" transferred all of us allegedly involved to districts a great distance from our homes. My new assignment was the 15th District, by far one of the worst in the city. My frustration grew intense. On my way to work, I actually passed six other police stations that could have been my assignment. This was a strict violation of the union contract. But when the "G" is involved, all rules get thrown out the window.

My assignment, in this pit of a police station, was working the desk. But first, I attended roll call to verify my attendance. I arrived early and one of the new young quota sergeants approached me in a robot-like manner. He reached into his briefcase and pulled out a Daily Bulletin. He shoved it in my face.

"Here you go, Officer; I know you're new in the district. I want you to familiarize yourself with this crime pattern. This offender has been a pain in the ass for our residents lately," said the sergeant.

I held the paper loosely in my hand and glanced at the print. It displayed a burglary pattern of ghetto garages where only pieces of pure junk were stolen. The sergeant strolled back and forth in front of me.

"Do you think you can catch this burglar on your tour tonight?" he asked.

"Are you fucking crazy? Do you have any idea what's up with me and where the fuck I came from?" I asked.

"Yeah, you're the thief from Major Accidents," he said.

"Fuck you and your smart ass mouth. I got the "G" trying to put me in jail on what they think and not on what they know. You've got no idea if I'm a thief or not. So back off!

Now, do you think I give two fucks about this asshole that burglarized these ghetto garages? They have no doors on them, anyway, and all he stole was broken down grass cutters and flat-tired bikes. Take this crime pattern and shove it up your ass!" I said.

"You're not going to last very long around here, Officer," he said.

"Yeah, you're right. I'll be outta here as soon as my clout can drop a dime," I yelled.

The sergeant left the room and slammed the door shut.

After roll call, I reported to my desk assignment. I noticed the unusual height of the structure. All the old police buildings had very high desks. This particular desk was chest high and there were no chairs to sit on. I lasted about an hour and made a beeline to the captain's office. He was very sympathetic to my problem of no prolonged standing, but no other work was available for me to do.

"I'll tell you what, Officer, why don't you just go over to the desk and sit down and relax," he said.

"What do ya want me to do, just name it, sir," I said.

"Oh nothing, just sit and that'll be fine," he said.

For the next seven hours, I sat at a desk and did absolutely nothing. What a waste of taxpayers' money, $148 a day to do nada. This fascinating job lasted for the next two days until I could not take it anymore. I limped into the captain's office and volunteered for anything. Well, remember how Jimmy the old-timer warned me never to volunteer for anything? Clearly, I forgot his advice. The captain gave me a royal snow job.

He asked me to work in one of the local hospitals. My job was to sit in a room and take walk-in police reports. My presence would lighten the workload for the beat guys, who would then be available for more radio assignments. The job did not appear that dreadful, so I complied. But, I had a problem. I was unaware the Supreme Court voted into law that an emergency room must administer minimal treatment to anyone, at any time, for any illness. The court defined minimum treatment as a mandatory examination by a doctor.

My hospital of assignment was quite elegant, air-conditioned; I had my own office and pretty nurses. Sounds great, does it not? Wrong! It was smack dab in the middle of the west side crime-ridden ghetto known as the Austin area. It was the month of August with the weather hot and sticky. The humidity jumps very high during this month and the dampness creates much discomfort in the ghetto. The poor people who live there just could not afford the luxury of an air-conditioner in every room. Most spend much of their time in the streets where the temperature was a lot cooler.

When it comes to accidents, August is one of the busiest months of the year. The hot weather puts young adults and children in a variety of mischievous modes. These little kids would nose-dive from trees, porches, windows, and all would end up in the emergency room with bumps, bruises, and scratches. They had the right to be treated, even though their medical dilemma could be solved with some iodine and a band-aid.

The problem became intense when Mama brought four other children, her sixteen-year-old daughter's children, and a couple of the neighbor's kids she happened to be baby-sitting. Numerous times a night, mothers walked into the emergency with six or seven kids at their side. Progressively, my office resembled a day care center.

Another problem also existed. At anytime, a neighborhood gang-banger could get shot or stabbed and be brought into the emergency room for treatment. Usually at his side would be two or three of his gang-banger friends. The only hitch was the opposition gang now knew where they could find other members of the rival gang, and all beneath one roof. Since the emergency room was so crowded with mothers and the kids, the gang-bangers waited outside as easy targets. I constantly ordered them to leave and move down the street. My concern was not for the gang-bangers, but the chance a stray bullet might find its way inside and some kid or I could be the next victim.

F.B.I. statistics support the numerous beatings, shootings, and stabbings in the ghetto daily. Contrary to what one might think, in approximately eighty percent of these crimes, the victims are either related or known to the offender.

One night, Tyrone and Willy got into a little humbug. Tyrone pulled a blade and stabbed Willie before Willie could pull out his roscoe from his purple velvet Seagram's Seven bag. While lying in a pool of blood, Willie got his shit together. He shot Tyrone with one to the back as he ran.

Remember, not all Chicago policemen are the most intelligent people in the world. It seemed two different officers brought both victims to the same emergency room. Pure confusion and insanity followed. In less than fifteen minutes, ten adults were present from each of the families. During the chaos, it took all of them awhile to figure out Willie could die from the stab wound and Tyrone could die from the gunshot wound. So, in reality, we had two victims, two offenders, and two crimes.

Shortly, the brothers from one side battled the brothers from the other side; the cousins from one side fought the cousins from the other side. Pandemonium broke out and I sat in the middle of it, bad leg and all. You notice daddies were not mentioned. That is because they were unknown or the tavern on the corner had a busy signal and the emergency phone call failed to get through. In any case, one of the daddies did show up. The fight was already over and everyone was gone. Daddy was dead drunk and I had to deal with him. The only way to get rid of him was to tell him gin was on sale at the liquor store two blocks down. I pointed him in the right direction and threw his drunken ass out of the hospital. Peace at last.

This emergency room job really sucked. I was a nervous wreck before and during my entire shift. It was not until late October when things improved with the start of the cold weather. Instead of twenty reports each day, the number dropped to five or six. Now the job was less nerve-wracking, yeah, for about three more weeks.

One morning, the phone rang at my home and it was the Police Medical Section. They informed me of my new assignment. With my head stuck in a fog from a J&B hangover, it was difficult to think. The message ordered me to report to the O'Hare Field Police Station. I hung up the phone and rolled over. I gave the bimbo lying next to me a kiss on the shoulder and went back to sleep. Could it have been a dream? Hours went by and my eyes popped open. The fog dissipated and my thoughts were now clear. I realized what just happened.

"Ah, fuck! I can't believe this shit. Those assholes from downtown are fucking with me again," I shouted.

I looked at the sexy lady to my left and discovered she was not a bimbo. I took this fact into consideration and began to think with my other head and stayed in the bed. We fooled around for about half an hour, and after I changed my oil, I reached for the phone to verify my transfer. Unfortunately, the I.A.D. pinned wings on me and my flight took me to my new assignment. What dumbbell sends an officer with a knee disability to O'Hare?

CHAPTER FOUR

TERMINAL ILLNESS

I arrived at the staging area and the captain issued my new assignment. There were some old friends present, mostly disabled, and on light duty status. All of us were in the dark with regard to the demand for our presence. Suddenly, the commander walked in. Unfortunately, he and I hit it off on the wrong foot immediately.

"Officer, what unit did you come from?" he asked.

"The Major Accident Unit," I said.

He stared at me as if there was a growth on my face. I knew the scandal and investigation underway by the "G" and the Internal Affairs Division ruffled his feathers.

"Officer, did they let you wear your hair that long in Major Accidents?" asked the commander.

"Never had any complaints from my bosses; after all, this is the eighties, sir," I said.

My comment rubbed him the wrong way. He ordered me to cut my hair. Next, I heard mumble from under his breath.

"My wife has shorter hair than you," he said.

My mouth clamped shut, but a thought entered my mind. His wife must be a real beauty if her hair is shorter than mine.

My first assignment was the limousine detail. What a joke. I supervised approximately two hundred limousines while they made their rounds throughout O'Hare to assure no driver committed any city ordinance violations. It was a real dangerous job. Often, I threatened to call in the heavy weapons team to keep the chauffeurs in line. What amazed me was how all the other police officers in the unit hated the limo drivers; they went out of their way to screw with them. Most of these guys were family men and were just trying to make a living. Sure, some of them were the biggest assholes around, but I know many policemen who are assholes, as well.

The limo detail consisted of a platoon of misfits. Remember, we were all on light duty and limited as far as our performance was concerned.

The problem the city had with the drivers concerned a tax issue. For some reason, there existed a loophole in the law and the limo drivers were able to avoid part of the city taxes. The police were ordered to deal with them and deal with them hard. The city did not care if they provided a crucial service for the people traveling to and from the airport.

Many of the high-ranking positions at the airport were politically appointed jobs that came right out of City Hall. Some lacked the intelligence to foresee that, without the limo service, there would be massive traffic jams at numerous times during a twenty-four-hour period. Even fifty more police officers added to the detail would not solve the traffic problem during peak time periods.

As time went on, the police and limo people seemed to cope a little better. Computer systems were installed to help eliminate problems associated with the limo detail and to keep track of the driver's limo runs. In six months, the job became a piece of cake. The only time it was unbearable was when the computers malfunctioned and the work had to be done by hand. It seemed my workload doubled in those situations, but what the hell; it was only for eight hours.

Well, one day led to two days, then two weeks, and finally two months, and still no computers after a shutdown. We labored like dogs, but many were afraid to complain because they would be transferred back to the patrol division. The thought petrified the officers at O'Hare. They all must have been stealing or something, because in my nineteen years on this job, this was by far my worst assignment. The status quo seemed to be, "Whenever you have bosses who are shaky about losing their jobs, they create poor working conditions for others to make your job just as shitty as theirs."

The mystery of the down computers went on and, finally, after three months, we were told the problem. It seemed the big shots at AT&T got a tip about the financial situation of the city around budget time. They installed a self-destruct computer chip in the whole system. Unfortunately, the AT&T people did not receive a dime in months, so bang, off went the system. The media got a hold of this information and airport officials were stunned and embarrassed. Six months of work and computer input went right down the drain. We were back to square one, at the cost of about four million dollars to the taxpayers. The city tried to keep it hush-hush, but the story was too big. City Hall was true to form, and police heads rolled, but this time, they left the little guys alone and the brass caught the heat.

The airport detail dragged on for months, and before I knew it, the holidays were upon the city. It is a well-known fact that the day before Thanksgiving is the heaviest travel day of the year at any major airport in the country. All manpower was used to direct the heavy flow of traffic, but due to my disability, I was unable to assist my fellow officers in this ordeal.

I browsed through the paper as I sat in a warm, cozy booth located just outside the lower level of the terminals. The other officers directed the heavy traffic. I watched them work their butts off in the freezing cold. They were not happy campers. Suddenly, a supervisor approached me. I did not recognize him as a regular member of the unit. For some reason, he was steaming mad and, with both nostrils flaring, he yelled at me.

"What the fuck do ya think you're doing sitting in here? Get your lazy, fucking ass out there and help those guys get this traffic through the terminal," said the sergeant.

"Sarge, you must be new around here. I'm a light duty officer and not allowed to direct traffic or stand for long periods of time, especially on snow and ice. I'm still recovering from knee surgery," I said.

"I don't care who the fuck you are, you get your ass out there and that's an order," he screamed.

"Maybe you didn't hear what the hell I just said? I can't do that."

"No, Officer, maybe you didn't hear what the fuck I just said. I gave you a direct order," he shouted.

I walked out and approached two officers who were outside in traffic. I asked them to return with me to the booth. The sergeant now sat in my chair and browsed through my newspaper. I flung open the door and brashly instructed him to restate his order in front of the two witnesses. He stood there dumbfounded and mute.

"Okay, smart-ass, you got the stripes on your arms. Order me to go out and direct traffic and I'll obey your order. But I am letting you know right now; I'm gonna slip on the first piece of ice I see right into the fender of a brand new Mercedes Benz. Then, I'll sue the driver, the city, and your dumb fucking ass for ordering a person with a medical disability to do a job police doctors say I cannot do. Okay, Sarge, I'm waiting. Just repeat your order nice and clear so my two witnesses can understand it perfectly," I said.

The sergeant's wheels rotated in his head. He could not figure out why I threatened his authority in such a flagrant fashion. He did not realize I was so tired of all the bullshit at the airport. I was stressed out and I finally let it burst from my body.

He did not utter a word. I walked in front of him and opened my newspaper. I started to read it, but ignored him. I heard the booth door open and I watched him walk away. The man never spoke to me again and I couldn't care less.

I lasted at the airport for about two years. Probably the worst two years of my career, but I did meet some real characters. People who first come to mind are airport live-ins.

They are individuals who actually live in the terminals of the airport. Everything they own is draped over the top of a baggage cart and is hauled proudly from terminal to terminal. They rarely bother any of the passengers because they know it is cause for instant arrest. Most receive some type of aid, and to satisfy the quick cash urge, they return baggage carts to their racks for a twenty-five cent return fee.

But, of all the live-ins I have met, there is one who should be mentioned and possibly applauded. This man was an employee of an airline for thirty years and happily married for twenty-five of those thirty. His name was Ralph.

After many years of marriage, Ralph's wife decided to leave him. He was about to lose fifty percent of everything he owned and the pension he worked for his entire life. Our live-in decided to retire, but not on paper. He left his pension in tact and took an unpaid leave of absence. He had no source of income for his wife to extort. Fifty percent of nothing is nothing. But Ralph did possess an airline gold pass. This benefit card allowed him to continue to fly free on the airline he worked for during his career. So every morning, Ralph would jump on a flight to the east coast. This would take care of breakfast with first class accommodations. He returned to Chicago on the late afternoon flight, once again in first class, and with dinner. If Ralph got hungry late at night, no problem, he would take a red-eye to Las Vegas and return in the morning. He flew first class both ways, with steak and eggs on his platter.

I spoke to Ralph a few times and he proved to be quite a character and highly intelligent. But, if you saw him at O'Hare, you would think he was just another bum or homeless person. Ralph was a man with a plan. He survived this way until he was forced to take his pension years later. That was his way to get even with his wife.

My employment at the airport as a do-nothing police officer really added stress to my already stressful life. I walked from terminal to terminal one day when I saw a high-ranking civilian employee in a verbal battle with a limousine driver. There did not appear to be any reason for the insults that blasted out of the employee's mouth. Suddenly, the driver told him to stick it where the sun doesn't shine and the airport official yelled, "Police."

Apparently, this official felt he had authority over police officers. In the past, whenever he instructed the police to act, they would comply. He accused the limousine driver of a violation he did not commit. I observed the entire incident. I refused his order to arrest the limo driver. He felt highly insulted and threatened me with a transfer. Ha! Ha!

At this point, I told him what to do with the transfer, mimicking the limousine driver. The argument heated up and a police supervisor arrived. The supervisor on scene was a real stand up asshole. It was apparent he traded in his two balls for the two bars that were sewed to his shoulders pads.

"Listen, Officer, this guy could get us both moved out of this cushy job. Why don't we just honor his request?" asked the captain.

I paused for a moment to think over the situation. My thoughts verified I had righteousness in my corner. He wanted to screw the limo driver and fabricate the circumstances to the captain.

"Boss, I don't care about a transfer. I'm right on this one. You better call a deputy to the scene," I said.

The captain was stunned. Supposedly, I was the only officer under his command who did not care about a transfer from O'Hare Field. The captain and the civilian now lacked the leverage to make me change my decision as far as the arrest of the driver. I held my ground. He did not get locked up, the boss still had no balls, and the airport honcho would eventually get me transferred downtown.

The one thing I will miss about the airport is the scenery and the wacko policemen I got to know. One who comes to mind is Officer Shane. He was an elderly gentleman with over thirty-five years on the job. The problem with Shane was that he gave you the impression he was soft as a marshmallow. Everyone thought he was crazy. My opinion was he was crazy like a fox.

Daily, we reported to work at 3:30 p.m. Shane would call the check-in officer at 3:25 p.m. and tell him he was in the airport parking lot and would arrive at his post shortly. He was no more in the airport's parking lot than you can get promoted without clout. This meant the postman could not go home until Shane arrived to relieve him.

The deskman would inform the post that Shane would be five minutes late. He usually showed up an hour late and gave some half-assed excuse. Next, Shane called a beat car and requested the officer to cover him while he grabbed something to eat. He used the excuse that he ran late and needed to skip lunch to cut down on his tardiness time. If you fell for the con, he would say, "Since you don't mind covering my post for me, do ya mind covering it a while longer? I would like to attend mass in the airport chapel." Who can deny a fellow officer a request to attend mass?

The newly assigned officers would agree because they were not aware of his con, and by the time he started work, 6:30 appeared on the clock. At 8:30, he would call for his dinner break, and at 11:00 p.m., he was on his way home. He would pull this stunt two to three times a month. Does anyone still think he was crazy? He worked a quarter amount of time as the rest of us and received the same quantity of compensation.

Shane continued to pull his stunts on the guys. It was time to settle the score with the old man. One day, someone altered the worksheet to read "Position #1" instead of "Post #1." Shane had no idea where Position #1 was located, mainly because no Position #1 existed. He looked all over the airport for the site. No one would tell him the truth, brass included.

Finally, one clown sent him to an old shack at the end of two live take-off runways. No one actually thought this softball would get into his private vehicle and drive to the post. Well, he did. He cruised down a live runway as a jumbo 747 was about to take off. The pilot avoided Shane and aborted the takeoff.

The control tower alerted the police to make the arrest of who they thought was a madman. The authorities were everywhere. The F.B.I. even got involved, but they showed up late because they could not find Post #1 either. The airport brass and the airline hierarchy were furious. They wanted pitiable Shane suspended for an honest mistake; they even sought to get the supervisor some time. Well, thank the Big Guy in the heavens for clout. Shane went to a payphone and got the entire beef killed. No one implicated received so much as a written reprimand for the incident. Now, that is some heavy weight copper.

Almost certainly, the best story of the airport is not a story at all. It is all about numbers and facts. The brass believed they could simply solve the problems of airport traffic by adding more officers. Someone should tell them the airport handled eight million more people in 1986 than they did in 1985. During that year, nothing occurred to improve the entrances and exits of the airport. You do not have to be an Einstein to figure out that twenty million passengers is far too many for an airport the size of O'Hare to handle. So, finally, in 1987, an expansion plan began, thus causing another predicament.

The construction made in and out traffic an even larger fiasco. The city searched for an answer to the problem. They chose the police department. The brass immediately added more cops. The travelers love to bitch about something and the first person they come into contact with is the men or women in blue. So basically, part of your everyday duties included listening to the gripes and bitches of people who traveled to and from the airport. It is no wonder policemen are so grumpy and stressed.

My fifty-two mile a day trip to the airport drove me wild. Daily, I traveled on two of the busiest highways in the country to get back and forth to work. The flooded roadways took its toll on my nervous system. My transfer, started by the hotshot civilian employee, had not been authorized yet. This was due to the high volume of seasonal traffic. But, it was still in the works.

My brother lived in the area of O'Hare Airport so I decided to spend many evenings at his home to cut my travel time to and from work. My jaunt was only ten miles each way. I did not wish to breach any department rules, being under investigation and all, so I completed a temporary change of address form to keep things copasetic.

I submitted the paperwork on a Monday to Police Headquarters Personnel Division. The form proceeded through normal channels. Could politics get caught up in a simple change of address? My guess would be "yes."

CHAPTER FIVE

YOU'RE ON THE AIR...
I'M LISTENING

I reported for work the following Wednesday. The watch commander requested my presence in his office. The conversation was very short and to the point. He received a telephone transfer order that reassigned me from the O'Hare Detail to Police Headquarters located in the southern portion of the Loop. My new assignment was the Police Communication Center, more commonly referred to as the C.C. Room.

I was flabbergasted. I had no instruction whatsoever in this field and did not know the first thing about the police communication. The orders were accepted because I had no choice. I turned abruptly and left his office. Then, it hit me. I punched the door with a loud bang.

"Captain, what the fuck is going on here?" I asked.

"Nothing is going on. I just received a call from Internal Affairs, I mean, the Medical Section, and they ordered the transfer," said the captain.

Again, the "G" or Internal Affairs Division stepped in to harass me while their investigation of the Major Accident Unit remained in its final stages. My travel time to work from my brother's house would now double. I found myself again caught in jam-packed traffic on the same two highways.

After all my personal belongings were returned to my original apartment, I went to the union representative to ascertain who dropped a dime. What a coincidence: one week after I officially changed my address to be nearer to my workplace, I was transferred out on a phone order. I presented this information to the union. They could not lend a hand because a provision existed in our contract that pertained to my situation, something about "urgent need of manpower." My adversaries were victorious, but the conflict continued.

My next tour found me surrounded by miles and miles of electrical wires, city maps, headsets, and telephones. I did not have a clue about my duties, nor did I have the skill to perform any function in this unit except to answer the phone.

My orders were to report to the overload room for my initial assignment. This is an area where 911 calls are automatically transferred to when the normal 911 calls are overloaded. One would think this does not happen very often, but it does. The iron clad rule of the C.C. Room was that no phone light could flash more than six times without being answered. This usually happened when the original phone operator was very busy or asleep. To avoid a buzzer alarm that alerted the supervisors, the system would transfer the incoming call to the overload room. This is where I enter the picture.

Comparable to the airport, this room overflowed with misfits hampered with all sorts of medical problems. Hardly an officer requested this assignment. It was either a punishment detail or a task you got stuck with when there was no place else to put you. Visibly, no imperative need for additional manpower existed. This was my punishment assignment, but from whom?

A full week elapsed, and to be quite honest, the job numbed my mind. I despised reporting for work. There would be nights when I would work my ass off because half the room slept. The only time they woke was when the supervisor materialized during his rounds. The second he vacated the room, pillows concealed under their desks materialized, and the men laid their heads back down. I needed to do something to rupture the boredom, keep the guys awake, and keep my own sanity.

On the eve of my next shift, I sat at home and watched TV. The station aired a comedy featuring Peter Sellers as the famous

Inspector Coluseau of the Paris Police Department. He possessed a slapstick style of humor, but what really made people laugh was his articulation of certain words in the English language. I actually laughed aloud at the movie. Abruptly, a thought pierced my mind. Why not? It would be awesome to telephone transfer Inspector Coluseau to the Chicago Police Communications Center.

I arrived at work that night and told my circle of friends my idea to liven things up in this dead zone. Of course, I would keep within police guidelines to avoid a suspension or reprimand. I did not want any more trouble.

Most of my fellow misfits anxiously waited to see my plan put into action. When time allotted, they would "plug in" and listen to my phone conversations to break the boredom. The first call received was a trivial theft report.

"Halloo, Chicago Police Department," I said in a heavy French accent.

The caller related she would like to make a police report of a theft. I did not completely hear or understand her words.

"Speak into the foon, the tele-foon," I said.

"Say what, motherfucker!" she yelled back.

The guys who were awake swirled in their chairs and roared with laughter. The room had not seen this much excitement since one of the fat-assed lieutenants tripped over an electrical cord and spilled coffee on the console, a mortal sin in the communication center.

My goal, as long as I was banished to this hellhole, was to use all the famous Inspector Coluseau movie lines throughout the course of my duties. Only one catch: a certain type of call must be received in order to use any particular line from one of his cinemas.

"Halloo, Chicago Police Department, may I help you?" My "French" accent was getting better.

"I's need a poll-ece car and an am-bull-lance right away. My boyfriend hit me upside da' head," she said.

Without delay, I leaped from my chair and raised my arms as a referee would to signal a touchdown. I did this to alert the other officers another Coluseau line was about to be verbalized.

"He hit you upside da head, ma'am?" I said.

"Yeah, I's already told you he hit me upside da' head, Officer," she said.

"Okay, ma'am, the ambulance is on the way. Oh ma'am, do you have a boomp on your head?"

"Do I have what on my head?" she asked.

"Do you have a boomp, a boomp, you know, that's what you get when someone hits you upside da head?"

"Oh, you mean a goddamn bump? Yeah, I's got a motherfucking bump and it hurts. Now get me a motherfuckin' am-bull-lance!"

She slammed the phone in my ear.

Once more, my audience roared with laughter. I rose from my chair and took a bow. My antics kept us alive for at least a couple hours, but then fatigue set in. This state put most of the men back into their napping positions.

My impersonation of Coluseau continued for weeks to come and as many lines as could be remembered from his movies were used for the amusement of the troops. But as in the past, my thespian approach as a 911 operator began to bore me. I was determined to use the one last line that dodged my 911 experiences. This Coluseau masterpiece was spoken to a hotel clerk while a very small poodle knelt at Coluseau's feet. Coluseau asked the clerk, "Monsieur, duz your daug bite?"

"No, my daug duz not bite," said the clerk.

As Coluseau reached to pet the puppy, his hand ended up on the other end of a vicious snap. He clutched the wound and spoke to the clerk.

"I thought you said your daug duz not bite."

"He duz not. Zat is not my daug," said the clerk.

Weeks went by and we were on the midnight shift once more and still no call from a dog bite victim. Suddenly, about four in the morning, my light flashed. I reluctantly pushed in the button.

"I's need a doctor, my neighbor's dog just fuckin' bit me," said the caller.

"Can you please hold on one second, sir? I'll be right with you," I said.

I leaped to my feet so quickly that my weight pushed back the chair into the console behind me. The bang woke the entire room.

"Attencione, attencione, there's a dog bite victim on line four. I'll give you guys a few seconds to plug in," I said.

The other officers plugged into line four and waited for me to pick up. Their expectancy of the outcome energized the room.

"It's me again, sir, did you say your neighbor's dog just bit you?" I asked.

"Yeah, I did, ya dumb motherfucker; didn't you hear me the first time? I need help."

I prepared a ticket to dispatch a police vehicle to my victim. I curiously asked the long awaited question, "Sir, did you ask your neighbor if his daug bites?"

I had no idea what the gentleman's response would be. The other officers were also baffled.

"Is you crazy? I had no motherfuckin' time to ask if his dog bites. His dog gots a piece of my ass stuck between his teeth, and I can't sit down. Just send me some mothafuckin' help," he shouted.

He hung up the phone with a raucous bang.

More laughter exploded in the room. The supervisors were bewildered why we were enjoying ourselves so much. The captain sent one into the room to evaluate the commotion. Leisurely, we returned to our duties. During his exit, the guys hummed a few bars of the French National Anthem. The sergeant stopped and turned for a moment, shook his head, and walked away. My sanity still remained in tact. I owed this phenomenon to Jim. I utilized one of the three traits he taught me years ago to accomplish this feat, a sense of humor. The shift ended.

A few months later, Internal Affairs Division contacted me and ordered my presence ASAP with reference to the Major Accident investigation. This was an unforeseen surprise. It was the first time in twenty-six months my input pertaining to the scandal was sought.

I appeared and an investigator brought me into a room located on the eleventh floor of the Ivory Tower. He shoved a report into my face. The paperwork was approximately three years old. At first, I did not recognize the content, but the bottom of the paper displayed my signature.

"Officer, you're going to the penitentiary unless you tell me what the fuck you know about the thieves in the Major Accident Unit," said the investigator.

"I really don't have anything to tell you. I was only in the unit a short time before you people or the 'G' me transferred out. You remember. I'm Italian and they think there's a Mafia tie," I said.

"That's not why the 'G' transferred you," he said.

"Then why?" I asked.

"Beats me," he said.

"Fuck you, you lying empty holster. You don't have anything on me because I didn't do anything. That's the bottom line," I said.

With those words, he snatched the report from my hands. Point blank, he informed me the offender in this hit and run accident accused me of accepting a bribe to fix his case. I grabbed the case back and gaped at the name.

At the time of this accident, only one black owned and operated ice cream company did its business in the Chicago land area. This particular case involved one of the owners' trucks and I specifically remembered every fact of the case right down to the female African-American who founded the company. I spoke to her personally and pondered the thought of what a great job this minority woman pulled off in the white man's business world. The outcome of the case involved a promise to repair the damaged autos, and in return, no citations would be issued. This was perfectly legal and accepted by the police department as standard procedure.

Most people only care about the damage to their auto and the cost of the repair. The owner personally guaranteed me she would pay for all damages and would satisfy the needs of the victims. Provided this was okay with the damaged parties, it certainly was okay with me. This investigator from the Internal Affairs Division lied to my face. His goal was to get me to fabricate facts to save my own ass. I knew the allegations against me were the investigators fantasies. I looked at him straight in his shifty eyes.

"You're the hotshot detective. If this person said I took money, arrest me right here and now. I'll take my chances in court," I said.

That remark caused him to bolt from the room. He huddled with someone who was obviously his boss. This person now entered the room and actually treated me decently. It was the old good cop/bad cop routine. I sat there and listened to his crap. Obviously, they had nothing now, and even less on me twenty months earlier to employ for my prosecution. Two years of harassment and not one piece of legitimate evidence surfaced against me. Dah, maybe I was innocent? I walked out of the room without even a written reprimand for a rule violation. Politics attempted to wage many battles, but the war was finally over. I emerged victorious.

These same two supervisors officially transferred me back to my old Major Accident Division a few days later. All this political bullshit for something they thought I did, and not one shred of evidence to prove it. Now, is it clear why I admire those guys from the Internal Affairs Division?

A secured transfer out of this hellhole would make one want to jump for joy, but I would miss Jeff and George very much. If anybody could make me laugh, "Crazy Jeff" was on top of the list. How he got that nickname is a mystery to me, but maybe this conversation between the two of us might explain it.

We were at the phones one night, ready to fall asleep. Jeff seemed highly irritated. The department had forced him to see a police psychiatrist. He never enlightened me on the department's rationale for such a decision, but if anyone would drive the psychiatrist nuts, it would be Crazy Jeff.

"Hey, Rich, I'm so fucking mad. I've got to see the police shrink tomorrow morning.

After working the entire midnight shift, I won't be able to keep my goddamn eyes open. How do they expect me to make an 8:30 a.m. appointment?" asked Jeff.

"Why the hell do ya have to see a shrink? I've been working with you for a couple of months and you seem as normal as all these other weirdoes," I said.

"Well, I really don't want to go into the reason why they're sending me, but I can tell you this bitch shrink really pisses me off every time I see her. I can't help but feel her last report will stool pigeon me out to the department as an alcoholic," said Jeff.

"Alcoholic? I've never heard you even mention the word alcohol," I said.

"Well, you see, it's like this. You know these psychiatrists come up with all these new theories every six months to keep their profession thriving. It appears if you have a couple of beers on a daily basis, which I do every morning to help me sleep, you are classified as an alcoholic. I explained to her this is the only alcohol I drink. But, she insists I'm an alcoholic because it's done everyday. I made one last effort to change her mind, but she didn't buy it."

"What the fuck did ya say to her to change her mind?" I asked.

"Oh, it's real simple. I told her if I'm classified as an alcoholic because I have two beers everyday, she might as well tell the department they have a shit-a-holic working in the Communications Center because I definitely shit everyday, too! She wasn't amused by my analogy."

Only Crazy Jeff could come up with this type of deductive reasoning to prove his point. I will miss that character.

Now George, on the other hand, was an old-timer with old school mentality. Appointed to the police department in the late fifties, I guess you could call him a dinosaur policeman. It was very peculiar that George still worked, as opposed to collecting his pension. He had almost forty years of service.

It seemed George married a younger woman with a child. His daughter only needed to complete one more year of college to graduate. George worked for about $160 a day, but if he sat at home, his pension compensation would be approximately $95 a day. The high cost of college tuition made things a little tight.

While on a coffee break one morning, George and I sat and discussed politics. I loved to hear his point of view on everything. We sat eye to eye for a long period of time. George possessed a huge frame and a gigantic above-the-belt beer belly. I would constantly glance at it and wonder how in the hell his pants stayed up.

That day, I noticed a peculiar tie clip that bound George's tie to his heavily stained police shirt. It appeared odd he would worry about the correct position of his tie while his top button remained unsecured with his clip tie dangling from the open buttonhole. I could not help but notice the lettering inscribed across the solid gold pin. They read K.M.F.A.I.Q. My curiosity grew. I could not hold in my thoughts any longer.

"Hey, George, what the fuck does K.M.F.A.I.Q. stand for on your tie pin?" I asked.

"That's my retirement clip, kid. Haven't you ever heard of the club formed by Officer Gilhooley of the 18th District? He's an old-timer like me and really has a hard time putting up with this computer crap, not to mention all these new college sergeants. You know how they like to fuck with us old-timers."

"Yeah, George, but you still didn't tell me what the letters stand for," I said.

"Well, it's like this, kid. You know, I could retire tomorrow if I want and there're tons of young bosses out there us old-timers can't stand. This tie clip represents 'he who laughs last, laughs best.' The minute one of these new sergeants fucks with an old-timer, the pin is handed to him as a parting gift. That's usually what will happen when an old-timer like me has had enough crap and wants out. When he fixes his eyes on the lettering, the obvious question is 'What do the letters stand for?' The last laugh would be 'Kiss My Fucking Ass, I Quit.' With those words, I would ride off into the sunset and start my retirement the following day."

"Well, shit, George, I've been on for just over twenty years, I could quit anytime, where do I get my pin?" I asked.

George rose from the table and his belly brushed against it. He spilled my coffee everywhere.

"I told you, call Gilhooly. He'll sign you up."

That was the last time I saw my disgruntled friend George.

The very next day, I reported back to my old unit. The change was drastic since the scandal. There were fifteen new investigators and all new supervisors. The department really cleaned house. Whether the house would stay clean or not is another question. But, for now, it was squeaky clean.

Still on light duty, the boss stuck me behind a desk responsible for odd jobs a skilled monkey could execute. It had been a long twenty years, emotionally as well as physically. Ironically, the pain in my leg throbbed more frequently when seated, as opposed to possibly working the street. But the police doctors and my own surgeon deemed fieldwork out of the question.

My ailment progressed and I required another surgery. Would I be able to return to my police stage and act again? My gut feeling told me no. Frightened, I decided to have the surgery anyway. With another operation, plus recovery time, came more pain and suffering. My sick days mounted.

Department regulations state, "An officer injured on duty is allowed 365 days at full pay. On the 366th day, he is required to submit paperwork for disability pension." That 366th day would soon arrive and I would have to leave the department as long as my injury persisted.

Now that my police career has ended, I could look back at the good times, as well as, the bad. What did I accomplish? Did I serve the community well? Were all my efforts in vain? Most of all, did I accomplish any of my young man's dreams during my career as one of Chicago's Finest.

As a teenager, I always fantasized about what it would be like to be a movie star. In my college years, my fantasy changed. I yearned to be an acclaimed university professor. But I ended up a Chicago Police Officer. Sure, I was a college graduate, but I would have cherished the thought of my friends referring to me as "Doctor."

At that instant, I experienced a full body rush. It felt as if a Mack truck had just hit me. I realized both of my dreams had come true. I have acted for twenty years and performed in many different genres. I envisioned my many department awards, the same way an actor would be honored when requested back on stage for an encore. The actor's ultimate achievement is to be the recipient of an Oscar. A college student's aspiration is to see the letters Ph.D. after his or her name.

After twenty years of vaudeville, I finally did it. Ultimately, I joined Officer Gilhooley's tiepin society and brandished the golden tiepin award of achievement on my chest. The tiepin was my Oscar. Lastly, a Ph.D. was in my possession, attained in life itself. Yes, I earned it the hard way, on the streets of Chicago, my kind of town.

CPSIA information can be obtained at www.ICGtesting.com
Printed in the USA
BVOW031648240613

324002BV00001B/1/P